Loose Watercolor

A Step-by-Step Painting Guide

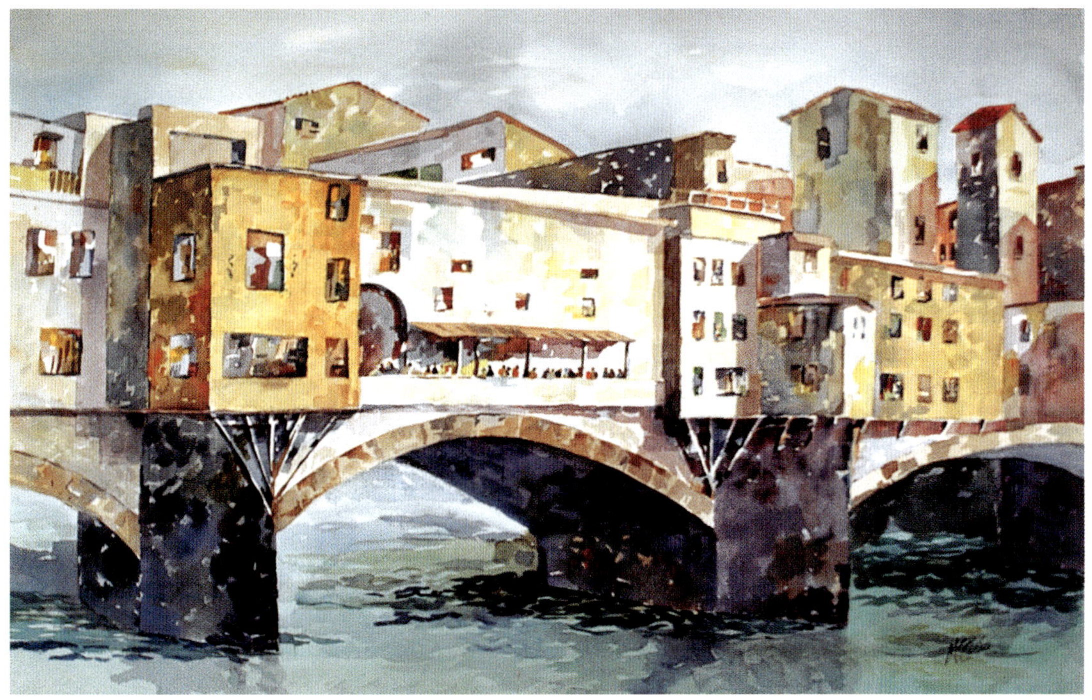

JERRY McCLISH

Published by Hand Books Press Rockport, Massachusetts USA
Distributed by North Light Books Cincinnati, Ohio USA

LOOSE WATERCOLOR
by Jerry McClish

Copyright © 2003 Hand Books Press
Text and photographs Copyright © 2003
by Jerry McClish

Published by Hand Books Press
2 Briarstone Road, Rockport, MA 01966 USA
TEL 978-546-3149, FAX 978-546-5862
E-MAIL handbooks@adelphia.net

Distributed by North Light Books
An imprint of F&W Publications, Inc.
4700 East Galbraith Road
Cincinnati, OH 45236 USA
TEL 800-289-0963

Editor: Herb Rogoff
Art Director: Stephen Bridges
Graphic Designer: Laura H. Couallier
Indexer: Ann Fleury

ISBN 0-9714010-1-2

07 06 05 04 03   5 4 3 2 1

Printed in China

Contents

Introduction

s you can see from looking through the illustrations between these covers, I paint my watercolors in a loose style, defined by an artist friend of mine as "slop and hope." This is a rather broad and played-down description of painting loose watercolors, because there are many watercolor painting procedures that you have to put into play if you wish your work to be successful. Painting in watercolor in any style is really very challenging and consequently frustrating because it *looks* so easy to do. This is a misconception, and one that's especially associated with watercolors done in a loose style. In the real world of painting, though, whatever style you choose to paint in and whatever medium you choose to express yourself with, the principles have to be respected. Watercolor is an intriguing medium. It's a demanding medium, too; it dares you to tame it and when you think you have it caged, it roars up to bite you. We will try, in this book, not to let that happen to you.

For me, painting loosely is extremely invigorating. It starts out very simply, then goes on a rampage of seemingly wild but truly well placed color patches and brush strokes that finally, and delightfully, end up in a picture. That picture, when seen from a short distance away may appear to the viewer to be quite realistic. When examined closely, however, this same watercolor painting is seen as merely indications of details, usually in a "lost-and-found" way, that casually invites those looking at it to put those strokes together in a recognizable picture. That is the excitement of loosely painted transparent watercolor.

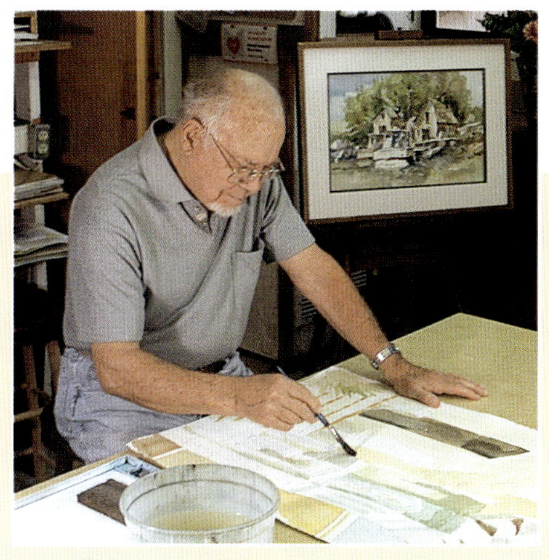

Why do I love loose watercolor? Many years ago, I grew tired of the "rake-and-scrape, roll-and-shake" methods being used and overused to paint dazzling watercolors. Alternate and uncontrolled techniques were used to inject a variety of textures into paintings. Among these were the use of credit cards or similar plastics to scrape a color wash, salt and other materials or liquids sprinkled into wet color for other effects, and Saran Wrap placed in a wet wash in an innovative manner. When the paint is dry and the Saran Wrap is stripped off, it leaves a pattern. What's more, we saw liquid frisket, an important and useful medium for masking out areas for details, being used instead to create multitudes of resists in an abstract and decorative manner. Furthermore, bottle caps, sponges, pieces of Turkish towels and many other objects for blotting or stamping techniques were overused to alter the look of a watercolor wash. My thinking was that we were inviting the intrusion of too many uncontrolled artificial techniques into what is a magnificent, tantalizing medium. Watercolor, I decided, needed no help from any of those tricks. All it needed was a happy brush dancing over a sheet of paper to paint positive and negative shapes while creating beautiful, spontaneous things. It took me some five years of diligent work to achieve anything that I was halfway proud of. And today, every time I pick up a brush, it invites me to find a better and more innovative way to make those transparent squiggles of paint look refreshing.

So, it's my pleasure to invite you to share this marvelous experience with me.

Jerry McClish
Bradenton, Florida

Materials for Watercolor Painting

Paints

A popular misconception among painters, especially those who are just starting to paint, is that there are different pigments for each painting material: one for oils, another for watercolor, yet another for pastels and another for acrylics. Here are the facts: *No matter what your medium of expression may be, the same pigments are used for all of them.* There's no such thing as an "oil pigment" or a "watercolor pigment" or different ones for pastels and acrylics. The substance that makes each medium different is the binder (or vehicle), which is the stuff that manufacturers mix with the pigment to make paint. Linseed oil is used, obviously, for oil paints; gum Arabic for watercolors; and an acrylic resin for acrylic paints. To make pastel chalks (or crayons) an aqueous binder is mixed with the pigment which, when dried and evaporated, leaves a stick of pure pigment. By the same token, to debunk another misconception, the manufacturer does not use one pigment for expensive paint and another one for a lower-priced grade. What makes one grade of paint (for professionals) more expensive than another (for students), is the ratio of pure pigment to filler that the manufacturer uses in each one: more pigment in the professional grades, less pigment for the student grades. This does not mean that I want you to think of student grade paints as being unusable; they do nicely for many phases of the painting experience. And most of the colors are permanent. Many artists of my acquaintance don't mind painting with them. I, however, prefer to stay with the more expensive professional grades of watercolor that are sold by all manufacturers. I also use only the large tubes of professional grade paints. The larger size goes a long way and the saving you experience by buying a less expensive smaller size tube is just not worth it. Of course, there are certain colors that you seem to have forever, such as some of the cadmiums and other highly intense colors. Even if you choose to buy mostly small tubes, buy the earth colors in large sizes because a painter uses more of them than any other color on the palette.

Watercolor Paper

Watercolor paper comes in many different grades, sizes and weights (the rarely used 72–pound is the lightest, the equally rarely used 400–pound is the heaviest). The weight of watercolor paper is based on how much a 500-sheet ream of imperial size paper (22" x 30") weighs. Popular weights among watercolorists are 140-pound and 300-pound. I have used both and find that each paper is nice to work with. The 300-pound paper is a little more than twice as thick as the 140-pound and normally does not have to be stretched to keep it from buckling or warping. Some artists stretch their 140-pound paper to keep it flat, but in most instances this is unnecessary. (You'll find more about stretching paper at the end of this chapter.) However, the 300-pound paper, in my opinion, is much thicker, and sized a bit differently and I feel it absorbs more paint than 140-pound paper does. As a result, it's been my experience that it requires more pigment to get brilliant results. Even with more pigment, the colors on 300-pound paper seem to be a bit muted.

Watercolor paper has three qualities: Hot Pressed (HP), Cold Pressed (CP), and Rough. Hot pressed paper is run through hot rollers after screening, giving a glossy surface. Cold pressed paper, the most popular texture among watercolorists, is run through cold rollers, which imparts some texture. The rough paper is just screened and, as its name implies, has a rather rough surface. Qualities of paper will vary from one manufacturer to another. After you have worked with a few of them, you will notice the differences for yourself and choose your paper accordingly.

The best and most expensive watercolor papers are hand-made using linen rag stock. You can always recognize a hand-made sheet by its uneven, ragged edges and the watermark that is present somewhere in one of the corners of the sheet. Watercolor paper is available in sheets, pads and blocks (where all four sides are glued to the bound edges). Even though some blocks may have papers the same weight and quality designation as sheet paper, they accept paint differently. They are close to the same price per square inch so I prefer to use the more versatile 22" x 30" sheet paper. Manufacturers of watercolor blocks claim that the paper has been stretched on each block, but in a wet-in-wet painting, I have found, the paper will usually end up with a crow's-foot in each corner as well as buckling in the center. For best results in serious painting, I suggest that you buy your paper in sheets.

Brushes

I can write an entire book about brushes alone. Instead, I will confine this segment of the chapter to only brushes that I employ in my watercolor painting. Almost all of my brushes are natural ox hair, but the supply for this type of brush, as with other natural materials for painting, is quickly disappearing. This hair comes from the ear of an ox, and the first cutting being naturally tapered (though not as sharply tapered as sable) makes a fine quality brush that is the equivalent of any good brush, even sable, according to a lot of painters, myself included. Subsequent cuttings with their blunt tips, however, do not produce brushes that are nearly as good. How a brush responds and the result it produces is up to the individual. A fact that everyone is aware of, though, is the difference in price between ox hair brushes and the exorbitantly priced red sable. Synthetic bristles are being taken more seriously today but as long as ox hair brushes are still available, they will enjoy the warmth and comfort of my studio. Of course, if you want to pay the price for red sable brushes (also known as Kolinsky, after the province in Siberia from where they come), you will enjoy the experience a great deal.

Most dealers have a cup of water at their brush racks. Dip the brush you're interested in into the water and shape the point or chisel edge. Bend the bristles and then check to see if it regains its shape when flipped.

Presented here are three veterans of my paint box: flat ox hair brushes (obviously shopworn), in sizes, from left to right, 1/4", 1/2" and 3/4". While these brushes, and others that I use, are more than twenty years old, they are in excellent condition.

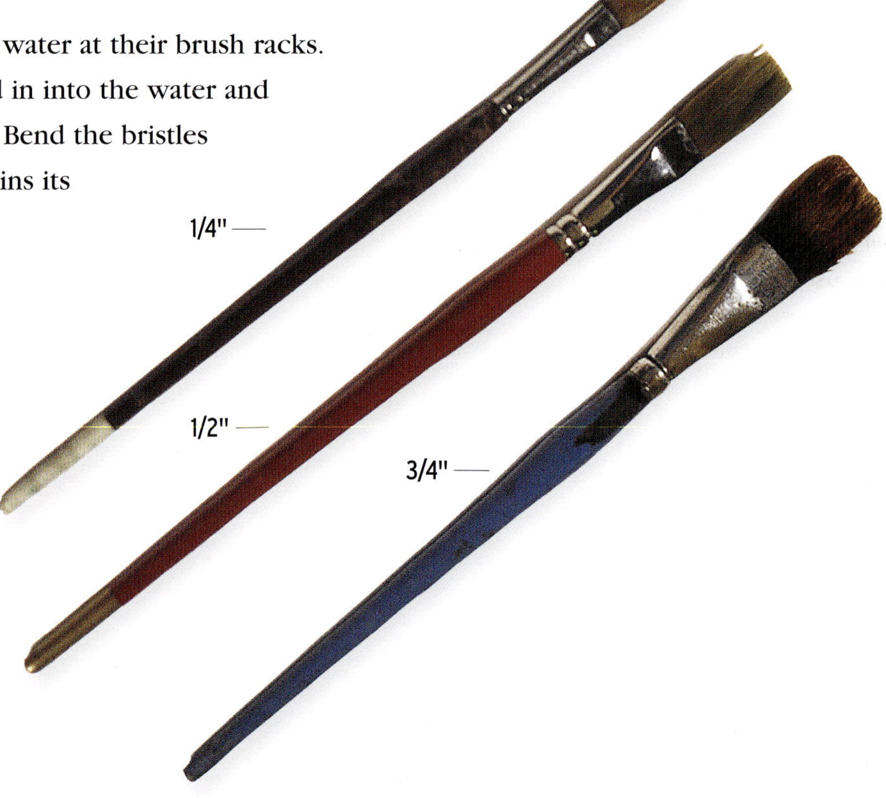

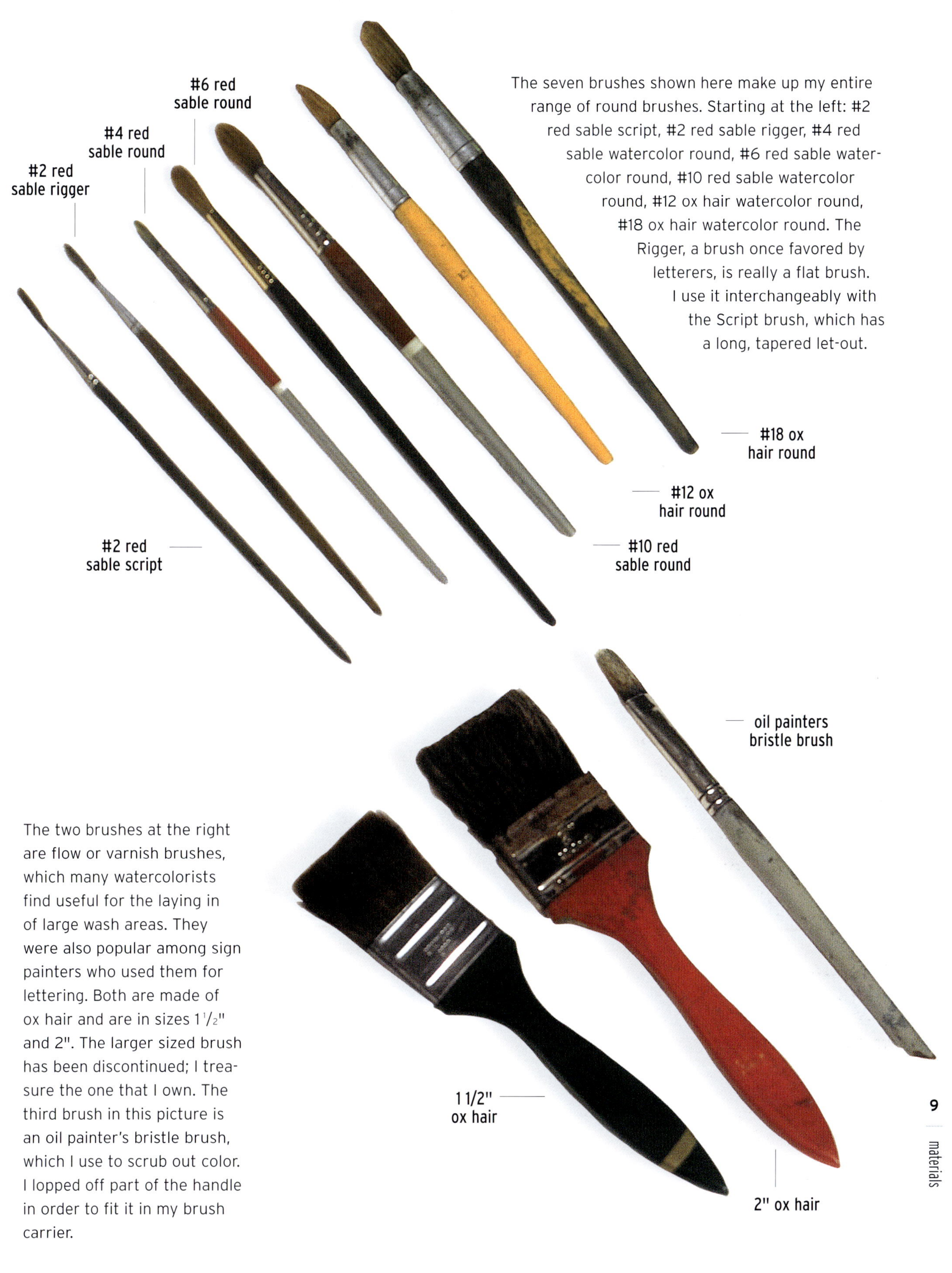

The seven brushes shown here make up my entire range of round brushes. Starting at the left: #2 red sable script, #2 red sable rigger, #4 red sable watercolor round, #6 red sable water-color round, #10 red sable watercolor round, #12 ox hair watercolor round, #18 ox hair watercolor round. The Rigger, a brush once favored by letterers, is really a flat brush. I use it interchangeably with the Script brush, which has a long, tapered let-out.

The two brushes at the right are flow or varnish brushes, which many watercolorists find useful for the laying in of large wash areas. They were also popular among sign painters who used them for lettering. Both are made of ox hair and are in sizes 1$\frac{1}{2}$" and 2". The larger sized brush has been discontinued; I trea-sure the one that I own. The third brush in this picture is an oil painter's bristle brush, which I use to scrub out color. I lopped off part of the handle in order to fit it in my brush carrier.

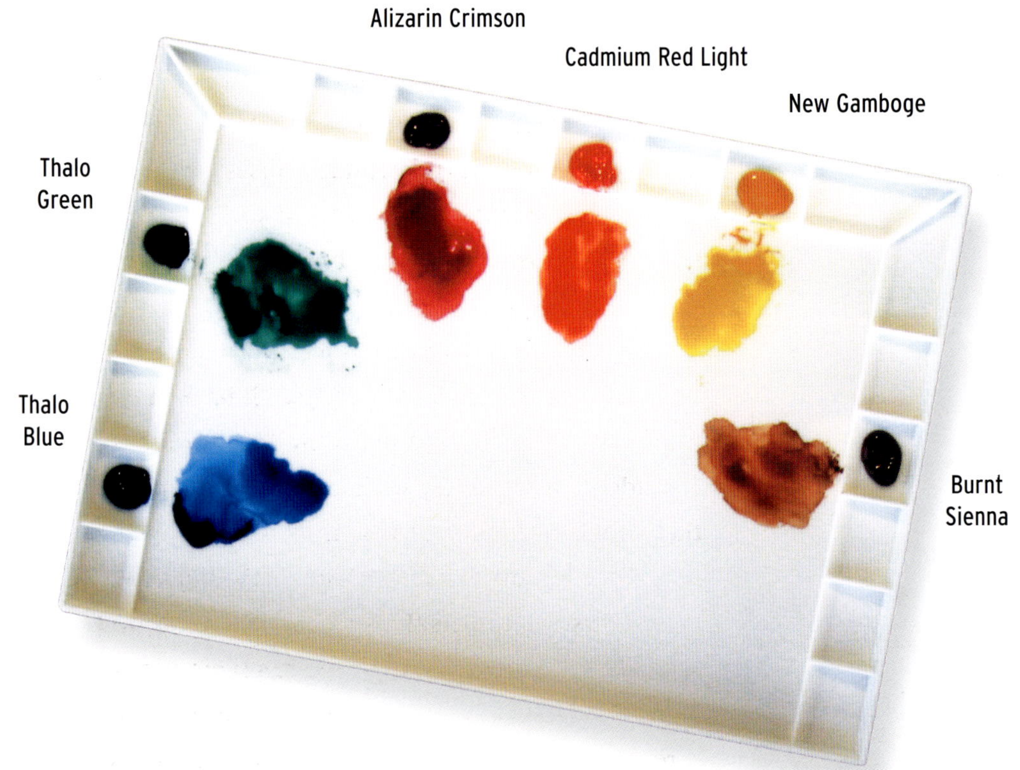

Palette

A palette is not only for mixing paints; it is also the artist's thinking place. I prefer the John Pike palette, created by the memorable watercolorist. It has adequate wells, is made from white plastic and has lots of mixing space. Placing a damp sponge in the mixing area and closing the palette will keep paint moist for a long time. This palette, as is the case with most plastic ones, can be cleaned with a sponge and a kitchen cleanser, like Comet or Ajax. This will even take out the stains from Thalo Blue and Green, Alizarin Crimson and other staining colors. A clean palette is a necessity when mixing transparent watercolors.

On this white palette, draw a brush through the mix and immediately behind the brush is the approximate color that will appear on the paper. My colors are arranged in a clockwise order starting on the left with Thalo Blue and Thalo Green. Alizarin Crimson, Cadmium Red Light and New Gamboge are on top. Burnt Sienna is on the right side. The range from left to right is, stain and cool to earth and warm. These total only six colors but most colors are mixed anyway and this group will make or approximate about any color necessary. I do have a few alternates. One is Indigo placed next to the Thalo Blue. It is used almost solely to darken the blue. The modern Thalo Blue does not have the deep pigment color that it once had. A little addition of Indigo gives it the deep blue that is so beautiful. Indigo is not a good mixer because it tends to gray colors but it does deepen the blue. Yellow Ochre is sometimes placed in my palette to mix with Cadmium Red Light to get a basic skin color. Yellow Ochre is a crutch color and overusing it gives a painting a yellowish opaque brick color. A real no-no for me is Paynes Gray. It is a beautiful color to use for a northern wintertime sky. However, it stays suspended in the water pail and imparts a gray look to all colors in the painting. The three sepias also should be watched closely although they are not as bad as Paynes Gray. There are many fad colors and more are coming on the market; they do little to produce a good painting. The artist has to do that.

Hardware

Here are some of the hardware items that are needed to paint a picture: the first option is a board to hold the paper with clips, tape, staples or other means. A box of some sort is needed to hold your painting paraphernalia. This can be a fancy paint box, it can be a simple fishing tackle box, or it can be any kind of simple inexpensive container. The kind of a container will make no difference in the quality of the painting that you do. In that box will be brushes, paint, pencils and eraser. Other items might include masking fluid, paper towels, a sponge, pencil sharpener and any other item that you wish. A water container should be white or a neutral color and it should be large enough to hold at least a quart of water. Bigger is better.

Procedures

Stretching paper is a debatable subject. Frankly, I think that it is a tremendous waste of time and is too often subject to failure. I'm sure I can paint a watercolor while other artists are waiting for stretched paper to dry. Furthermore, paper on a stretcher takes up a lot of room, especially if you are going out to paint. Another thing: if you don't get a perfect stretch at the beginning and if it is not kept during the entire painting, wrinkles will appear. The way I work, I paint with the paper lying loose on a table and do not have a wrinkle problem. That way, I can manipulate it in various ways to aid in drying or chasing pigment around. To flatten out a wrinkled watercolor, place it face down on a clean surface and lightly dampen the back or topside. Then cover it with a clean sheet of paper weighted down with books. When dry, it will be perfectly flat. It's generally believed that 300-pound paper never wrinkles; this is only a fantasy. It does wrinkle or take a bend and to correct that problem is very difficult because of the thickness of the paper.

One of the repeat questions in a watercolor class is how much water to use. I have never found an answer to that question. After a mixture is made in the palette, some artists have a rag in their non-painting hand that they use to dab the brush to remove excess water. This does two things. First it deforms the shape of the brush and secondly, it wastes the paint that has been mixed. After the dabbing, you have to return to the mixture to reload the brush and you are back to the same problem. To clean a brush, dip it into the upper portion of the water supply and rake it up the back inside of the pail. When clean water runs out, the brush is clean. One or two more wipes on the lip of the pail and the brush is ready to use. Never swish a brush on the bottom of the water pail. That is where the dirty pigment is resting. Also rubbing the brush on the bottom of the water pail may damage the hairs of the brush. To clean a brush, use kitchen detergent soap in a cup of tepid water. Dip the brush into the soapy water and then caress it in the palm of your hand, rinsing until clean water appears. After the brush is clean, point it up and let it dry. When mixing paint in a palette, make small-contained puddles that can be kept separate. Too many mixes mingled in a palette can come up with a dreaded mud color. When paint is mixed, take a little on the brush and dab a small bit on the picture. If it is not quite the right color, go back to the palette and adjust the puddle. Return to the picture and paint right over the test dab. It will disappear into the new mix.

Getting Started in Watercolor

Every picture painted presents a challenge that may require the use of different techniques during its execution. A picture painted in watercolor may be difficult to do exactly as it is planned because of the arbitrary nature of the medium. Watercolor refuses to be tamed and consequently will go its own way many times. It is a constant battle to adjust to the ever-changing ways of the watercolor medium as a work of art progresses. I believe that every painting is in constant flux while it is being painted and perhaps a better way to look at it is to say that a painting should be built starting with the first stroke of a brush. In this book, I want to point out various ways to approach the frustrating medium of watercolor.

I believe that there should be no set palette of colors to use, no single type of subject matter, no special techniques or ways to paint, and no special type of composition. Before you question my approach to watercolor, I wish to point out that you have to learn the basics of drawing and painting in order to understand the things that can happen with watercolor and how to deal with them. With those basics, you will soon discover that a brush held in your hand can be an educated tool that will happily dance over the paper. It will flit here and there in the composition adding and adjusting washes and details all over the sheet. For it to do this, you have to work using the basics and learning how to vary them. You may get a little despondent as we all do but if

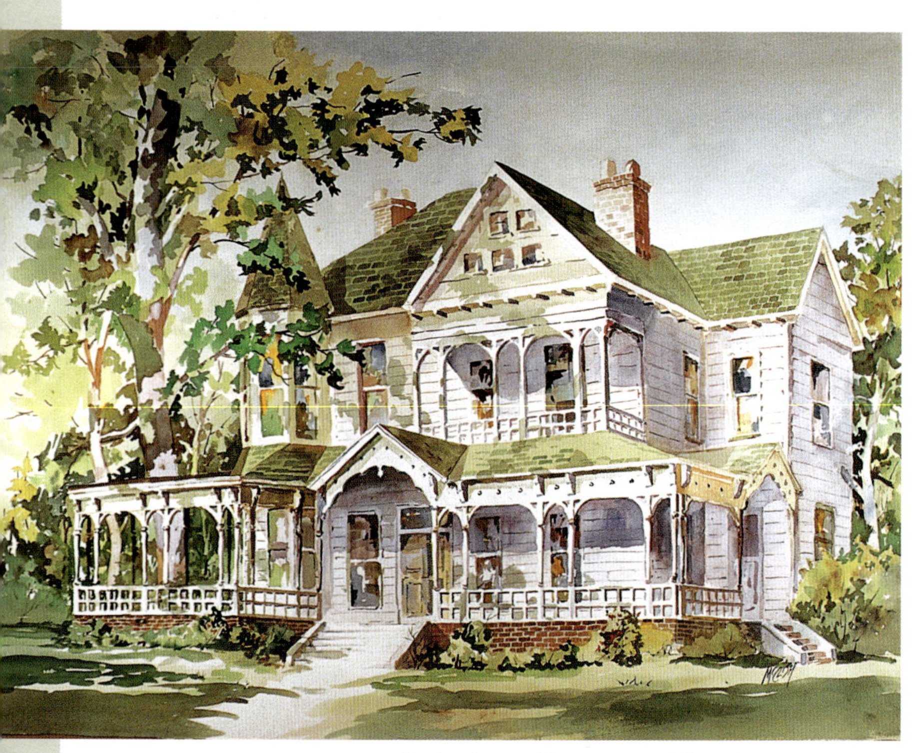

The Southern Belle, 32 x 44", 140 lb. Arches

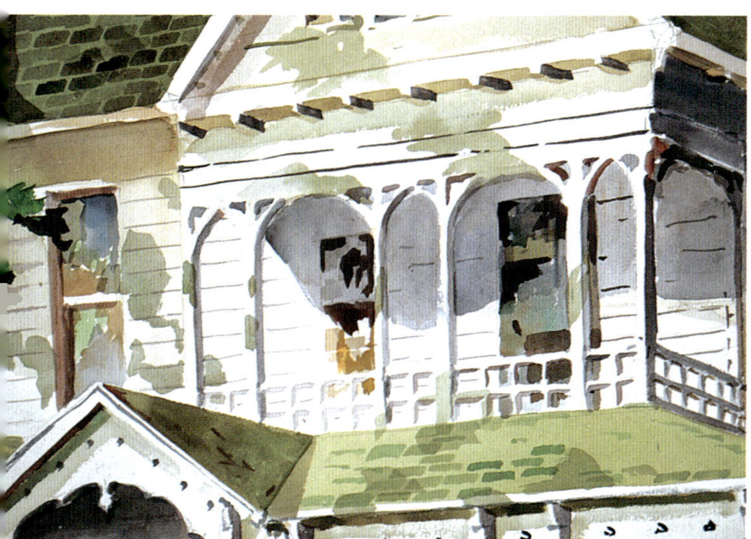

you stay with this delightful medium, there will come a special day when something nice and unexpected happens. When it does, the elation is worth all that you went through to make it happen.

Preparing Paper

Many watercolorists prepare their papers prior to painting. You may want to do this for your painting. If so, here are some tips: Thoroughly wet the paper (placing the sheet in a bathtub filled with water is a good way to do this). When the paper is so wet that it is sloppily floppy, stretch it over some canvas stretchers or on a board, such as thin plywood. You can then secure the paper to the stretchers or board

On location: Arcadia

On my many travels between Bradenton and Fort Lauderdale, I drive through Arcadia. It is a typical Florida town, and a far cry from the concrete-studded resorts on both coasts. The delicate Southern architecture of this house finally said, "Paint me." It was not an easy challenge because it took a lot of expertise to get the perspective right. On location, I made a value sketch, a half-sheet watercolor, and, for good measure, I took a photograph. Later, back in my studio, I decided that it needed a large size painting to do justice to all the bric-a-brac that the building contained. From a roll of 140-pound, cold pressed watercolor paper, I cut a 32 x 44-inch sheet. The large size demanded more accurate perspective than in the drawing and watercolor that I made on the site. I finally set up a card table a distance away from my painting table. Using a string, I extended the eye level line on the sheet across to a nail in a board clamped to the tabletop. Now with a string attached to that nail, the left vanishing point, I could stretch it across the picture area and get correct perspective on the front of the house. The vanishing point for the right side was very close in but still was not on the sheet, so I set up a second piece of wood with a nail in it that was also on an extended horizon line. With a string on each side going to their respective vanishing points, I could now get reasonable accuracy in the perspective of the house. The architecture of the house required a balance between a loose and a tighter technique in the painting. In the detail, you can see that it took a lot of negative painting (painting around areas) since the house was white. I did this by leaving the white of the paper to serve as the house color.

with staples, thumbtacks or tape. When dry, it will be tight as a drum on stretchers and will be nice and flat, ready to paint, on the board.

I do not like to stretch my paper. I lay it loose or clip it to a board if I am painting on location. I just lay my paper on a table so it can expand or contract at will. If you are careful with the amount of water in your palette and on the brush, the paper will lay flat and dry flat when painted. On the other hand, if a stretched paper breaks loose or gives a little, the stretch will not be successful. Even if the stretch is successful, the paper may wrinkle when painted in a wet manner. Since all four sides of the paper are being held to the board, when hit with a watery wash that totally soaks the paper, a crows-foot may form in each corner. If your watercolor becomes wrinkled after it has dried, don't despair. Moisten the back with a sponge, lay it face down on a clean flat surface, cover it with a barrier sheet of paper, and then load it down with a few books. When dry, it will be nice and flat. To sum up: To stretch or not to stretch? It's entirely up to you.

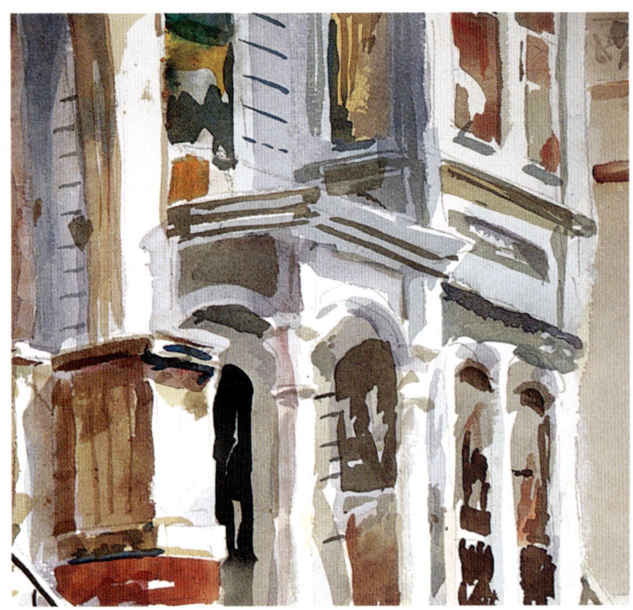

San Francisco splendor

There is a row of gorgeous, colorful houses in San Francisco that's called "Painted Ladies." They exude an architectural charm that exists nowhere else. There are many other scenes like this one in that foggy town that say the same thing. I just had to capture this townhouse in watercolor. It was a warm day, for that frosty town, when I opened up my bag of paint-on-location things and set up for painting. I never erased the quick sketch that I made and it remains in the painting. I used a number 10 round ox hair brush for most of the painting. The windows were just loosely suggested, as were many of the other parts of the building. This picture was painted in a loose carefree manner but it still needed the basics to put it together. I debated putting a figure or two in the painting but decided that it would take away from the beautiful period architecture. It was a fun picture to paint and looking at it when finished, it seemed to add to that treasured old song, "I Left My Heart in San Francisco."

The windowpanes were painted with different color patterns for each one. Their spontaneous display of varied color made the loose watercolor technique flow better.

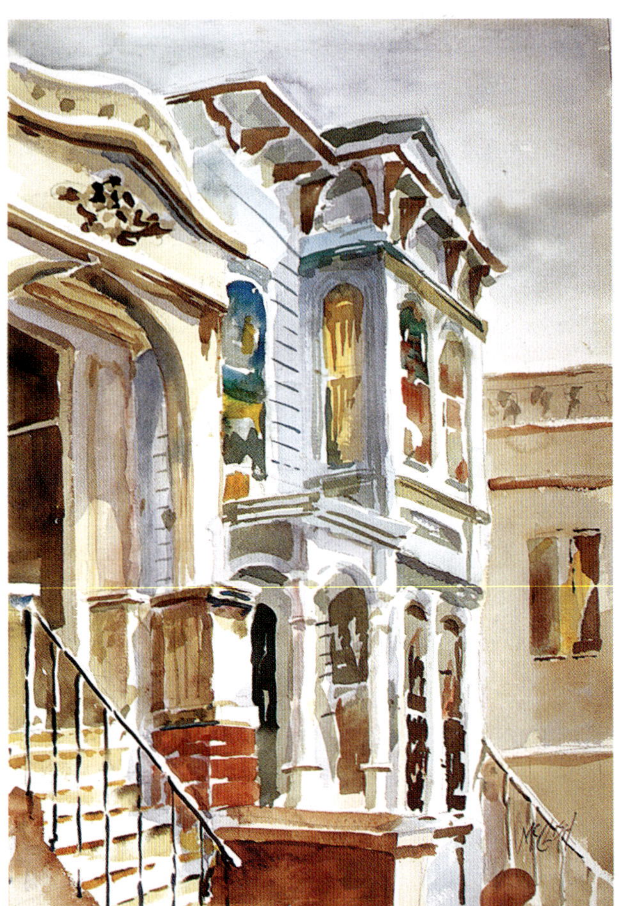

Painted Ladies, 15 x 23", 140 lb. Arches

A Hoosier autumn

I remember, from my boyhood years in Indiana, the beautiful fall season there. The foliage just exploded with brilliant colors. The poplar trees were a little different in that their colors were brilliant yellow while other trees had a display of reds, oranges, browns, yellows, and, of course, there were always a very few renegade leaves that remained green. If you have never painted fall's colored foliage this is your opportunity to break loose and play with the brush as the tree takes shape. Keep in mind that if the sun is not hiding behind a cloud, there will be shadow areas in the mass of foliage, as seen clearly in the detail of the painting. Finally, I added a split rail fence to the picture. The fence injected some human interest since it became the one thing in the picture that was not made by nature.

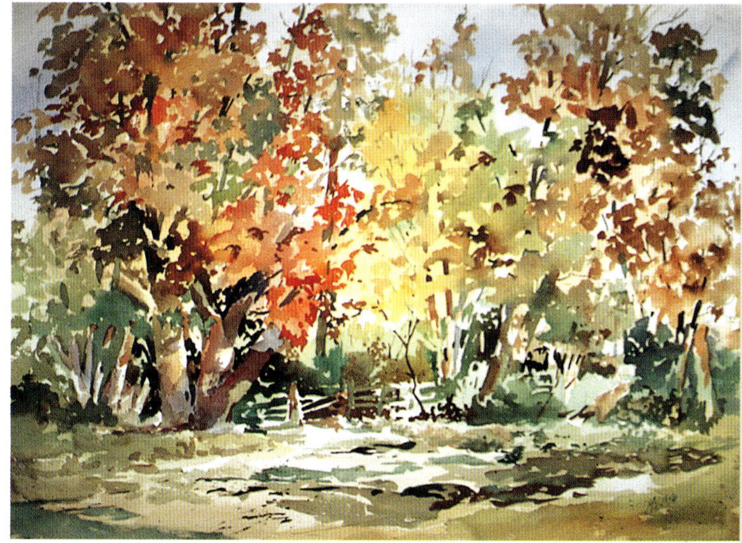

Hoosier Autumn, 22 x 30", 140 lb. Arches

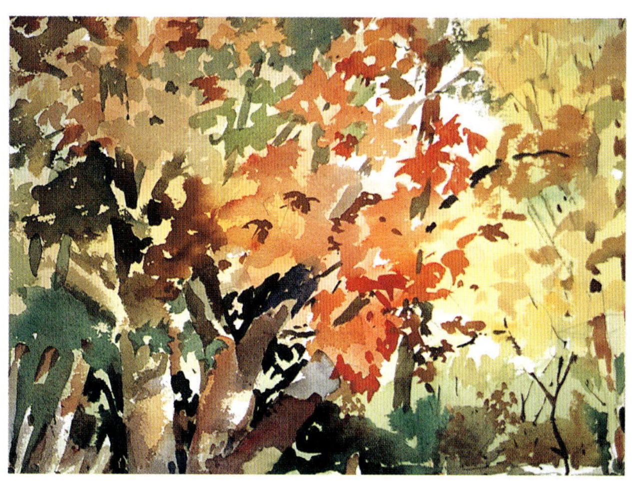

How to Handle a Brush

A brush has to be totally wet before using. Quickly dipping it into a water pail and then going to the palette to pick up paint will just not work. To get enough water on your brush, you have to swish it through water several times, and then rake it up the far side of the pail. You do the same thing to clean a brush. When raking it up the far side of the pail and you see clean water running out, you are sure the brush is clean.

Now, how do you know that the brush will have enough water to paint with? I just swish the brush through the water several times, raking it a couple of times up the far side of the pail. Then I gently wipe it across the near side of the top of the pail and it has just the right amount of water left to paint with. I never go to the bottom of the water pail with my brush. That's where all the sediment has settled; it's a sure way to get muddy colors.

Some palette instructions tell you to rake the paint out across the lip of the well that holds the color. What's wrong with doing that is that if there's any previous color in your brush, it will contaminate the color in the well. I prefer to slip the brush in the bottom of the color well and pull out color. This leaves the top with pure pigment when needed. I may also have two or three separate colors in a brush. I load the center of the brush and then dip a corner in and pull out just a bit of different color. The colors are mixed somewhat on the paper, not on the brush.

I prefer to mix or adjust a color prior to putting the brush to the paper. I seldom use a full strength color. My palette is usually sparsely filled with small pools or puddles of different mixes. Each puddle is isolated. You can run a finger around each puddle in my palette and not get it wet. If two puddles somehow get together and are not compatible, I take a sponge and wipe out both. Indiscriminate mixing of too many colors is an easy way to get a muddy look to a painting.

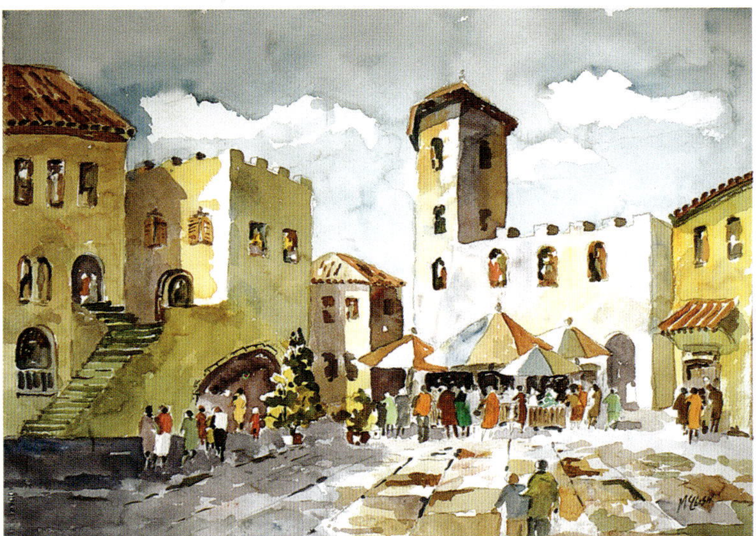

Starting a Watercolor

I start a watercolor with some random washes all over that do two things: 1) they get rid of some attention getting white areas of the paper that are not needed; 2) they set up the background or under painting to start saying something. Each puddle in my palette is adjusted and maybe added to many times. A golden rule: when mixing colors, don't mix the life out of them and don't mix too large a puddle. Just mix and paint. When the puddle runs low, add to it. While the color may vary slightly if added to a wet wash, it will blend perfectly and give a welcome variation in color and value.

Todi, Italian Market, 15 x 22", 140 Strathmore Imperial

Finding a picture within a picture

There are many times when you can find a picture within a picture by using two pieces of L-shaped mat board to frame different areas. That is what happened with this market scene that I painted in Todi, Italy. Over on the right side, away from the center of interest in the original picture **A**, there were two ladies standing in front of a building. I guess they could be called a minor or secondary center of interest, which balanced the large group in the right center of the market. It looked interesting, and **B** shows the result of a picture within a picture. At first, the composition looked a little dull, so I added a third story dormer to the building, and that helped. This is a splendid example of a simple loose watercolor. I added warm color to the face of the building. I felt that the red-striped awning grabbed too much attention and tamed it down. For the windows, I merely suggested them rather than painting architectural details. All of them have different but interesting color patterns. The sun streamed in, which created definite shadows of the two ladies and, in the lower left, there was a shadow from another building or maybe it was a tree. **C** is a close-up view of my new composition, which shows the two ladies in conversation. They became my center of interest in the new picture.

Tricks or "Trickniques"

For some reason, watercolor painting encourages the artist to use all sorts of tricks and materials for special effects. A few of the unconventional aids that artists employ for "flashy" textures and strokes is sprinkling salt, making patterns with Saran Wrap, scraping with plastic credit cards, rolling rollers, scratching with knives, pre-coating with various resists, dabbing on with sponges, the use of paint additives and many other things that creative brains may come up with. Using these tools, that were never designed to produce paintings, the artist does funny things to the paper and he can't really control what happens. In my opinion, a painting that uses these techniques is not true watercolor although it may appear decorative. Leaving white areas in a painting (negative painting) will beat any kind of liquid frisket or resist and, what's more, it looks like an artist did it. Little random white blobs that are created when salt is sprinkled into a damp wash will invite a competent judge to toss out a painting or relegate it to a back seat in an exhibition. It is much better to take a brush and paint rather than wait for a resist to dry or a get a wash through use of a trick.

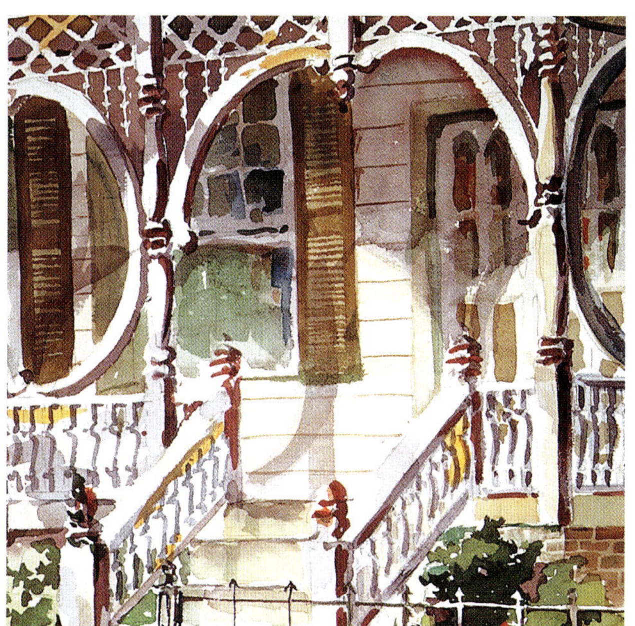

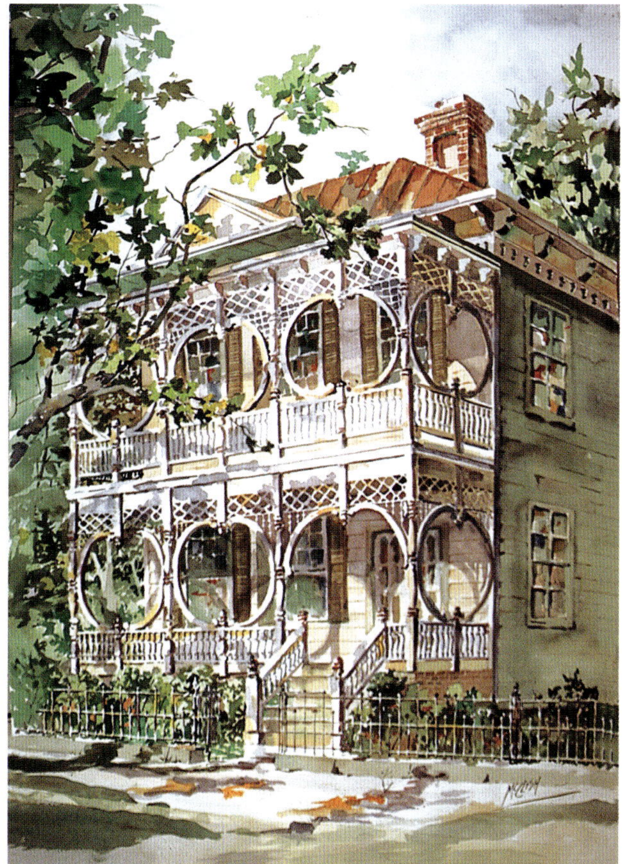

Savannah Lace, *32 x 44", 140 lb. Arches*

Savannah Lace

In downtown Savannah, Georgia, there is a large historical area that is filled with old period homes. Just outside the perimeter of that area, I came upon this house that I nicknamed "Savannah Lace." It appeared to me that the architect went wild on the design of the front of the house. I studied it and finally sat down and made a value sketch. In the small scale, all the details were lost. I finally took some photographs and decided to paint it once back in my studio. When that time came, I again looked at the photograph and value sketch of that house and decided that due to all the details it would take a large sheet of paper to do it justice. From a roll of 140-pound Arches cold press, I cut a 32 x 44 sheet of watercolor paper and started work. The basic drawing in this picture was very time consuming, even though it was intended to be a loose watercolor. Finally, I picked up a brush and went to work with more negative painting than positive. By negative, I mean that I had to paint around all the crosshatch, circular, and other white areas because I do not use Chinese White in my palette. When that was done, various areas were treated as planes and were glazed over. In the close-up view, you can see the negative painting.

Set-up for Painting on Location

Painting on location should be a fun experience. Of course, there are a few drawbacks, such as bad weather, especially with rain or a wind that can blow away your easel and painting. Some other nuisances can be: a hot, relentless sun, insects that bite, and passersby who stop to watch you and want to chat. You can easily deal with nature's irritants (see item 10). However, it takes some doing to put up with those people who insist on looking over your shoulder as you paint, and, worse, break your concentration by talking to you. I know some artists who are bothered by these rash interruptions and don't hesitate to let these spectators know about it. I just ignore them. If you find that hard to do, then a good way to deal with this problem is to find a remote place where you can paint in solitude. I very often do that.

Once I settle on a spot and set down my bag of tools, I survey the scene and pick the area that looks interesting, a vista from which I can decide on an interesting composition. I then unpack and go to work.

I have been over much of the world to paint and to teach. While packing for my painting outings is now second nature to me, I still approach that task with a great amount of care. In fact, I have a checklist that I pack with my

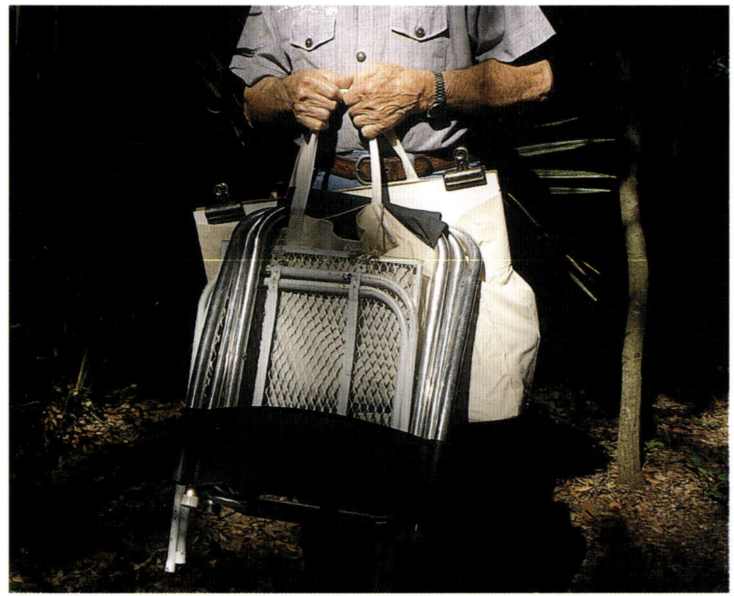

My On-location Bag of Tools

Here is a view of my bag all packed for going outside into the big wide world to sketch and paint. Yes, it does look cluttered but it is organized clutter. Back in the studio, when everything is put away, the bag flattens out and is easily stowed.

supplies. I check off each item before I leave to make sure I don't omit anything. I have had students show up with all the bells and whistles only to discover that they have forgotten their brushes and, yes, even a palette. Here's a list of what I take with me when I go out to paint:

My Checklist

1. ☐ Lightweight stool or folding chair
2. ☐ Lightweight easel
3. ☐ Container for water
4. ☐ Small box for paints and brushes
5. ☐ Small bag for sketching pencils
6. ☐ Sketchbook
7. ☐ Lightweight board for paper
8. ☐ Clips to hold the paper to the board
9. ☐ Palette (preferably plastic)
10. ☐ Materials for the elements (i.e. hat, sunblock etc.)
11. ☐ General cleanup materials
12. ☐ Portable table
13. ☐ Carryall tote

1. *Lightweight stool or folding chair.* Art supply shops also stock folding chairs that are reasonably priced and quite light in weight. I sit on a folding camping stool to paint. Sitting down puts me close to my water supply container and any other items that I've placed on the ground. Art supply shops stock folding chairs that are reasonably priced and quite light in weight.

2. *A simple lightweight easel.* My easel is one adapted from a camera tripod. Four metal clips hold the paper on the board.

3. *Container for water.* The mouth of the container should be large enough to get at the water with any size of brush. I use two wide mouth plastic containers with tight covers to prevent leaking. Why two? Sometimes your water supply gets dirty and may contaminate your washes. When that happens, you'll want to have a clean supply.

4. *A small box to hold one tube of every color.* I also recommend a

rolled container, such as a mailing tube, to hold brushes. In the absence of one, a plain box will do.

5. *A bag to hold several #2 and 6B pencils.* A sharpener and a kneaded eraser are also necessary to have on hand.

6. *A sketchbook.* It should have a hard cover and be roughly 8 x 10 in size. With any book smaller than this, it's difficult to get any details. Anything larger is cumbersome, takes too much time to sketch and is difficult to carry.

7. *A lightweight board for your paper.* It should be cut to fit a half-sheet (15 x 22") of watercolor paper. The thinnest commercial plywood is 3-ply (1/4" thick). While you could get other different kinds of plywood that are many layered and of different thickness, the standard plywood I have just referred to is ideal and holds its shape. You need a board that has a little bit of weight and is sturdy. Even a slight breeze will lift a light board, such as Foamcore, off into the atmosphere.

8. *Clips to hold the paper to the board.* There are all types from which to choose.

9. *A palette, preferably made of plastic.* My palette is wrapped in a plastic bag to prevent any colors from leaking.

10. *Materials for the element.* You'll need a hat, sunshade, sun block and insect repellent.

11. *General cleanup.* I use paper towels to blot color, to mop up spills and to use for other cleaning purposes. Rather than carry a full roll, I usually tear off a number of sheets, fold them and stick them in my carryall.

Going Outside to Paint and Sketch

I may look like a carpetbagger of years ago but, actually, I am an artist going out to paint on location. My carryall bag may look cluttered, but I have not found any way to make it neat without adding considerable weight and size. And though the folding camp style seat with the back is a little bulky, it is a necessary item, as is the folding table made of aluminum. That seat back allows me to lean back and take a look at my picture every once in a while. On the minus side, my hat could have a larger brim; on the plus side, though, a larger brim would make it easier for the hat to blow off. Everything necessary for a location-painting trip is inside or hanging outside on one of the handles of the bag that's pictured here. That even includes a very light jacket. The bag does get a bit heavy when walking for a long distance. For that reason, I had metal rings sewn inside the top opening to accommodate a shoulder strap. It's somewhere in the bag.

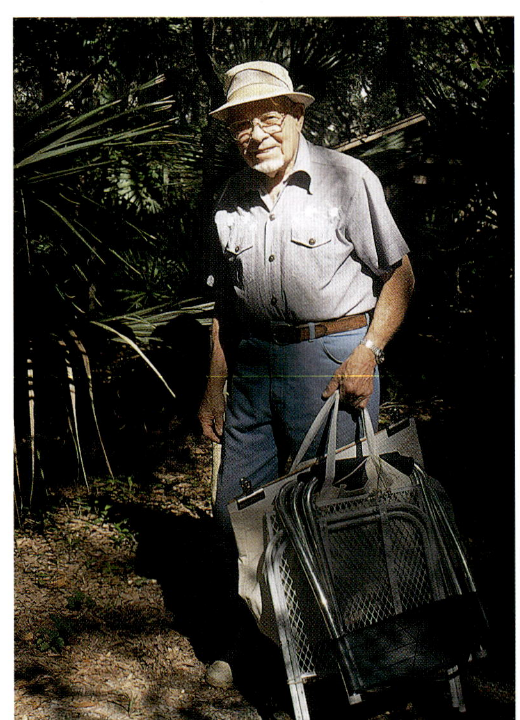

12. *A portable table.* This is for your palette and other items you customarily place on your painting table. Make sure to get the smallest, lightest folding TV-type table you can find. I have a small, lightweight, metal table that folds up quite compactly.

13. *Finally, you need a carryall.* Quite adequate is a canvas bag that is large enough to hold all of the items listed. Better yet, if it has a pocket on the outside for your sketchbook and pencil bag. Try to get one with a clip-on shoulder strap to make it easier for you to carry the whole shebang.

Summing Up

When going out to paint our beautiful world, try to take just what you will need and nothing more. Since it's important for me to be comfortable, but not to the point that I will start dozing off, my lightweight folding stool, which is far from a leather recliner, will prevent that from happening. I've clipped my watercolor paper to the board at the top and bottom and I have placed it on my easel that I've set at a slight angle. My very small folding table is on my right side to hold my palette and brushes. The water container is on the ground directly in front of me. My carryall bag, with everything else in it, sits on the ground at my left where I can get to it easily. Everything that I use will fit either in the bag or hang on the outside. My hardcover sketchbook fits in a pocket on the outside of the bag along with my pencils. In a matter of minutes, I can set up, be drawing and then busy at work with brushes and colors.

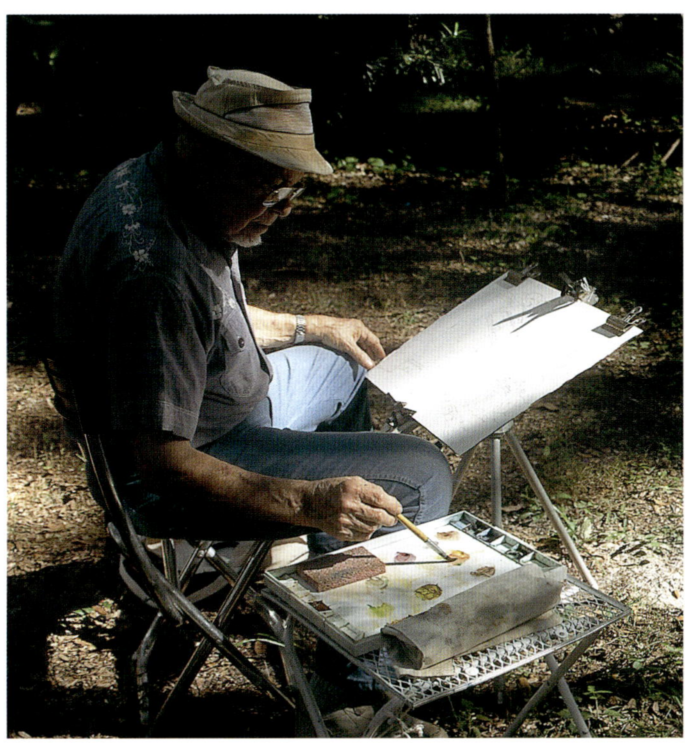

With Materials at Hand, I am Ready to Paint

Here I have just finished a sketch of a Florida scene with a palmetto as my center of interest. With brush in hand, I am ready to paint and have fun. This is the time when many artists get intimidated when someone walking by stops to look. Always remember that you are an artist. The person standing at your side, looking on, is probably not an artist but is interested in what you are doing. Whether it's drawing, painting, or both, it's probably something that's something he or she can't do. Go at it with confidence.

Simplify Your Composition

Finding something to paint along Rocky Neck, the picturesque artists' colony in Gloucester Harbor, isn't very hard. All of Gloucester, and neighboring Rockport to boot, teems with paintable vistas. While walking along the neck, I saw two dories tied up at a dock; they intrigued me. I made a quick sketch of the scene. I immediately saw that it took in too much. The structures on the dock competed for attention with the two dories moored below. Was my painting going to be of two dories or would it feature the buildings with the two dories docked nearby?

The dories as subject matter were what initially had intrigued me so I decided that they would be featured. I consigned the dock and building to subsidiary roles. Another problem: it was dead low tide, which left a boring expanse of pilings showing. Not willing to take the time to wait for the tide to come in, I took some artistic liberties and changed low tide to about half, shortening the pilings in the process. The harbor was calm with just a few wavelets playing on the surface. To be able to show a few reflections in the water, I decided on a high horizon, which made room below the boats to show the reflections. That moved the dock and its structure back and up in the scene, thereby eliminating most of the building, with only a hint of its presence in evidence. Now with a better plan in mind, I started the drawing over. The two dominant dories were sketched in not quite two-thirds of the way up on the page. A ladder was on the extreme left of the dock almost out of the picture. I moved it over a little, left of center behind the dories.

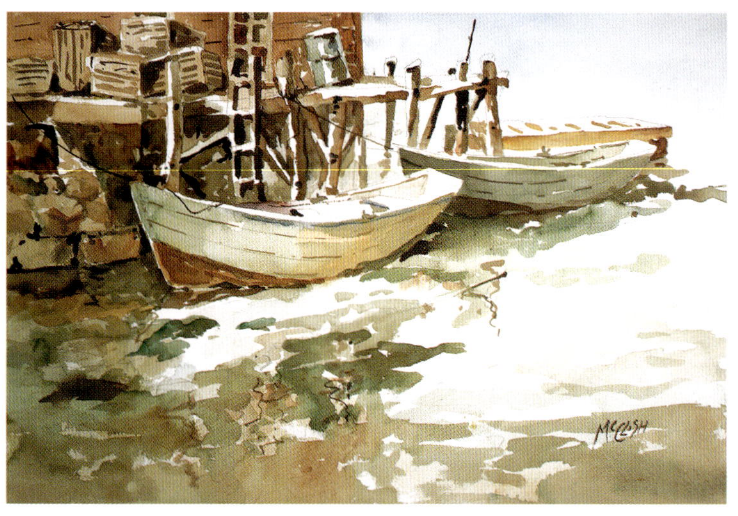

4

Two Dories
in Gloucester, Massachusetts

In the first sketch that I made of the two dories in Gloucester, I felt that the composition was too busy.

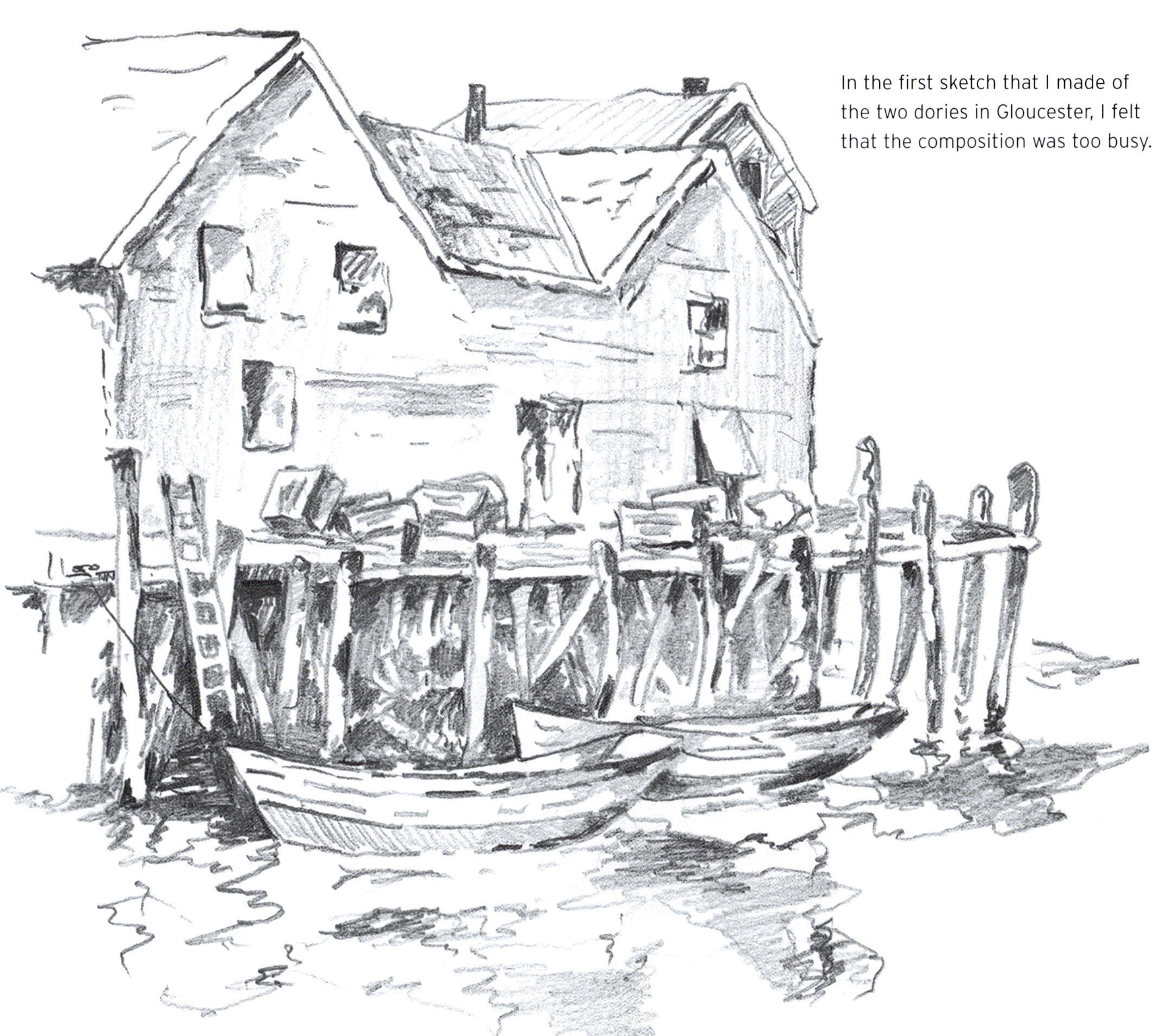

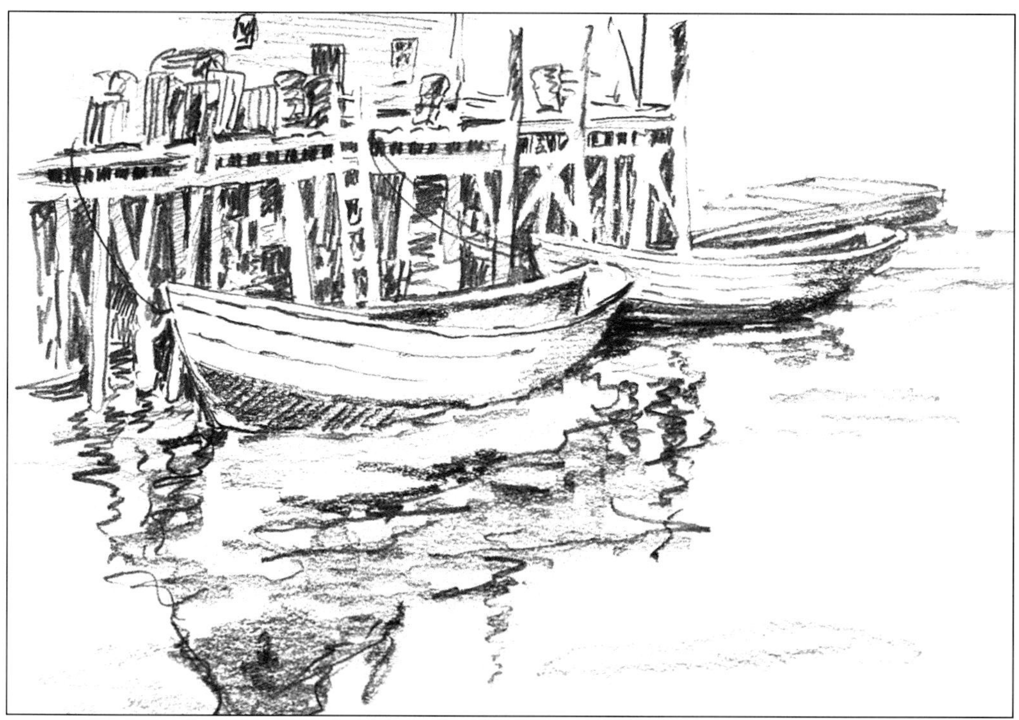

My second sketch shows the dories as the major elements. I was convinced to use it for my painting.

Most of the docks in Gloucester Harbor have random spaced pilings, with some leaning in a jumbled pattern. This one was no different and I did have fun helping out that pattern in my sketch. The top of the dock was drawn in next, followed by the portion of the building that was still in the picture. To make the dock more interesting, a group of lobster traps some distance away was moved to the left end of the dock. The next important item was to decide on the direction of light. It was almost noon with the sun high in the sky, and the shadow pattern did not read very well. I decided on having the light come in from the left front. With all those details in mind, I added values to the drawing, which helped to give it a sense of three dimensions. Also helping to get this effect was the way I overlapped objects in the composition, and, along with the use of perspective, I created that third dimension.

The perspective in the dories did its job, even though the lines of the boats curve in many directions and do not go obediently to a vanishing point anywhere. It is the overall mass of the boat that suggests perspective as it recedes. Even if the dory had some straight lines, probably none would recede to an orderly point as in most perspective drawings. Boats are always in motion even in very light breezes and the planes, curving or flat, are constantly changing direction. They just do not conform. I liked this sketch; I was ready to transfer it to the sheet of watercolor paper. It was a simple procedure to simplify the tonal sketch into a minimal line drawing that would be ready to paint. I saved the values and details to be put in with a paintbrush.

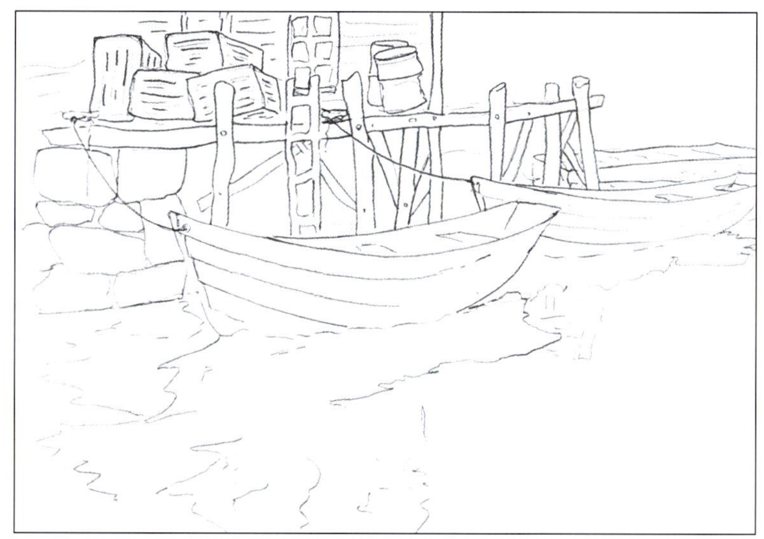

STEP 1 ▶

Using my second sketch of the two dories as a model, I made a line drawing for the watercolor. Even though it was a simple drawing, it still conveyed the two dories tied to a dock. Details under the dock between the pilings were only hinted at. I did not want to do a "paint-by-numbers" in that area. It would be a looser watercolor if I were to ad lib, and, I might add, it would be more fun to do.

STEP 2 ▼

With the sketch done, it was time to start painting. I made a very light puddle in the palette, mixing green and blue, and with a large number 20 round brush, I started the painting. Helping to relieve the monotony of white paper, the blue-green tint was started in the upper right sky area and continued down and across to the left, leaving the white of the paper for the dock, float and boats. Notice that I ignored the horizon. It was just implied. A random shaped area was left white in the water below the dories for reflections to be added later. As the wash continued, a little more green pigment was added to the puddle. It is important to keep the first wash very light. You can always make it darker but it takes a scrub-out to go lighter in value. The wash looked a little monotonous so I dropped a touch of Burnt Sienna in the lower center of the still wet wash. It is hardly noticeable, but it does mute the green dominance of this wash.

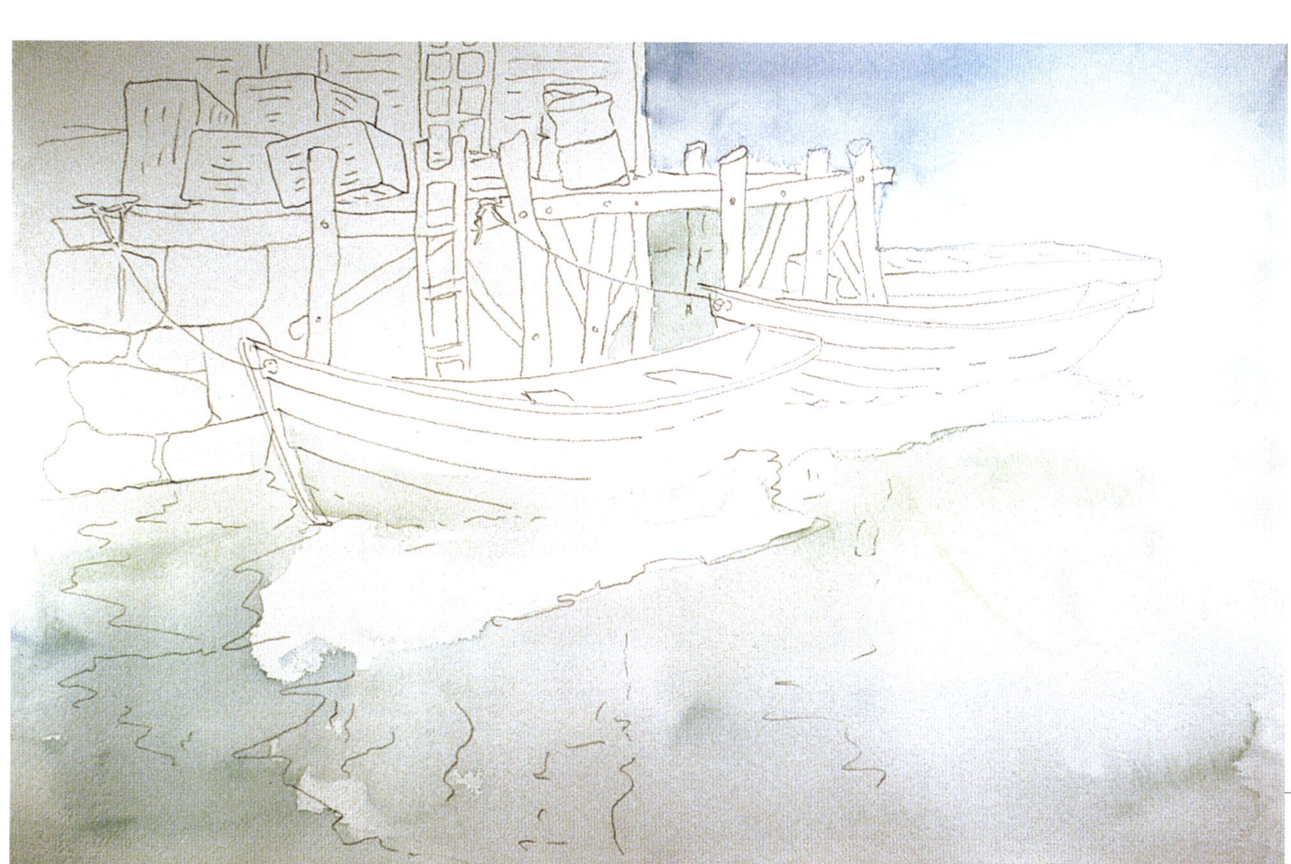

With a 3/4-inch flat brush, a pale mixture of New Gamboge with a little tinge of Cadmium Red Light and Burnt Sienna was made and applied to the side of the forward dory. The center of the side of the dory seemed a little deep in value so I blotted it with a paper towel. This will be a highlight in the completed painting. Adding some Thalo Blue to the puddle, I painted the rear of the side of the boat where it turns under and blended it up into the first wash. A small amount of Thalo Green and Burnt Sienna was added along with some water to lighten it. I painted the rear dory. It looked just like the color for the stone jetty to the left so I gave it a base coat. Adding more Thalo Blue to the puddle to cool it off, I painted the areas behind the ladder under the dock. A little more Burnt Sienna and water was mixed into the same puddle and it was just the right color for the shadow side of the lobster pots. On the foremost pot, I just painted in between the slats leaving them white. Up to this point, I used only two small puddles of paint by adjusting them many times. This gave me color harmony.

With a mixture of Thalo Green and Burnt Sienna, I painted some of the reflections in the water of the underside of the dock and the main dory. To help separate the boat from its background, the dark mixture was carried through under the stern of the same dory. That dark patch looked so good that I continued it along the waterline of the rear dory. I painted the area between the pilings with that same dark color. The backside of the dock was sitting on a pile of boulders that ended about even with the right end of the building. This is where the dark shadow area under the dock stopped. We cannot paint the pilings light over dark background because watercolor is a transparent medium and we have no opaque light colors, as in other media. In oil painting, adding white to colors makes those colors opaque. Our white is the white of the paper. This means that to have the pilings in sunlight, we have to paint around them. Leaving objects as the white of the paper is called negative painting. On the right end of the dock, where there was a light water area behind the pilings, they were painted

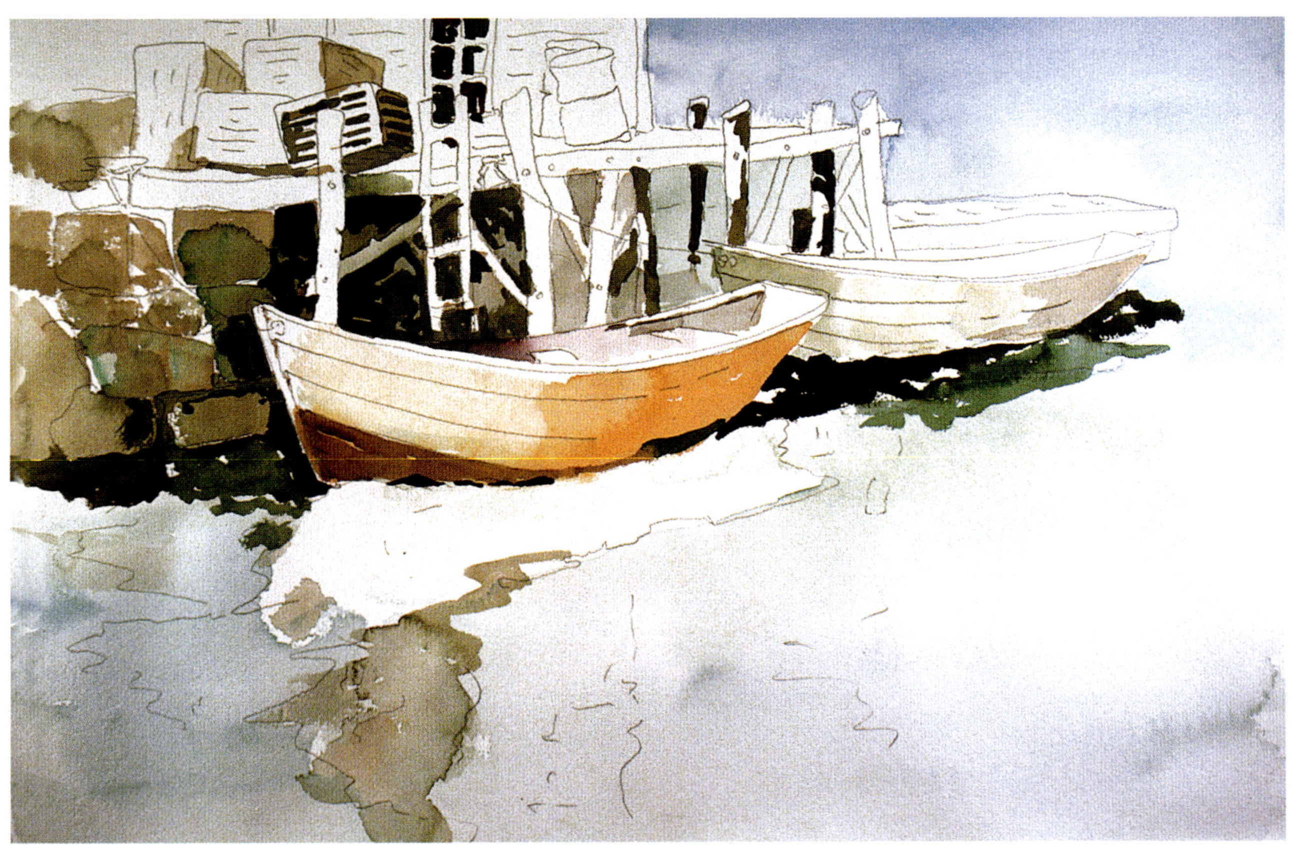

positive, that is, dark against light. This light-dark, dark-light variation is called alternation. It livens up a painting and creates interest. At this point, I had done enough background painting. It was time to start modeling the dories. The sides of the boats were built with overlapping planks running lengthwise and they needed to be at least partially defined. The plank lines were defined better at the bow, the closest point of the dory. As they faded away toward the rear of the boat, they could be only suggested with broken lines. With a rigger brush picking up some dark value, I painted the lines in a lost-and-found way.

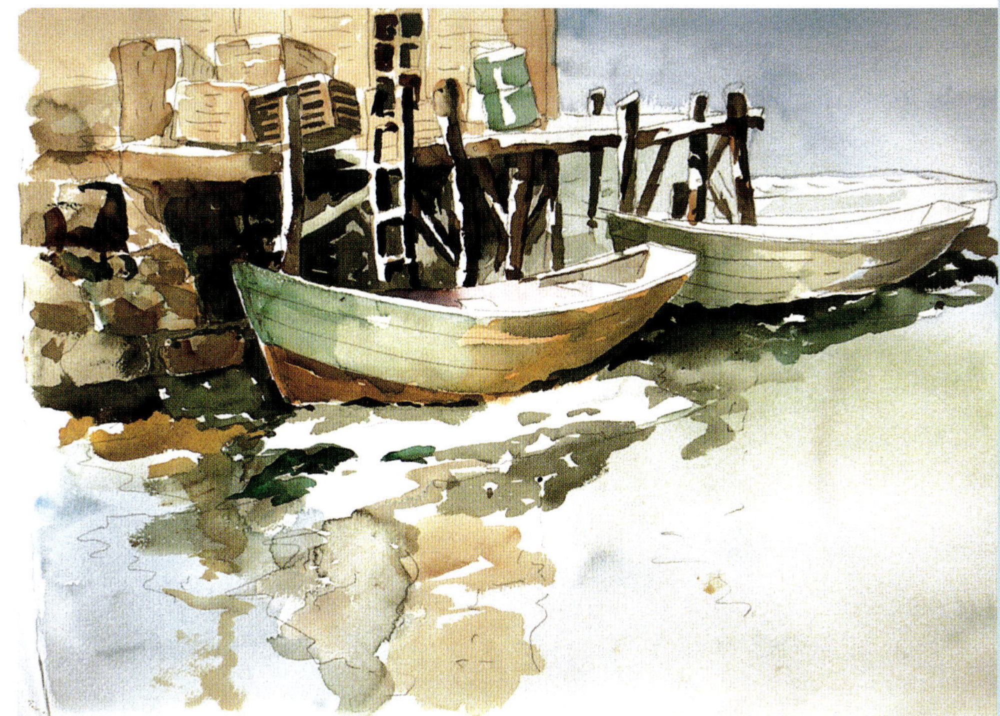

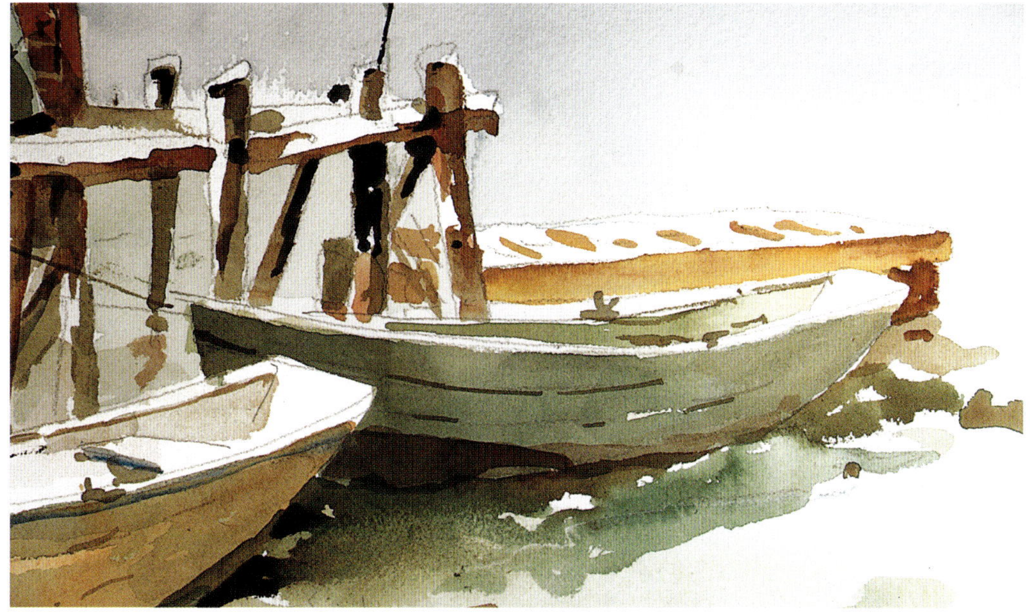

STEP 5 ▲

As a plane recedes (the side of the boat is a curving plane receding to the right) it has to change in some manner, so I had it lose some definition and texture. The bottom paint on the topsides shows along the water's edge. It is interesting to note that the upper edge of this reddish paint does not follow the waterline. It follows the plank lines and sweeps up forward and aft. I used a combination of Cadmium Red Light, Burnt Sienna and just a touch of Thalo Blue that was dabbed in while the wash was still wet. It would be confusing to use the same red mixture on the right dory. I mixed a dominant blue in the red puddle and painted the waterline on the right dory.

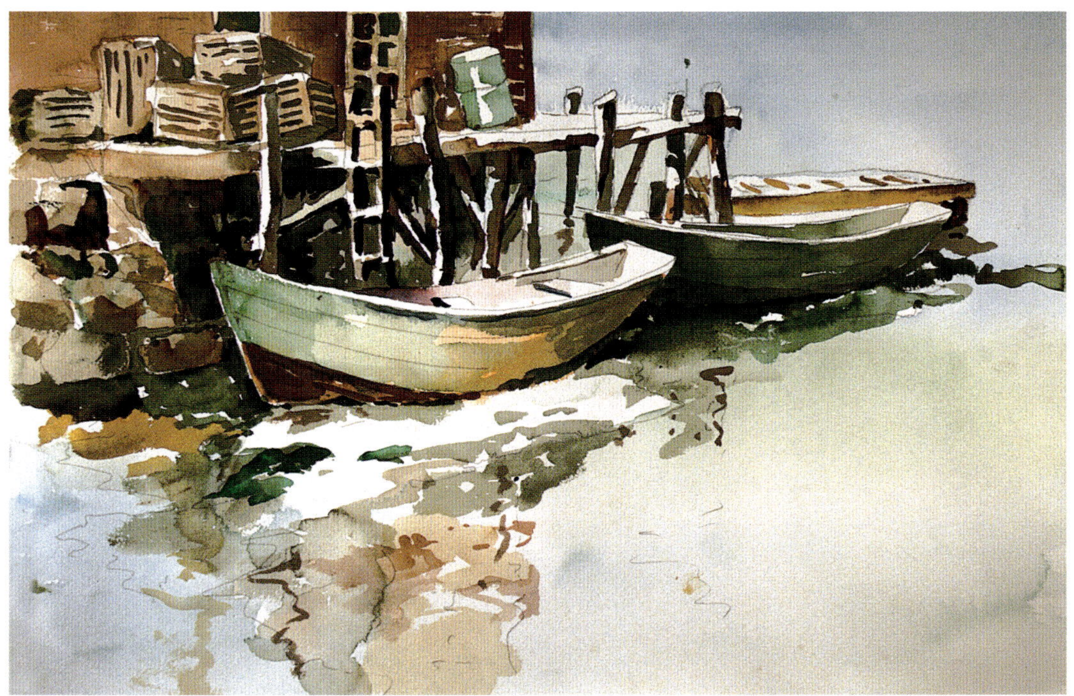

STEP 6 ▲

Since many of the fishing
boats in the northeast are painted a green
color, why not paint the dories to match?
Using Thalo Green with a little Burnt Sienna
mixed in to get the passive green color, I
painted the front boat. The bow received the
darkest value that faded into the highlight
area that was blotted out a little left of the
center of the side of the boat. The stern, or
rear, of the dory was partly in shadow due to
its curvature; its color was muted or grayed
with the addition of some Alizarin Crimson. I
tamed down the same gray green puddle
with Burnt Sienna and painted the side of
the rear dory.

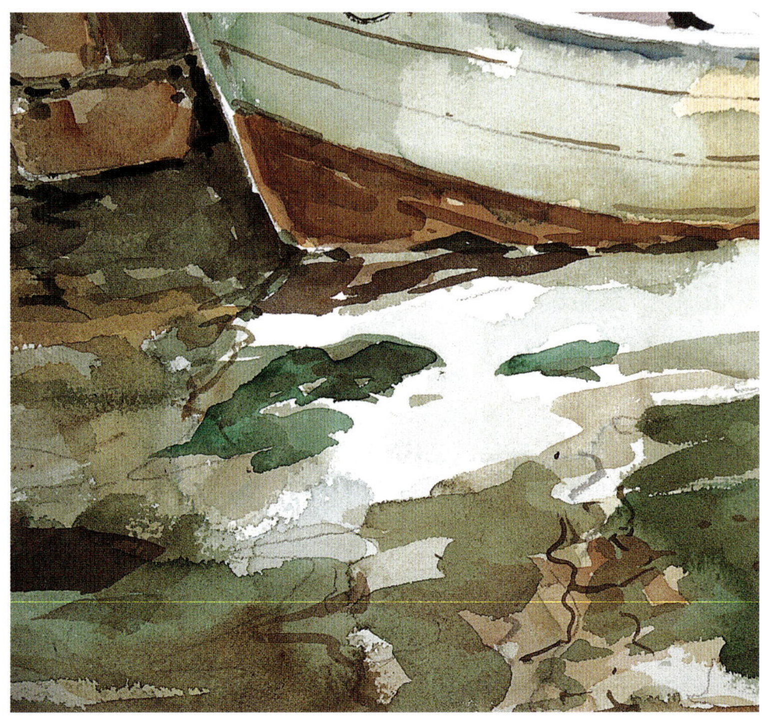

STEP 7 ▶

It was time to step back and
take a look at the picture. The lower right
corner was a little too light and it competed
with the center of interest — the dories.
Covering it up with my hand, I got into
the picture much better. Mixing up a fairly
light green-blue-Burnt Sienna color, I
added some details to that section of the
foreground water.

STEP 8 ▶

Moving up to the shadows behind the ladder, I strengthened the mixture making it very dark and negatively painted that area. In the same puddle, Burnt Sienna was added. The color was thinned with some water, and I reinforced the rest of the shadow area under the dock using varied values for interest.

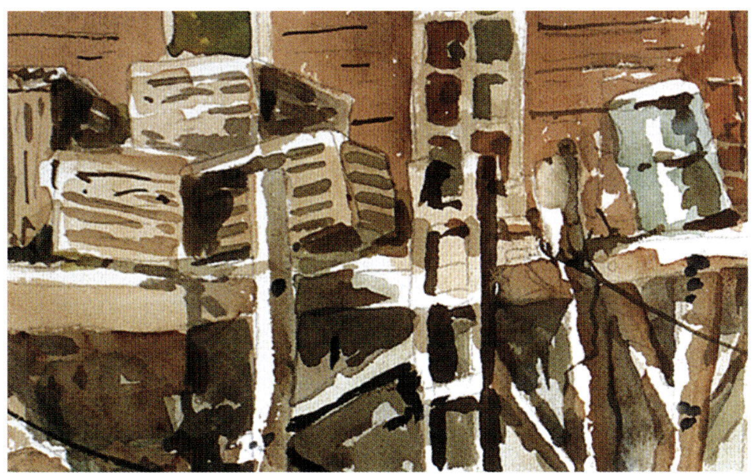

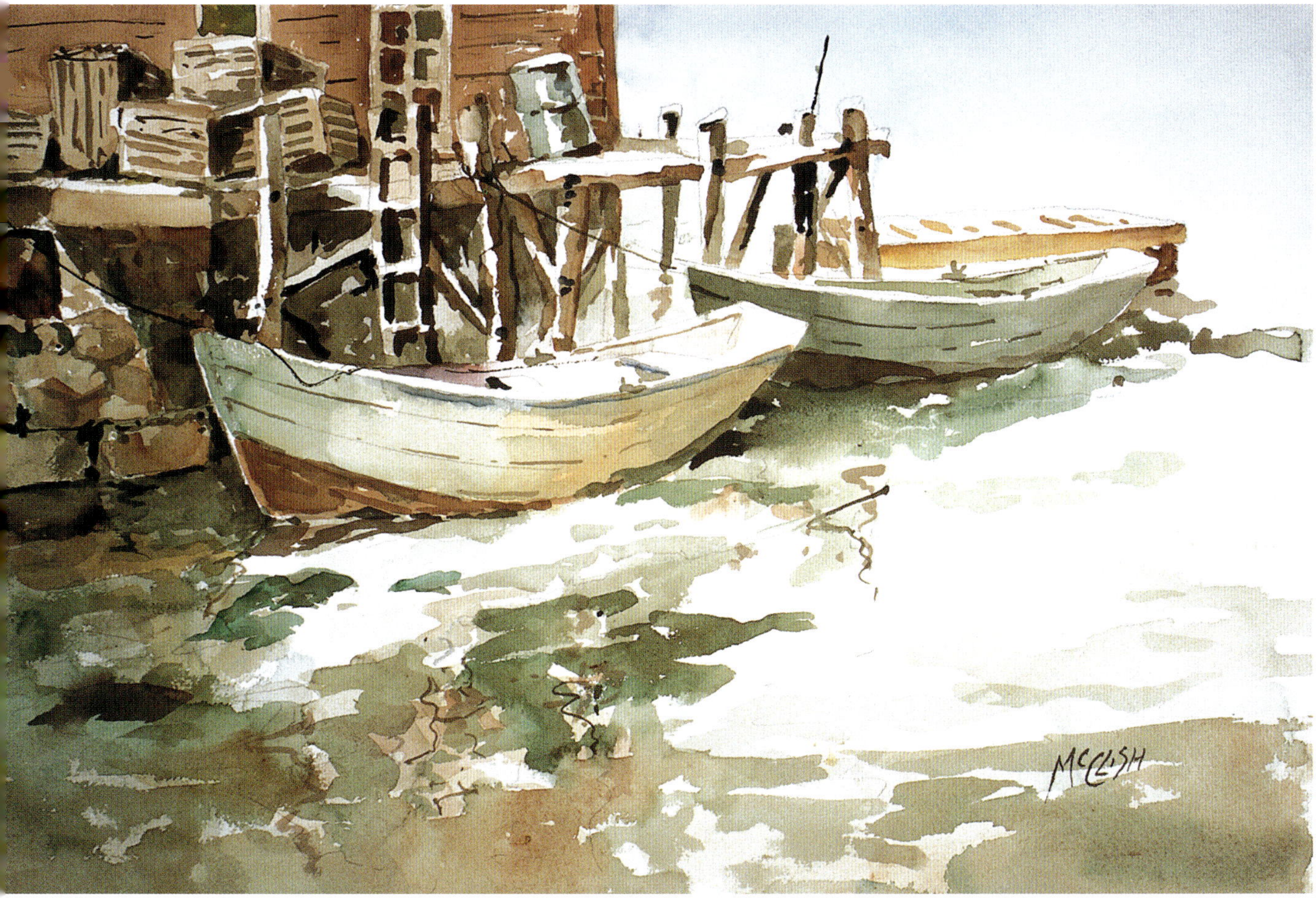

Gloucester Dories, 15 x 22", 140 lb. Arches

STEP 9 ▲

The finished painting. Using Burnt Sienna, the slats on some of the lobster pots were emphasized. One of the main rules in watercolor is to quit while you're still ahead.

Working with a Low Horizon

Pemaquid Lighthouse sits on the rocky Atlantic shoreline about halfway up the Maine coast. I decided on a low horizon view for my painting. My vantage point was on the rocky ledges down below the scene on the ocean side. Just the top of the lighthouse was showing. I made a value sketch in my sketchbook. It seemed to make a better composition by emphasizing the height of the bank in front of the lighthouse. Tucking the lighthouse and other structures in its area down behind the rock and foliage, I thought, would give a little intrigue to the scene.

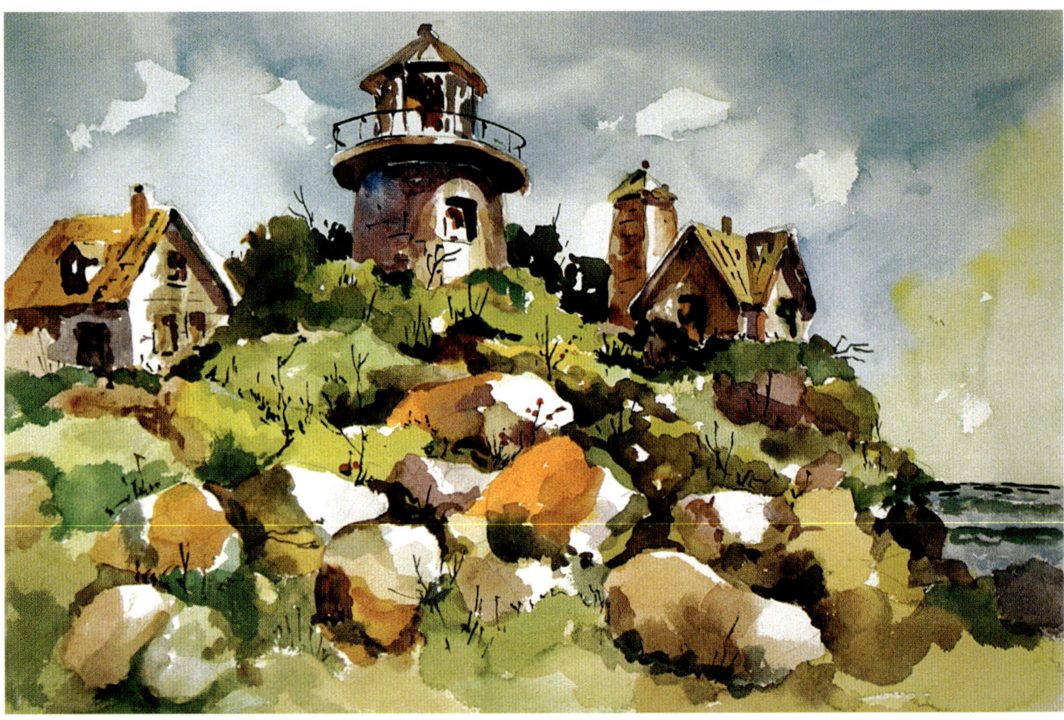

5

A Lighthouse
in Pemaquid, Maine

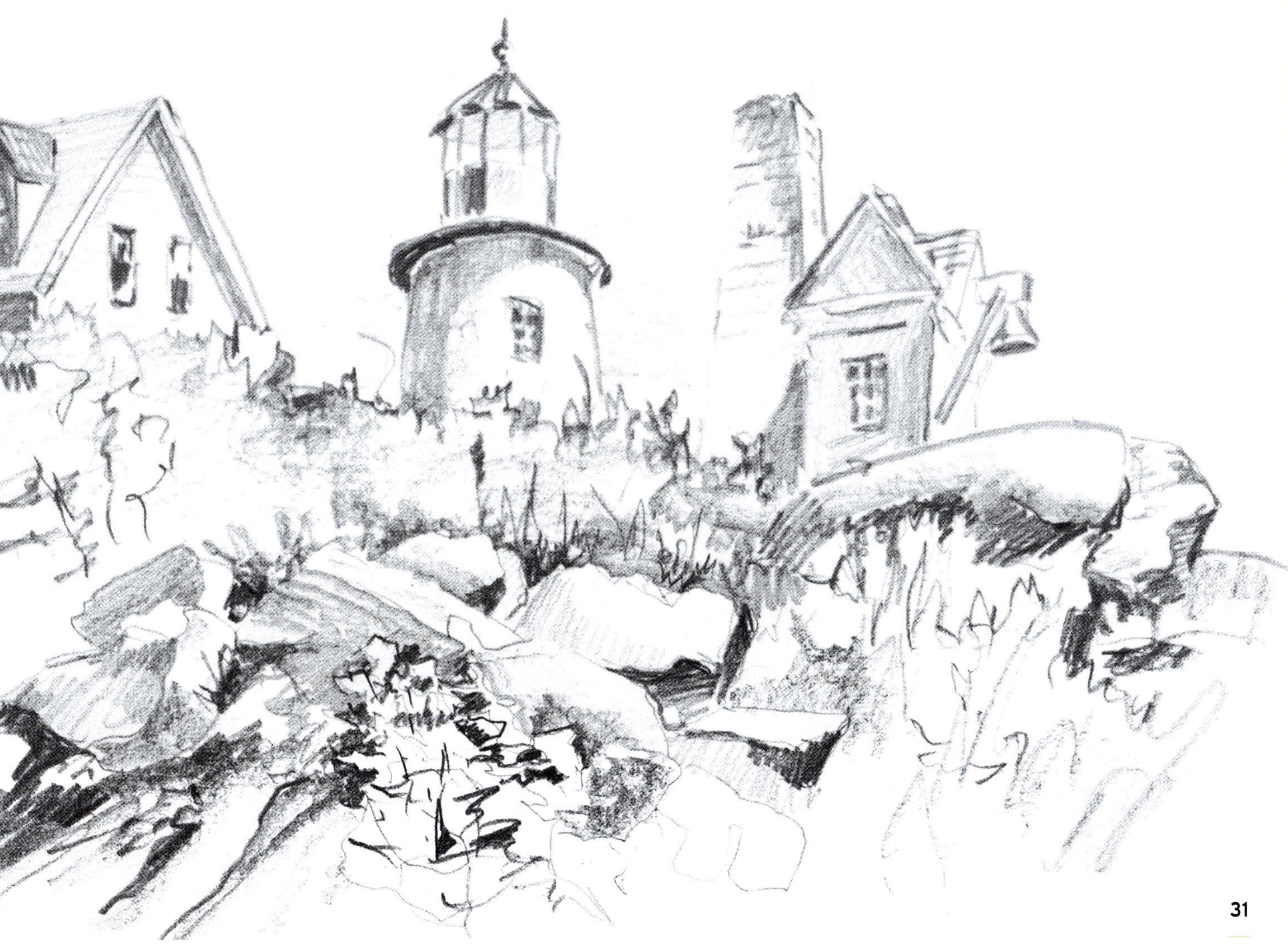

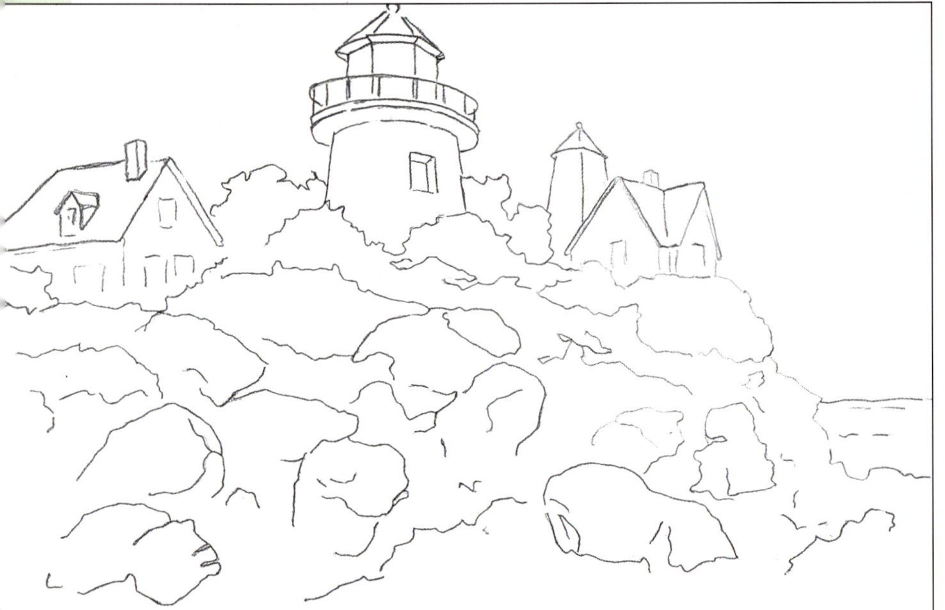

STEP 1 ◄

To begin the watercolor, I captured the scene in a very limited line drawing made on 140-pound cold pressed paper. The pencil drawing was minimal, with just the right amount of detail needed to guide me through the painting. Too many beginning painters feel that they need a finished pencil drawing over which to paint their color. What you see here, and in other sketches in this book is all you need.

STEP 2 ►

My first washes were placed on Pemaquid Lighthouse. The sky in this picture was secondary to the lighthouse, the main focal point, and the associated buildings. It should say "sky" but not stand out. With this thought in mind, I dampened the sky area with a number 18 round brush, and I left some areas dry. As the painting progresses, some of these dry areas will be washed over and some might be left light for clouds. This prior wetting of the paper helps to keep me from having overlapping and unwanted brush strokes. Mixing up a fairly light mixture of Thalo Blue, I started to lay in a wash from left to right. Instead of a smooth, even wash, I tried using a scrubbing motion to vary the intensity of the blue paint. The sky is a receding plane and it must change in value, definition, texture, or color as it goes back. To get this effect, I dropped a little touch of New Gamboge in some areas. I also introduced some Burnt Sienna to mute the sharp color of Thalo Blue paint. On the left side of the lighthouse structure, the sky wash was painted right over the edge of the lighthouse. This is one of the tricks of loose watercolor. It always helps to have color harmony as your painting progresses. Next, I mixed a green puddle on the palette using Thalo Blue and New Gamboge. It was painted in loosely, forming the line of foliage just under the lighthouse. Adding some more New Gamboge to the puddle of green along with some water to lighten its value, I washed in a second row of foliage just below, leaving an irregular white area in between. I hoped, as the painting progressed, that this would be worked into something like a stage set. On the left side, I added more water and continued the wash down to the corner. From there, moving across the paper to the right, I continued the wash with more water to lighten it and I also added a small touch of Burnt Sienna. In the lower right corner, I pulled in some more paint to the mixture and another irregular area was painted in. I then deepened the original blue mixture that I used in the sky and painted in the sea on the lower right side of the paper. With this last addition, much of the picture had received some varied light value washes leaving only some random white areas. In this first stage of the painting, green and blue dominated.

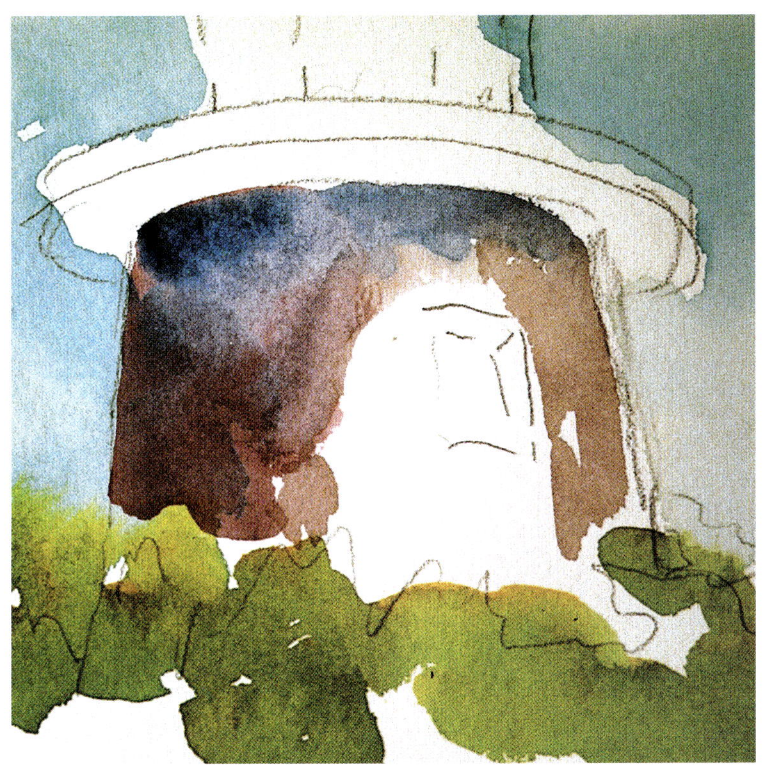

STEP 3 ▶

Here we see a close-up of the first lavender color that I painted on the shadow area of the lighthouse. A little of the complementary color, New Gamboge, was casually added to some areas of this wash to make the shadow area of the light-house a little more interesting. While it was still wet, I painted a bit of Thalo Blue in just under the walkway. On the right, or sunlit side of the structure, there was a thin watered-down pink value placed vertically on the wrap-around area to help get a three-dimensional effect.

STEP 4 ▼

The next stage was the addition of the first major darks in the painting. These darks may have seemed to be a little intense, but with the addition of other slightly lighter darks and various half tones, they melded into the picture. Also, by establishing major dark values early in the painting, it was much easier to get those half darks later on. I mixed Thalo Green with Burnt Sienna and New Gamboge until I achieved a warm dark green. It was then laid in on the foliage next to the lighthouse on its lower right side. Notice that by putting this very dark wash next to the lighthouse, it separated the sky, lighthouse, and the green foliage, which gave a feeling of depth to the painting. Working progressively down from the initial dark value, other lighter, warm and cool darks were placed. I adjusted the original dark green mix several times with additions of New Gamboge, Burnt Sienna and Thalo Green, changing this puddle alternately from warm to cool and the reverse. I lightened its value by adding water and then I darkened it with more paint. I took great care when I added water to this mix. It was very easy to get a watery light value puddle that would look vibrant when wet but would fade away when dry.

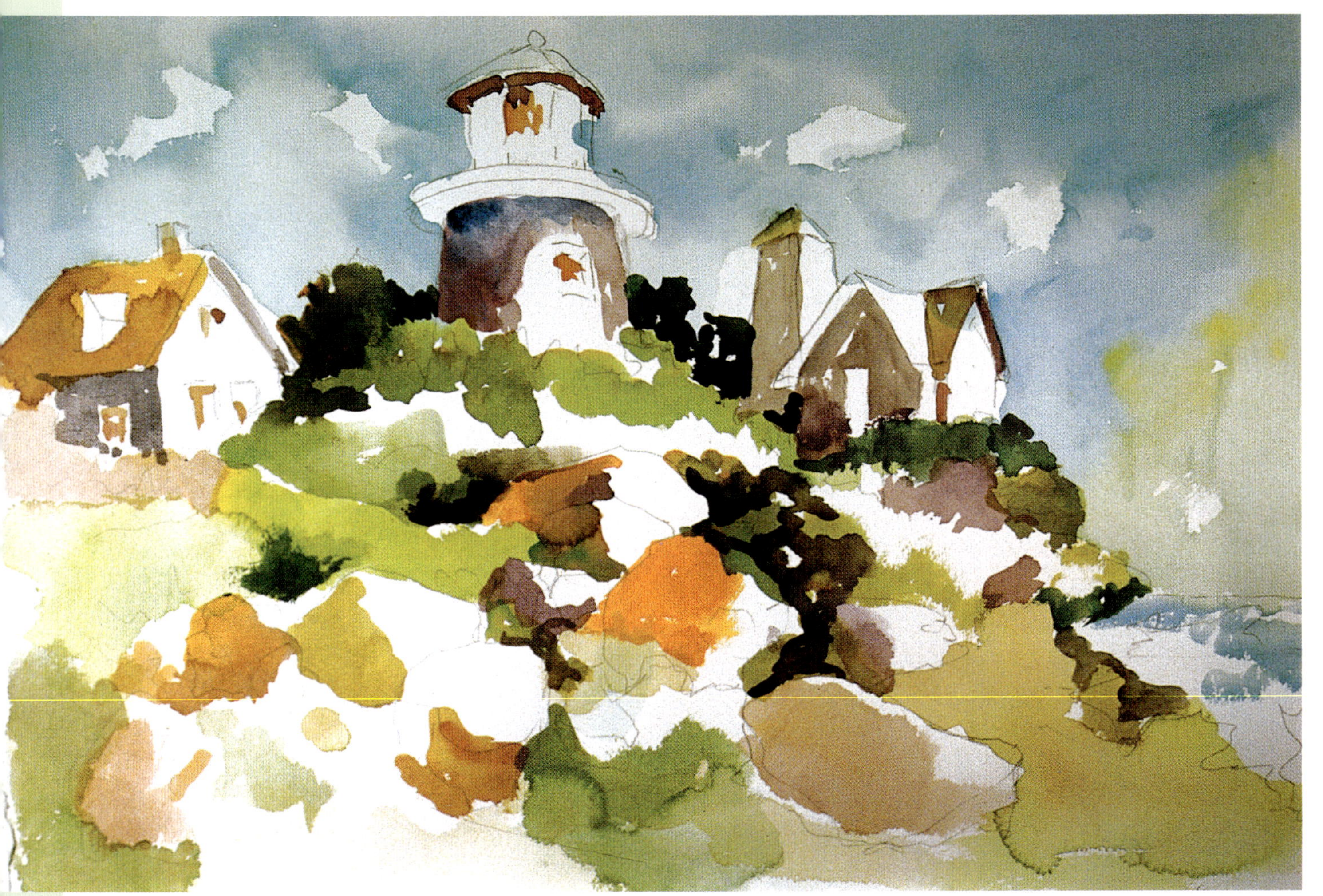

STEP 5

At this point in the painting's progress, I started modeling the rocks with negative painting around some areas using varied warm and cool greens in the middle of the composition just under the lighthouse. Putting a fairly dark value green wash in the foliage next to the white sunlit area of the large central rock separated it from the background. I used this painting style in various places down through the jumbled boulders to the lower right corner. On the shadow side of the rocks, values of those areas were varied from light to medium dark using a puddle of Burnt Sienna to start. Then, with alternate additions of Thalo Green, Thalo Blue and New Gamboge, I had fun alternating the shadow areas from warm to cool and back again. The intensities of these washes were also varied, giving lighter changes of value in the foreground. In the lower left corner, I used light values with subdued and watered-down mixtures of some of the puddles. This gave me color harmony. Underneath the walkway that went around the upper portion of the lighthouse was an area in complete shadow. I painted it using dark lavender with a fair portion of Thalo Blue in the mixture. I used this same dark value in the upper and right interior walls of the window just below. To carry this color outside the immediate area, I used it to paint the shadow side of the dormer on the house to the left, under the eaves on the tall slender building on the right and then under the eaves of the building in front of it. I used a slightly watered-down mixture of the same color with a little Burnt Sienna added in the shadow side of the windows in the house.

I reached the step that most beginners get to too soon—adding the details. I was ready to add the smaller details of the picture. For this, I switched to a number four round brush. But first, I finished the top of the lighthouse roof and refined the walkway around the top of the lighthouse. I then painted the outer band of the walkway leaving a small white area where the light hit. I placed color in some sections of the panes around the area that housed the lighthouse's lights. Under the eave of the roof, I painted a dark value strip, and placed a stronger shadow area on the shadow side of the tall structure to the right of the lighthouse. On the left side of the lighthouse, spots of the green foliage were deepened in value; I worked my way down through the rocky slope, and increased the value of certain areas of shadow in the foliage.

I painted dark washes around the rocks in some areas pushing the background back and bringing the rocks forward. There was a group of competing white areas on the rocks. Some dirty water from some of the paint puddles tamed that down. In this taming of the whites, I was sure to use watered-down color from varied puddles to create interest. Any color is usually better than a dead gray in shadow areas, either in cast shadows or the shadowed side. In the small building on the right, there was a bit of confusion on its left shadow side. Because it was still wet, I chose to let it dry. Once dry, the side of the house would have to be separated from foliage and that would take either a change in value or color or both on either the plane of the house or the foliage in front. I was ready to use a number two rigger brush to add the finishing details.

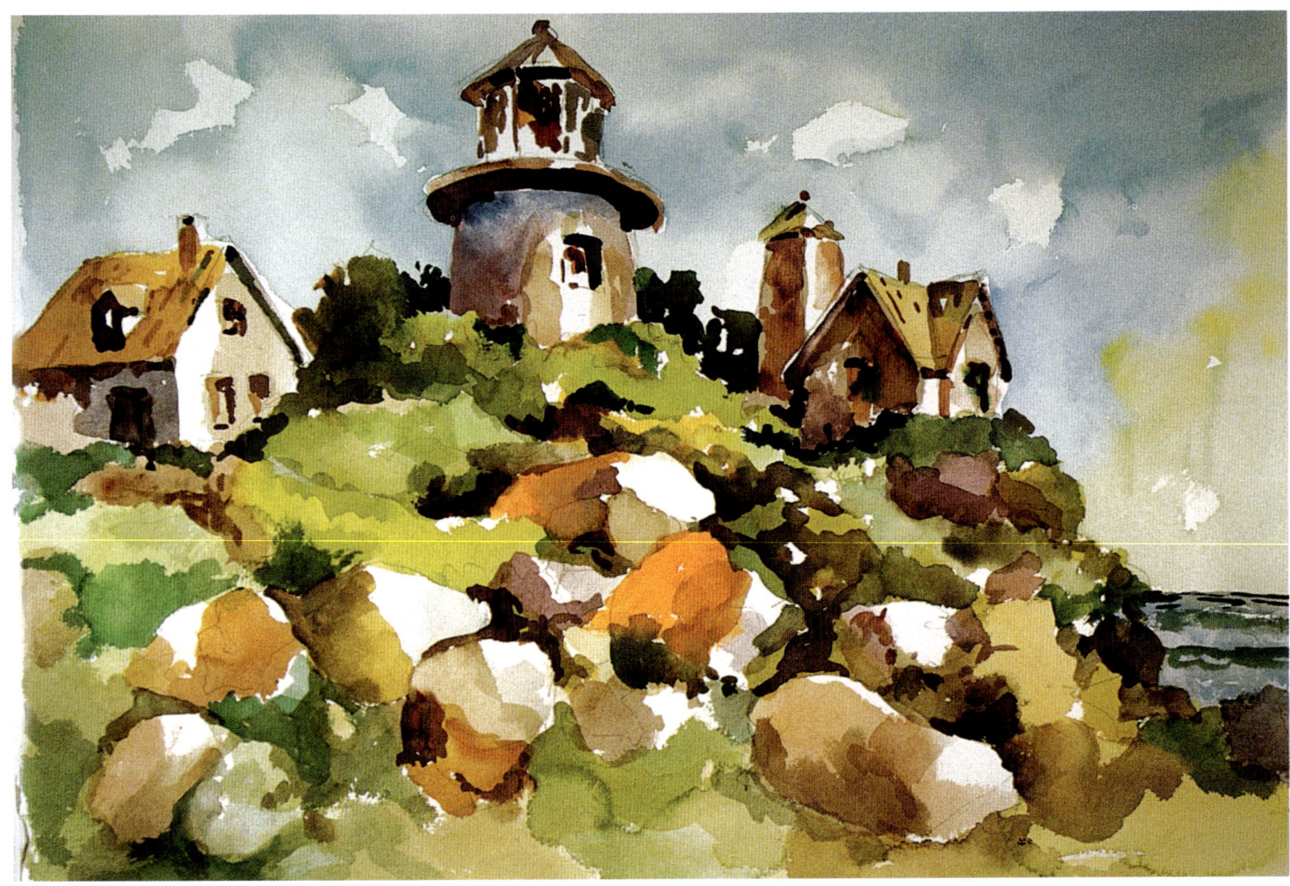

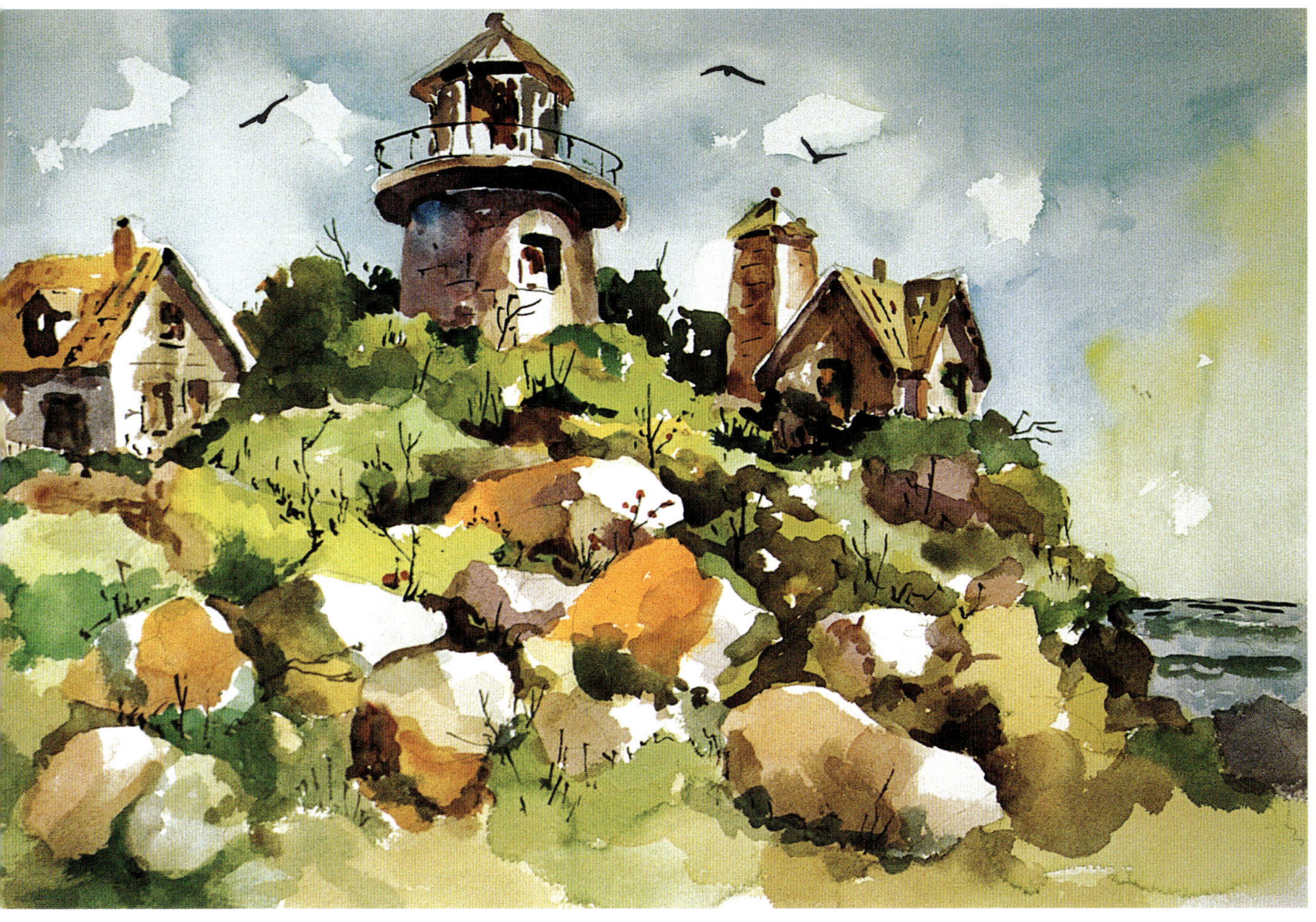

Pemaquid Lighthouse, 15 x 22", 140 lb. Arches

STEP 7

Using a fairly dark mixture of Burnt Sienna and Thalo Blue, I let the brush "dance around," which means that I scratched in little branches and weeds in and around the rocks. Then, I painted the railing on the walkway around the light. Please note that on each side, the arc of this railing continued around as it started to complete the oval. Next, I put little accent lines in places like one side and maybe the top of a window, and added branches in the foliage. In this outlining, I only suggested details, using a lost-and-found technique of hard-and-soft edges. In the foliage, some of the larger stems overlapped objects like rocks or structures that were above and behind them, which created a third dimension. On the skyline, there were some leafless branches that extended above the foliage line. Since there are always birds soaring around at the sea-shore, I placed two seagulls near each other in the sky on one side of the lighthouse and then put a lone bird in another location in the sky. **Please—do not make them all look like check marks.** There are three basic wing positions: up, down, and level. When birds are in flight their wings flap up and down or are stretched out almost level as they soar. Furthermore, birds do not always remain in level flight; they turn or bank at times. I always have fun giving them some action with strokes of my brush. Finally, in this picture, before I washed out the last brush I used, I placed the picture in a mat and viewed it from a distance. I spotted some obvious corrections that I then made and signed the picture.

Using Cast Shadows to Advantage

t was a beautiful sunny day on Majorca when I saw this little church. It looked lonesome sitting out in an isolated area of the island. There was a covered gate leading into the church entry. The garden that I could see over the gate seemed to say, "Draw and paint me." I made a value sketch in pencil and then a line drawing for a half-sheet watercolor. The sketch that I chose for my painting is pictured here. On the left side, I didn't finish all of the trees and foliage. At the time, I thought that none of it would have added anything of importance to the painting. I was right.

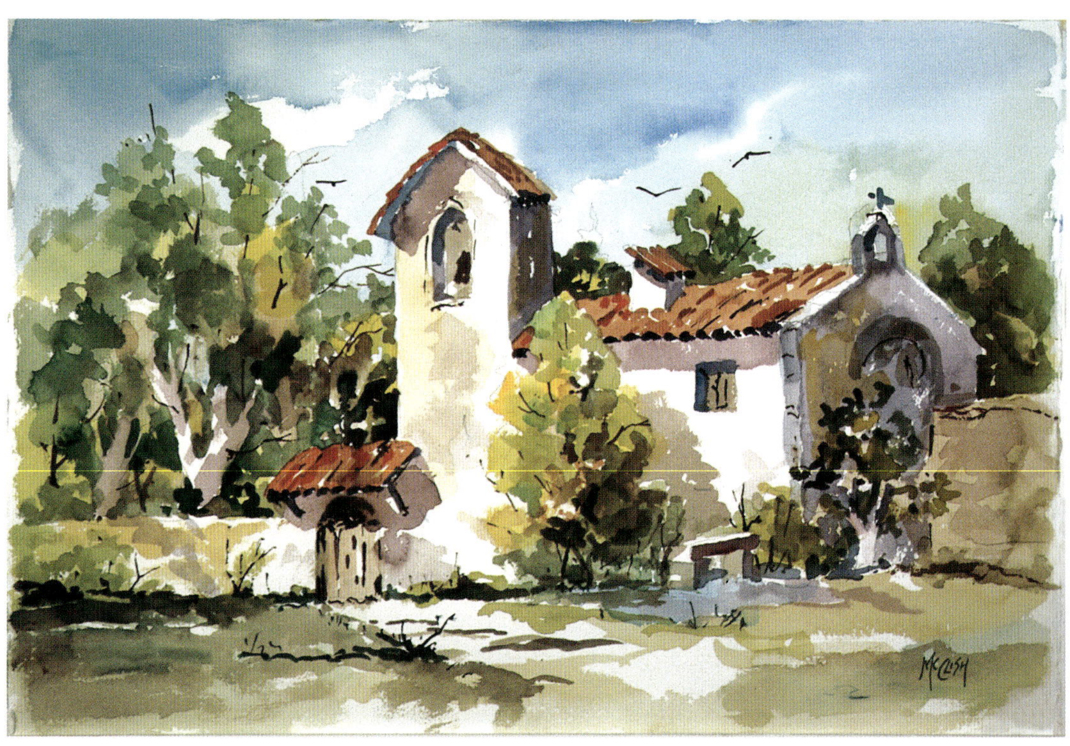

6

A Church
in Majorca, Spain

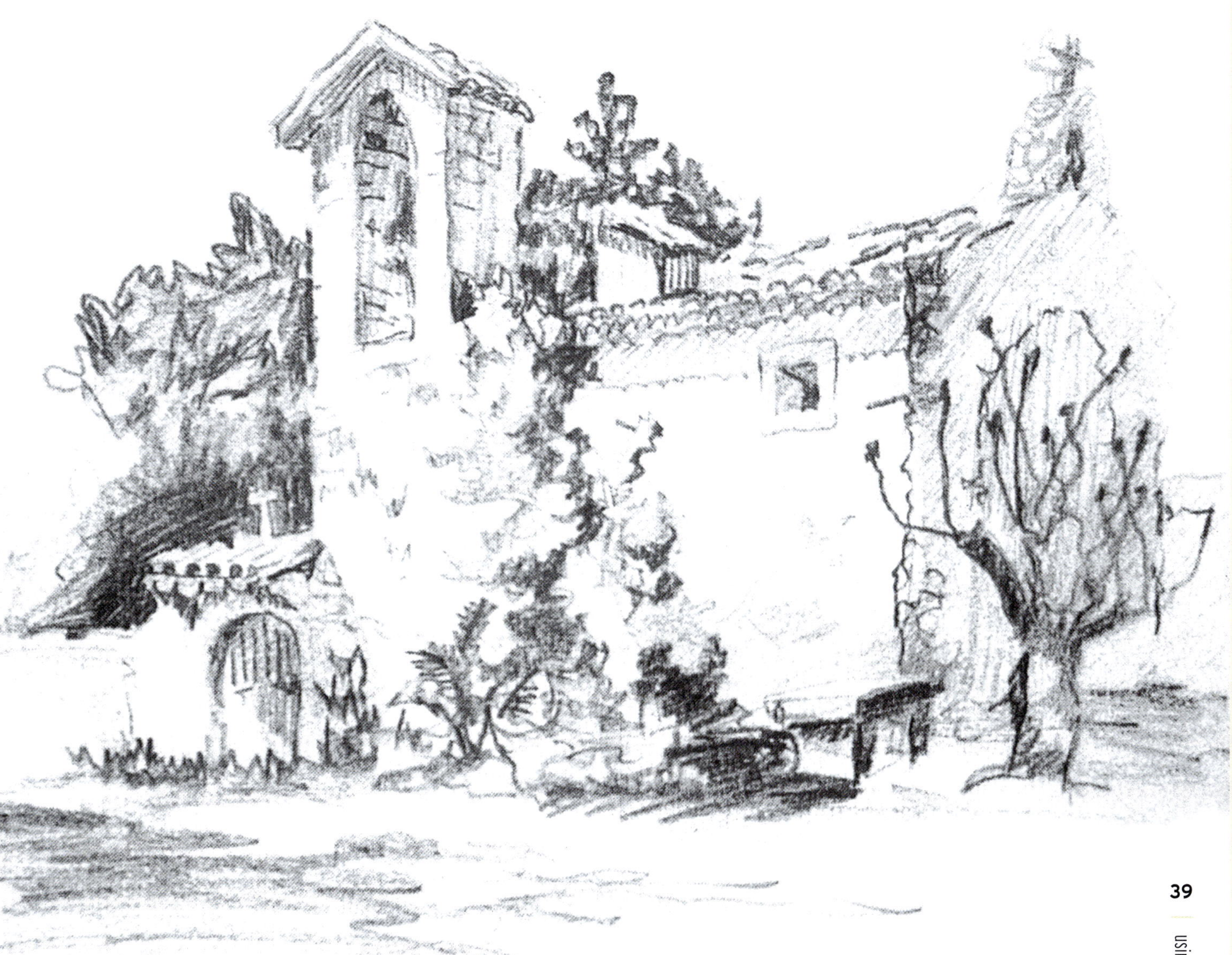

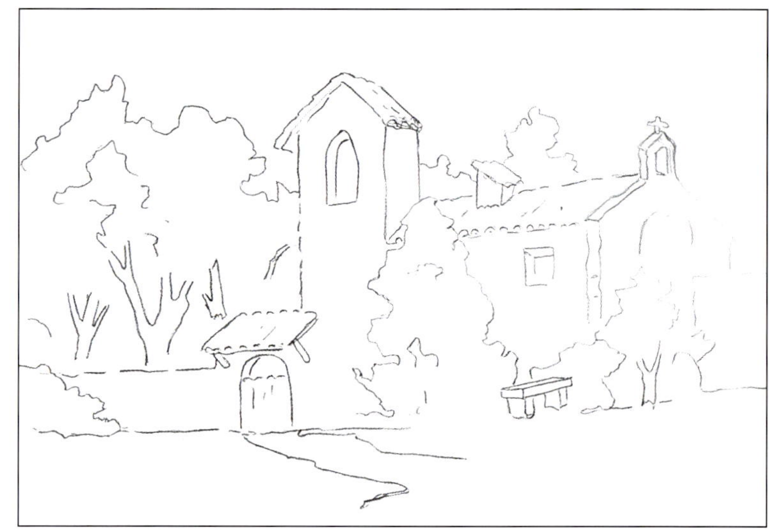

STEP 1 ▶

On 140-pound cold pressed paper, I drew the composition with pencil. This drawing was a carefully drafted line rendition of the scene. Putting in the important elements of the subject, except the values, of course, was as far as I wanted to carry it. The drawing is shown here, awaiting the full-color steps that will follow.

STEP 2 ▼

With a number 18 round ox hair brush, I dampened the sky area of the paper. Some areas that I wanted to function as clouds were left dry. Loading the brush from a puddle of Thalo Blue, the sky was painted, starting in the upper left-hand corner and then working across to the right side. Using a scrubbing motion, I painted the sky, leaving some white clouds and some other lighter blue areas for variation. On the right side, I added a touch of New Gamboge to warm up the cool blue. The light was coming in from the left front quarter so I put in a little darker blue next to the left side of the tower to contrast with its bright sunlit side. Since the sky was secondary in importance to the church, I left it rather plain.

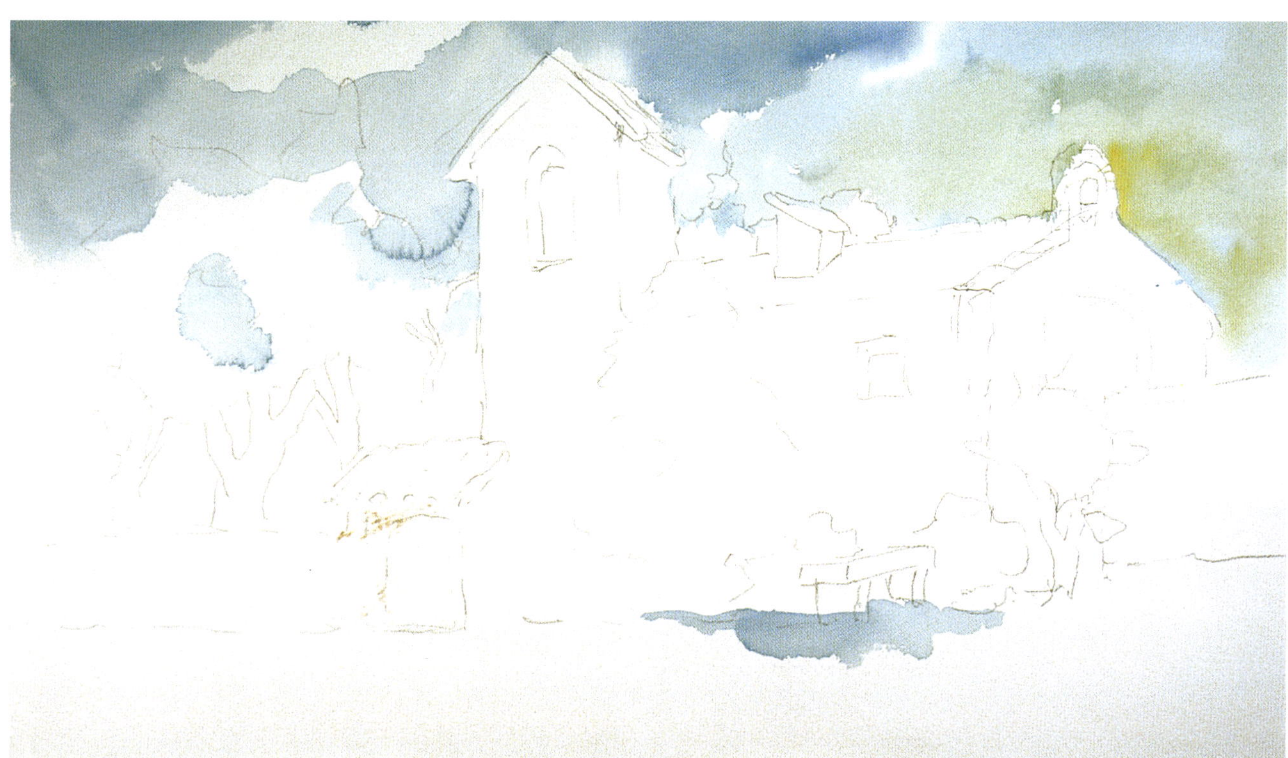

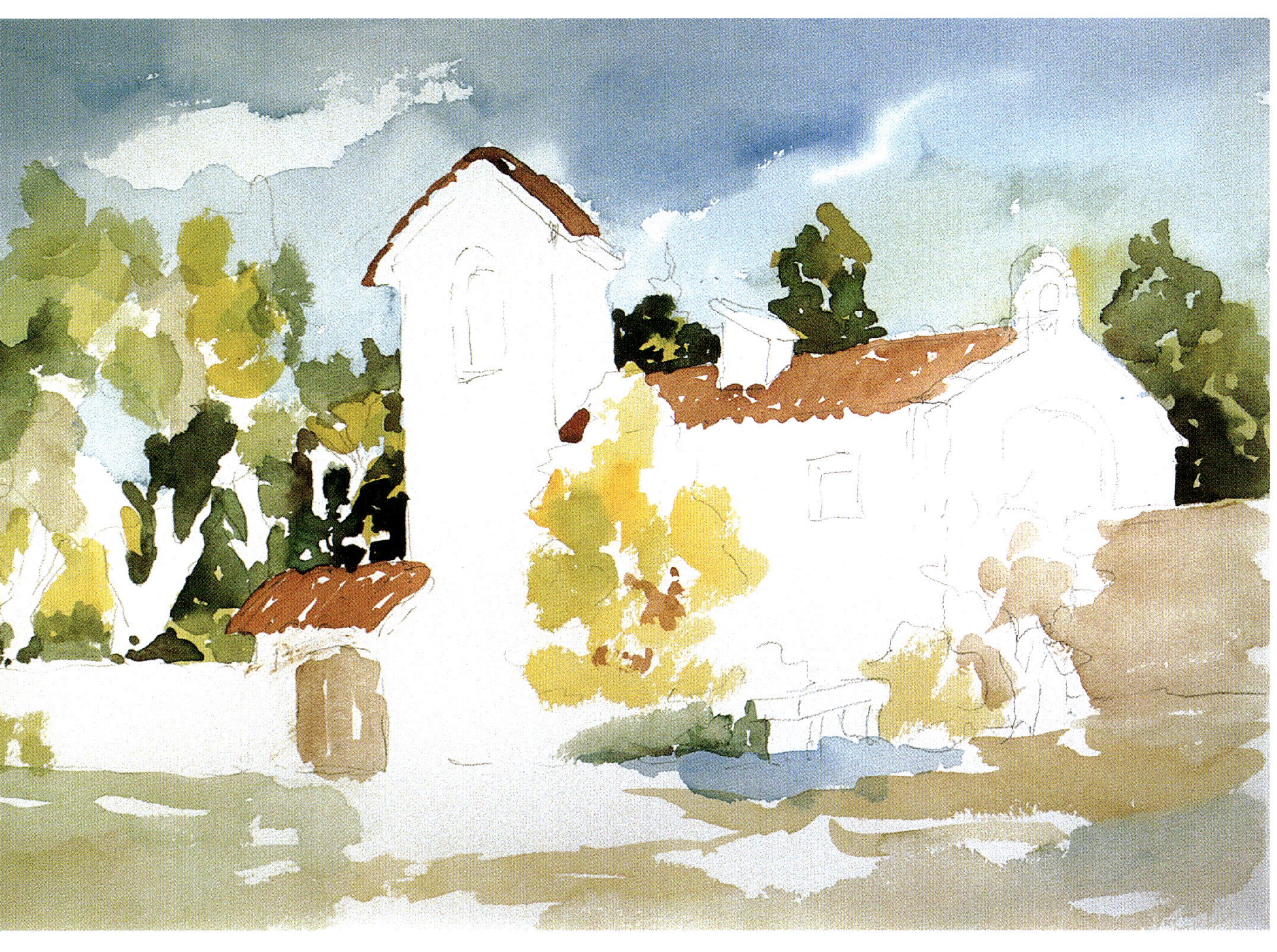

STEP 3 ▲

On the mixing area of the palette, I created a puddle using Thalo Blue and New Gamboge to get a very light yellow green. I then added some Burnt Sienna to modify the green. Switching to a number 12 round ox hair brush, I painted in some random areas in the foliage while leaving most of the visible sections of tree trunks white. In some of the upper areas, the latest wash overlapped the sky creating an area of deeper green. By alternating this mixture back and forth, using New Gamboge, Thalo Blue and Burnt Sienna, I varied some of the areas, changing color and values. Note that on the left side of the painting above the fence, the green wash was cooled off with a little extra blue. In the center foreground to the right of the gate, I dabbled in almost pure New Gamboge as an under painting for the bush. Adding some blue into the shadow areas varied this wash. On the right side, I gave the wall that runs out of the page a very light Burnt Sienna wash. Using the same Burnt Sienna in a little deeper value, I painted the vertical planks on the gate. There was also a little of the New Gamboge in this mix. In the foreground, where the terrain was mainly sand with a few blades of grass and perhaps a little moss, I brushed in an under painting using a cool light green mixture on the left and then adding New Gamboge as we moved to the right side. Note that up to now most of the washes were no deeper than a number one value on a scale of zero being white and three being dark.

It was now time to establish a major dark, and in this case it was green. I mixed up some Thalo Green and Burnt Sienna to make a warm-neutral dark color. I painted the foliage, starting in the area next to the tower above the entryway. I recalled that there was a cross over the entry portico; I painted around it and left it white. I then proceeded to work out gradually from this area lightening the value and varying the color by alternately adding New Gamboge, Burnt Sienna, and bits of Thalo Green in random amounts. The upper left portions of the foliage got lighter in value because they were farther away. On the right side of the tower, the dark green mixture was lightened a little and painted across the top of the roof and around the little structure that sits on the roof. This wash was continued on the right side of the picture above the wall, but I made a change in values to reduce it because it was not near the center of interest. I brought the brush around to ground level under the central bush and made a couple of marks that would indicate shady areas.

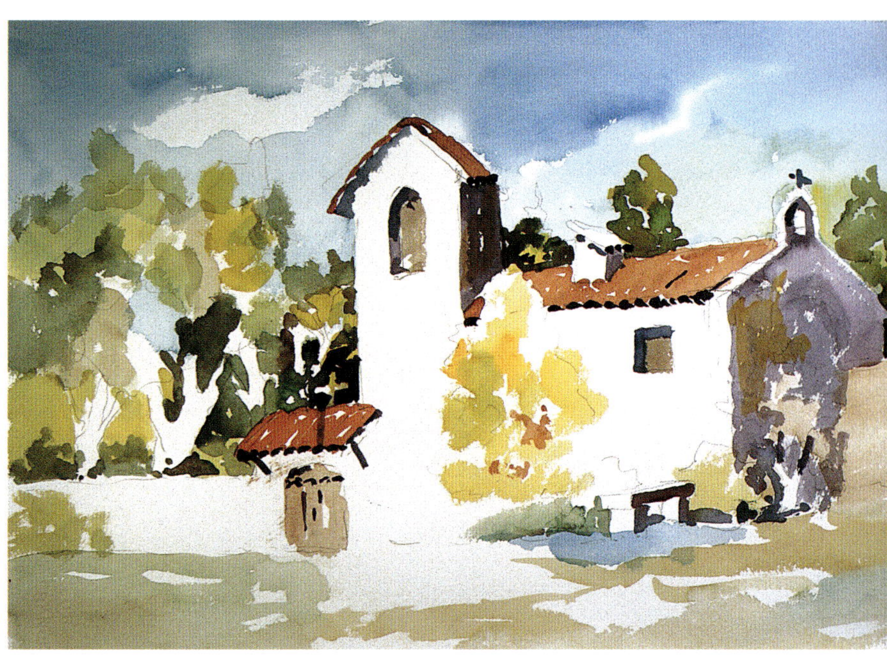

At this point, it was time to add more color. Wanting this color for the tile roofs, I mixed a little Burnt Sienna into a Cadmium Red puddle. After watering it down a little, I placed it on the sunlit roof over the gate. My brush strokes the angled lines of the tile roof, leaving a few white streaks that will be incorporated in the tiles when they are merely indicated later on. Since the main roof was also in sunlight, we used the same vivid color here. The right side of the tower roof got only a glancing light along with a little light from the sky so it could be made a little darker than the other roofs. To repeat the red tile color, I dropped in a few small spots in the bush in front of the church. They could serve as blossoms or berries.

The picture was now at a stage for me to separate the planes of the building. With light coming in from the left front quarter, the planes receding to the left were bathed in light and the planes at the right were in shadow. I mixed Alizarin Crimson and Thalo Blue to get a lavender. Using a little extra blue in the mix, I made sure that it did not end up too prominent. Since the center of interest of this picture was the tower and gate entrance, I planned to paint the darkest shadow area on the right side of the bell tower. A golden rule is that the darkest dark abutting the lightest light will be somewhere in the center of interest. Anywhere else in the composition, there may be an equivalent dark color but the light area next to it will not be as light. There also may be white areas, but the dark values next to them will not be as dark. In other words, the contrast will be weaker. Next, I painted the shadow side of the small structure on the roof and then lightened the lavender to paint the right end of the church. While still wet, a little touch of New Gamboge was dropped in some sections of these shadow planes to warm them up. Using deep lavender, I painted in the arcs of the ends of tiles along the eaves. Still using

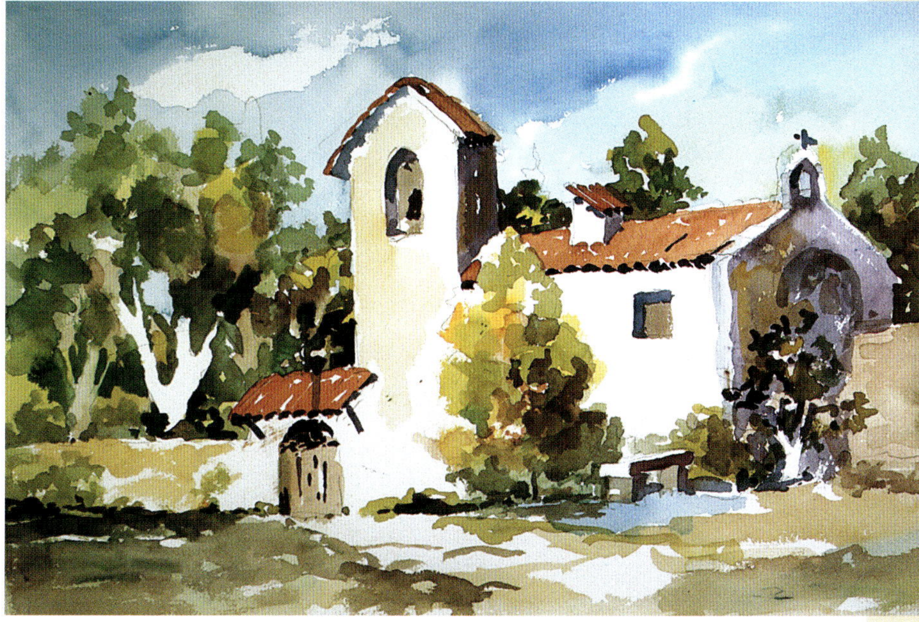

the darker lavender, I merely indicated a few brush strokes in the opening over the gate, and put two props under the small roof over the gate. I randomly painted small areas of shadow on the tree trunks, especially where they tucked up under the foliage and disappeared. The shadow sections of the bench in the foreground followed, and then, finally, I started modeling the small tree or bush on the right side of the picture.

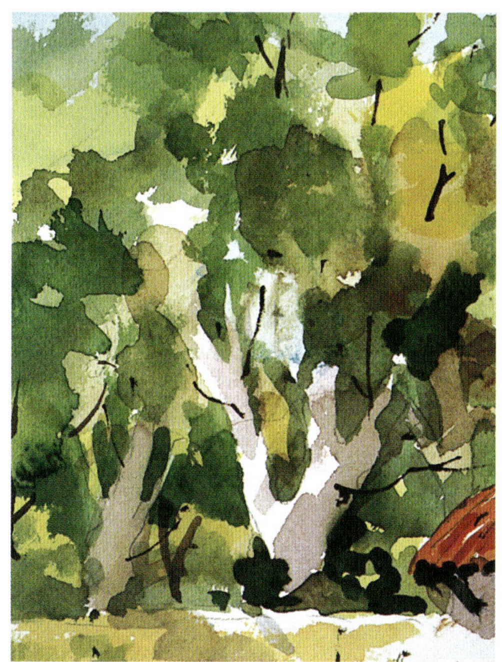

Next in my painting plan, I had to work on the foliage. Mixing up Thalo Green, New Gamboge and Burnt Sienna to get a warm sultry green, I painted areas of the foliage. I realized that there were several random areas in the green foliage that were in full shade, some in half shade, and those in full sunlight displayed a strong yellow-green color. Along the fence where it met the ground, some dark green weeds were dabbled in where the vertical fence ended and the flat foreground started. The prominent central bush also received shadow areas but, being in the center of interest area, the green shadows were mellowed with New Gamboge. The small tree on the right side in front of the shadow plane of the right end of the church received a dark pattern running through it. Using one of the lighter values of dusty green paint, I put a few accents up through the foliage on the left side of the gate.

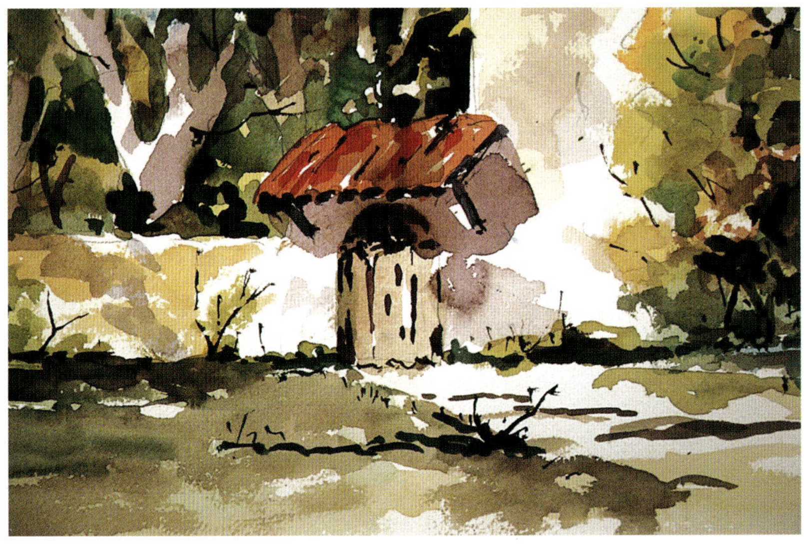

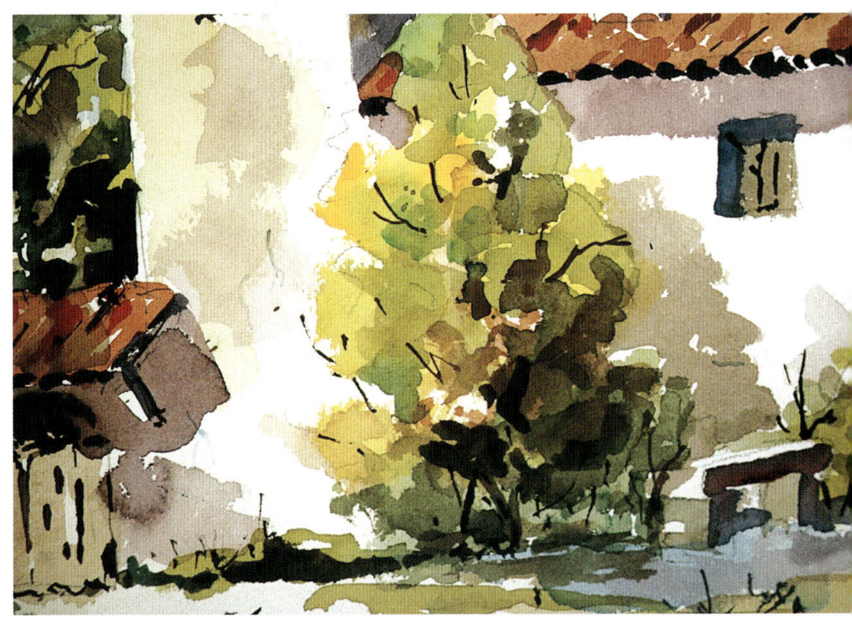

STEP 8 ▲

Almost every picture is usually adjusted at some time in its progression, and the time for this one was now. The foliage seemed to be a little too green overall so I painted a light wash of Burnt Sienna over some areas to give it a warmer cast. I also added a light wash of the same puddle with some New Gamboge to tone down the glaring whites of some of the tree trunks that competed for prominence. It was also placed on the wall to the left of the gate to add texture to the blank area. The entire front of the church, bathed in sunlight, was basically a receding plane going off to the left. A receding plane, I believe, should vary in some way as it recedes: it may vary in size, value, texture and warm and cool color. In this case, I tinted the lighted plane on the left side of the bell tower with a very light value of yellow-orange. Some of this color was added on the wall to the left of the gate. Looking at the gate entrance, I sensed that it seemed to be a little too low. With almost full strength Burnt Sienna, mixed with a small amount of Thalo Blue, I brushed in an arc, thereby enlarging the area of opening above the gate. Using the same dark Burnt Sienna, a portion of the bell that might be seen in the tower window was suggested. A fairly deep Cadmium Red Light, with some Burnt Sienna mixed in, emphasized detail on the tile roof of the small structure in the middle of the church roof. I reached the point where I was ready to concentrate on details like shadows, branches and texture.

STEP 9 ▲

Shadows that are cast by buildings or other objects, such as roof eaves, add an interesting and necessary touch to a picture. In this little church, the addition of those cast shadows helped immensely to define the building. I prepared to put them in by mixing a warm lavender that I placed in the palette and then adjusted to be just a little bit on the red side. With a 3/4-inch flat brush, I paint the angled shadows from the eaves of tile roofs. On the central tree, just to the left of the gate, I put in some shadows on the trunk, leaving an interestingly shaped light sunlit area. Finally, the tree trunks that were left as white paper were toned down with dirty water.

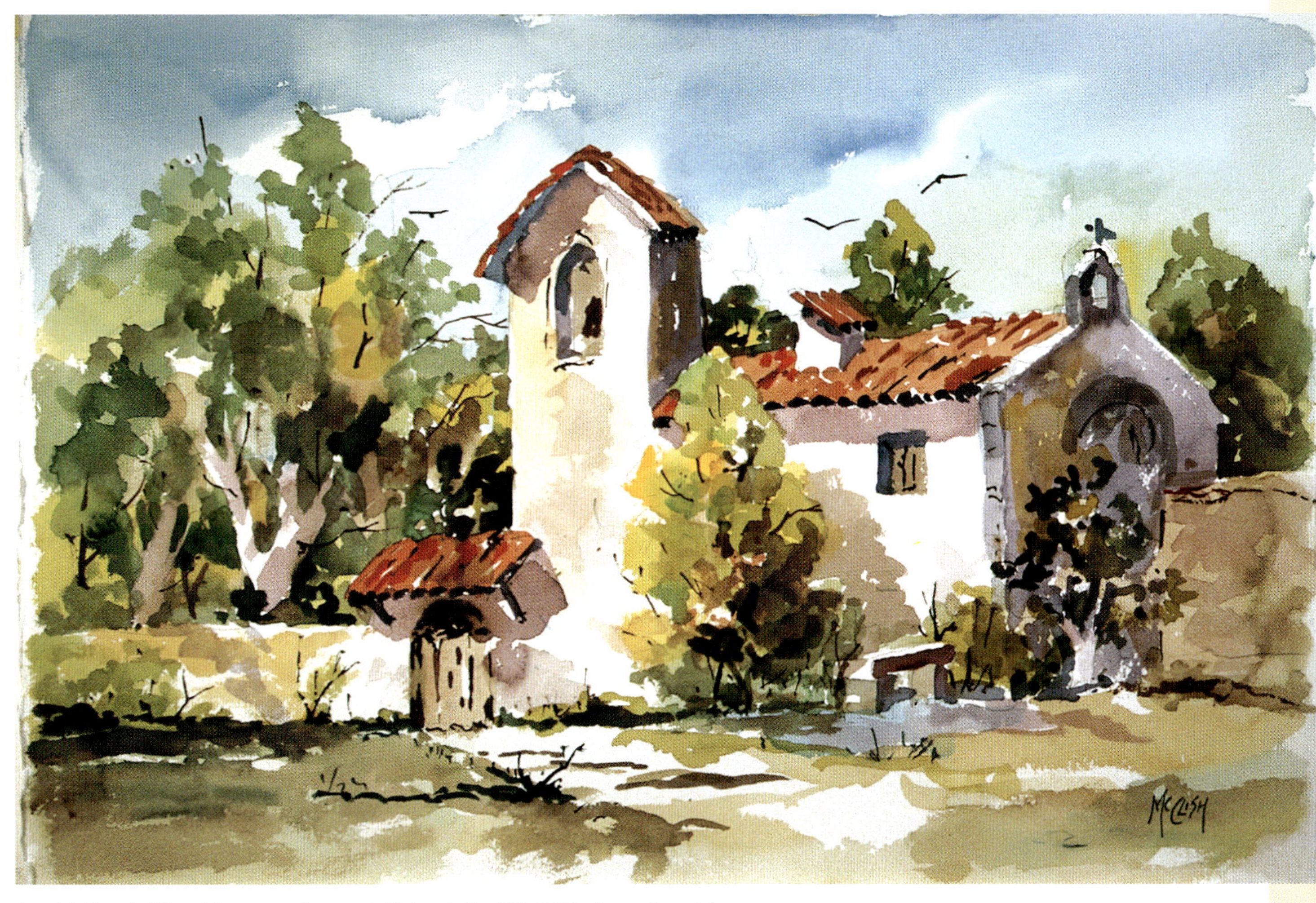

Spanish Church, (Missa Riumenges, Camponet, Majorca), 15 x 22", 140 Strathmore Imperial

STEP 10

With a number four round brush that's been loaded with Cadmium Red Light and a touch of Burnt Sienna, I proceeded to lay in some strokes of varied lengths in the same direction as the rows of tile on the sunlit roofs. Up until now, most of the brushes that I used were fairly large. At this point, I switched to a small script brush to add details. Using a mixture of Thalo Blue and Burnt Sienna, I whisked in the smaller branches and twigs in the foliage. Branches and the larger trunks of the trees were visible for a distance, and then they disappeared into the foliage only to reappear in some other place. I painted sprigs of grass in the foreground and along the fence base. I added some lines on the wooden gate to indicate vertical planks, and I suggested details of a frame to the small window on the side of the church. The bell tower window also needed a hint of a frame and sill. There are no figures showing in this picture, so I added three birds to give life to the scene. Two birds on the right side with one on the left created a balance. Birds in flight have their wings down as often as they are up so the right-hand bird was painted in this way. For variation, the lone bird on the left had its wings almost level to soar. I had been working close to the picture during most of the painting, so I placed a mat on it and set it up to view from a distance. I liked it. The next and final step would be my signature in the lower right corner.

Light and Shadow

ight is the life of most watercolor pictures and watercolor is what this book is about. However, the basics of painting in that medium apply to all other mediums as well. The juncture of light and dark values is the catalyst that sets off the sparkle in most watercolors. Correct use of light and its associated shadow planes is probably one of the most important things in painting a picture. There are several different origins of light that we have to deal with as artists. There is sunlight, moonlight and artificial light along with different directions of each. Where there is any kind of light, there are shadows created. There are two distinct types of shadows, a shadow side on an object and a cast shadow from that object. Where the shadow side meets the lighted side of an object, there is a change of plane. The shadow side is darkest where it abuts the light plane and it gets lighter as it recedes. The light plane is lightest at this junction and it gets darker as it recedes. A cast shadow is usually darker where it starts than the object casting it. As it recedes, it reverses and becomes lighter than the object casting it. It is also well defined at the start and then loses definition and value as it recedes. The shape of a cast shadow varies depending on the angle of the plane that it is falling on. A foliage shadow cast straight on the front of a house will be sharply defined depending on how far away the tree is. Falling on an angled wall, it would be elongated and will probably change in definition and value. The angle of cast shadows should be consistent with the direction of incoming light. Here are descriptions of the different kinds of light.

In this scene of Eastern Point Light in Gloucester, Massachusetts, we see the affect of lighting that is head on.

7

Front Light.

This is what you get when taking a flash picture with the flash unit mounted on the camera. Everything is bathed in full light and shadows are hidden. However, when front light comes from the sun flooding down on the scene, there may be shadows created. Due to the height of the sun every eave, overhang, or protuberance will cast a shadow straight down. How far down depends on the height of the sun.

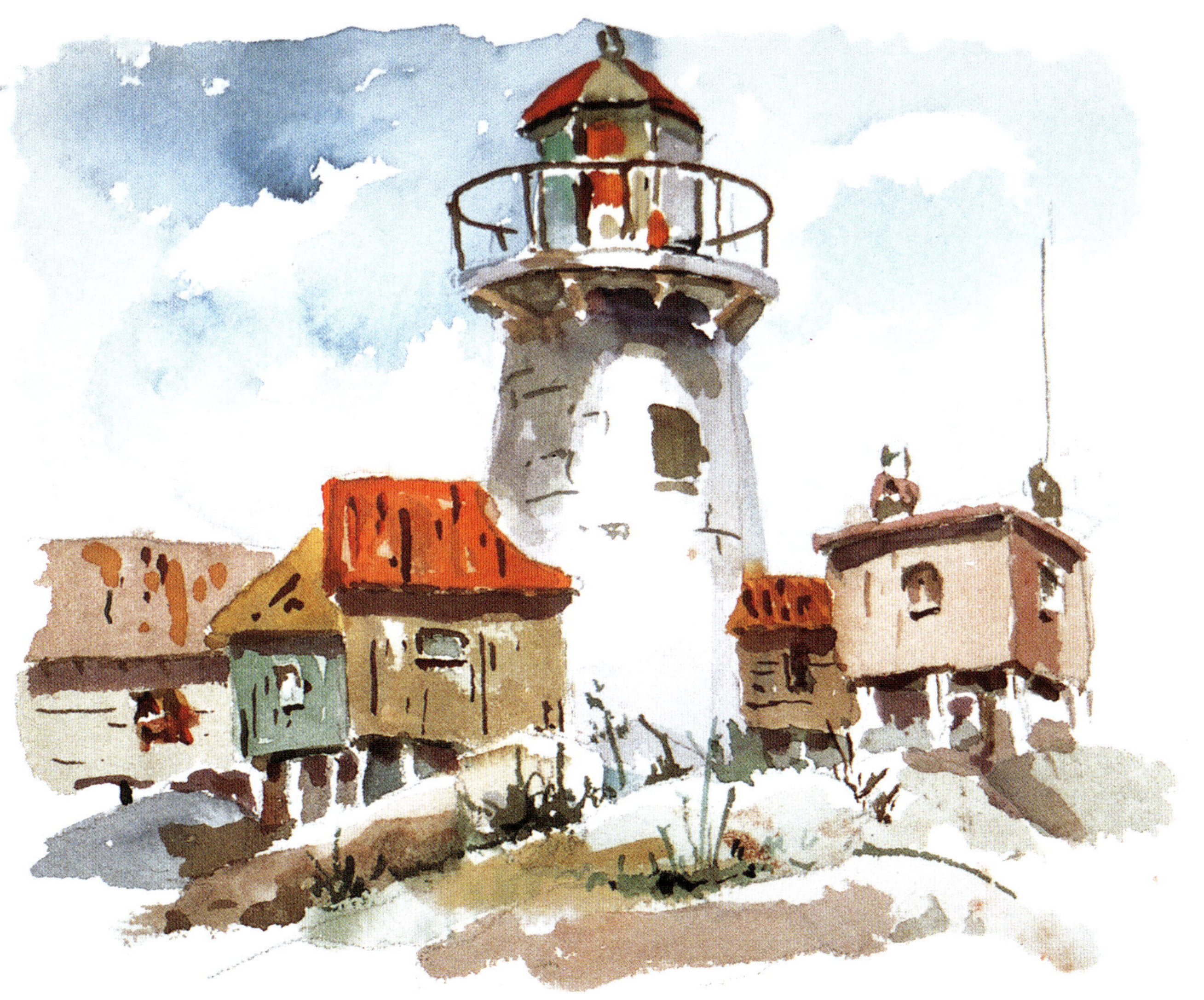

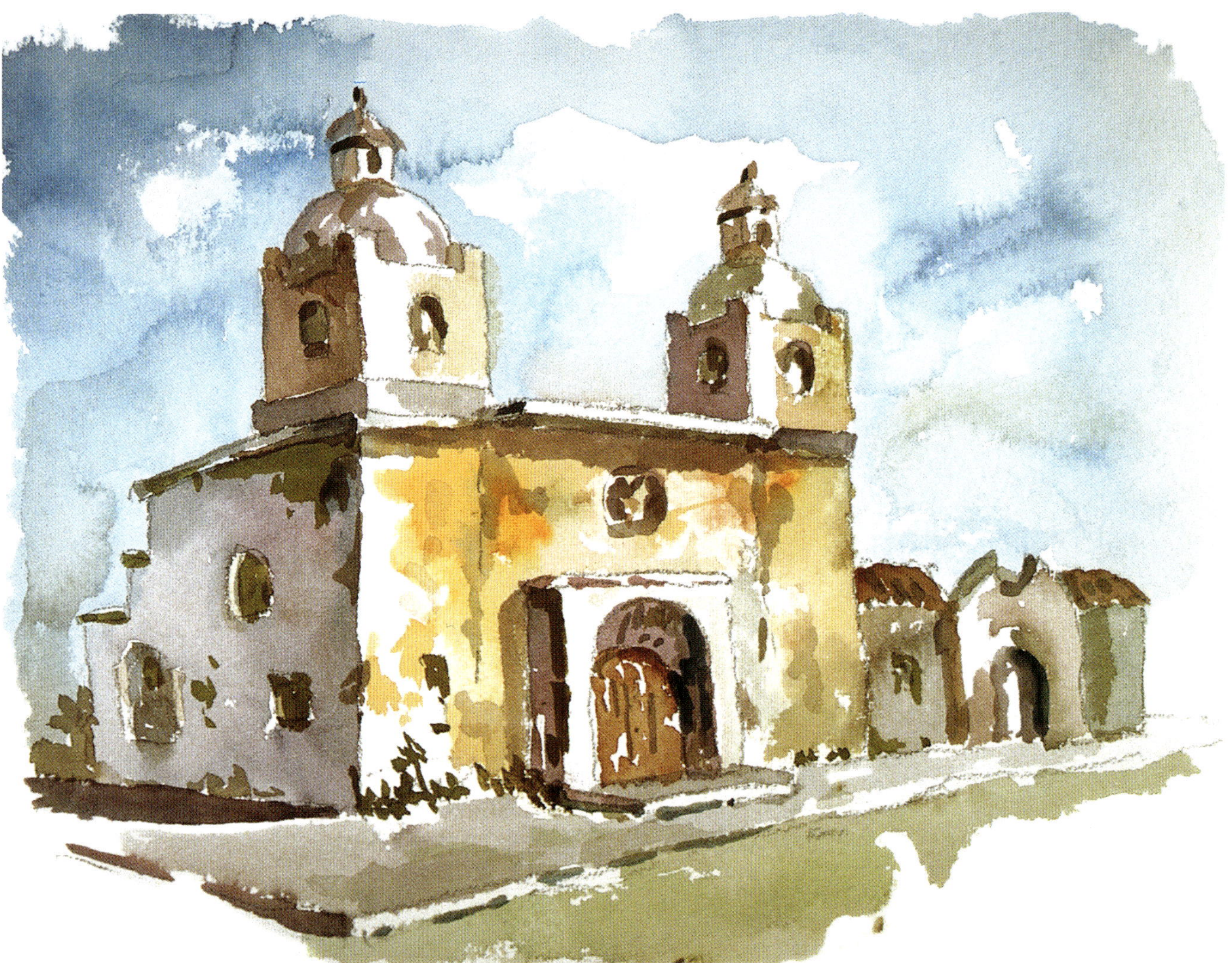

One-quarter Front Light.

This light is the painter's friend. It gives a light side and a shadow side to objects in the picture. This light can be from the sun or it can be from an artificial origin such as a street light. Make sure that the angles of all cast shadows are the same. Shadows cast by the sun can be assumed to be parallel. When by an artificial light, they will splay outward on an angle from the light source.

Side Light.

With shadows marching right or left across the picture, this becomes a mood setting light. You should take care in using this light source that you keep your composition from becoming monotonous. In the wood scene (next page), I varied the positions and size of the trees. I also kept the light source quite low so very little shadow would be cast from the foliage.

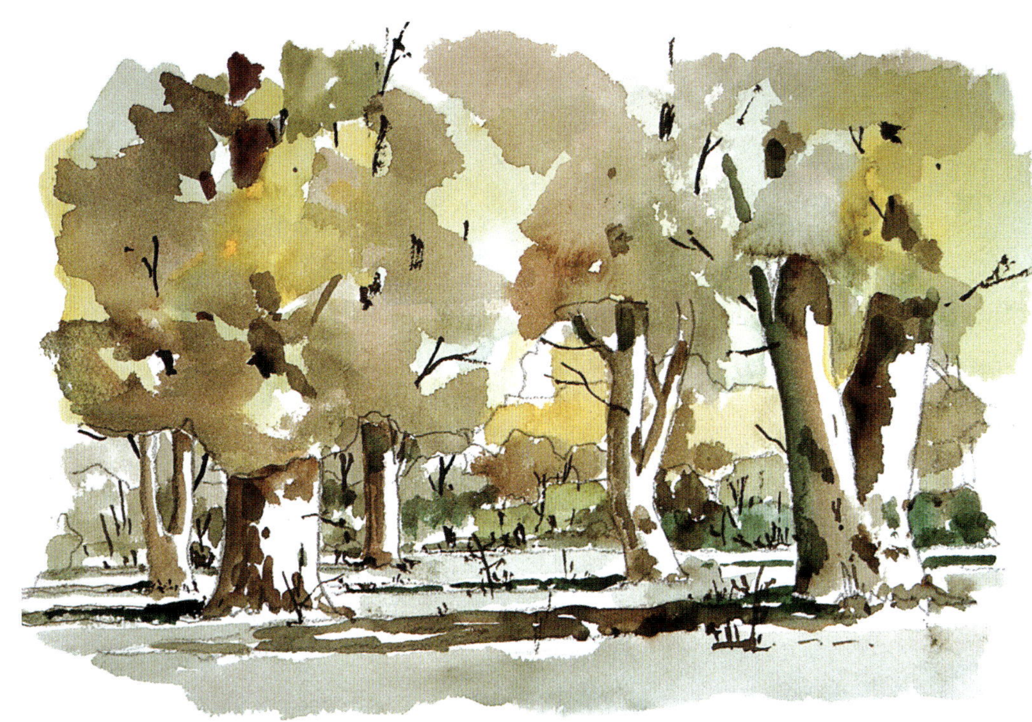

Three-quarter Back Light.

Here is an intriguing light; it leaves just a sliver of light on objects while putting the rest of the scene in shadow. It is a near silhouette with the light plane coming toward you making it brilliant and dramatic. There is still detail and definition, however faint in the shadow areas.

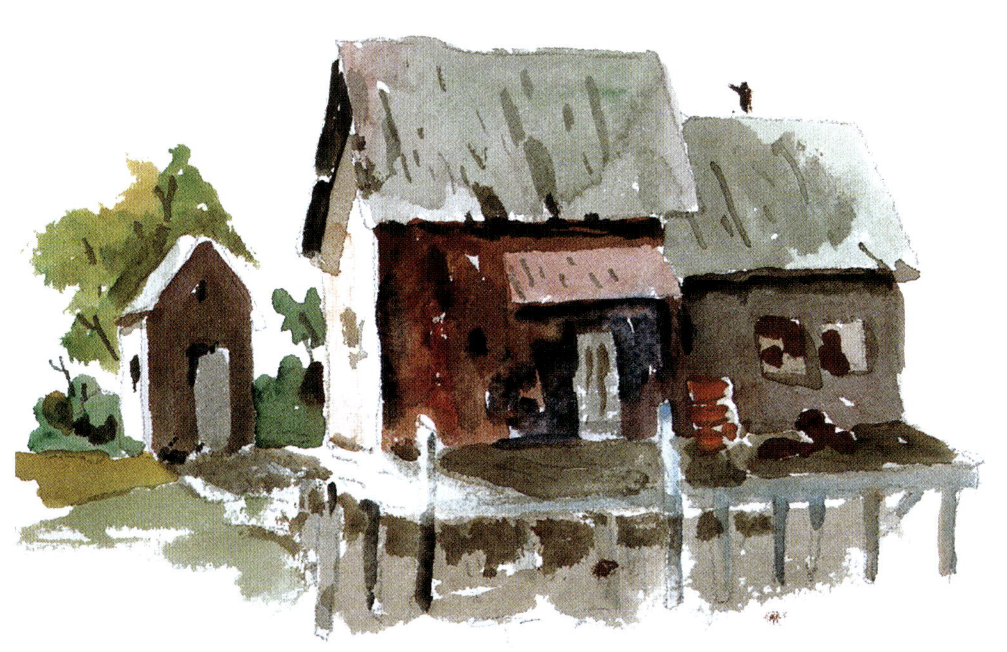

This little fishing shack in Gloucester, Massachusetts, is more in shadow than in light due to having only one of its sides being illuminated by light coming forward. That leaves the front in shadow.

Back Light.

This light gives a silhouette with shadows coming straight forward. In back lighting there are no light planes on objects. You should take extreme care when planning a composition using this type of light. With all of those dark areas, you can easily create muddy colors. Keep in mind that even in dark shadows, there are still details with subtle changes in color and value.

Top Light.

I call this light "High Noon on the Prairie": picturing a building in the desert with the sun directly overhead causing all four sides of the building to be in shadow. There is a cast shadow from the eaves all the way around it. This is an unusual light in our country because the sun never gets far enough north to be overhead at noon. However, it can approach top light.

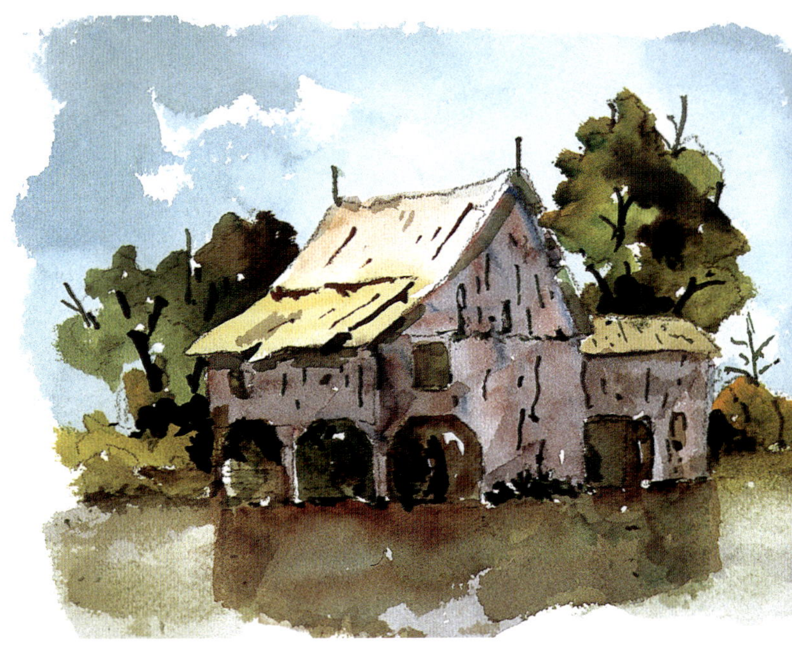

With the sun completely behind the subject, the sun's lighting appears only on the side that the viewer can't see, thus creating a silhouette-like effect.

When the sun is directly overhead, as in this scene, all four sides of the building are in shadow.

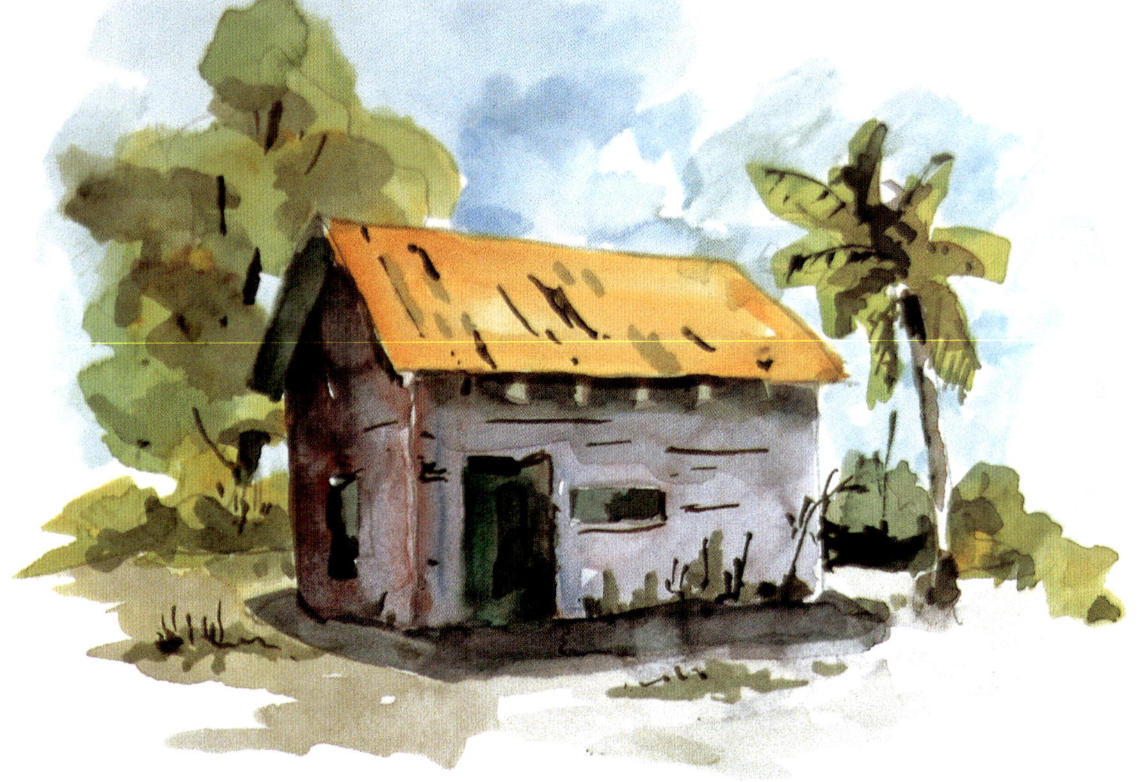

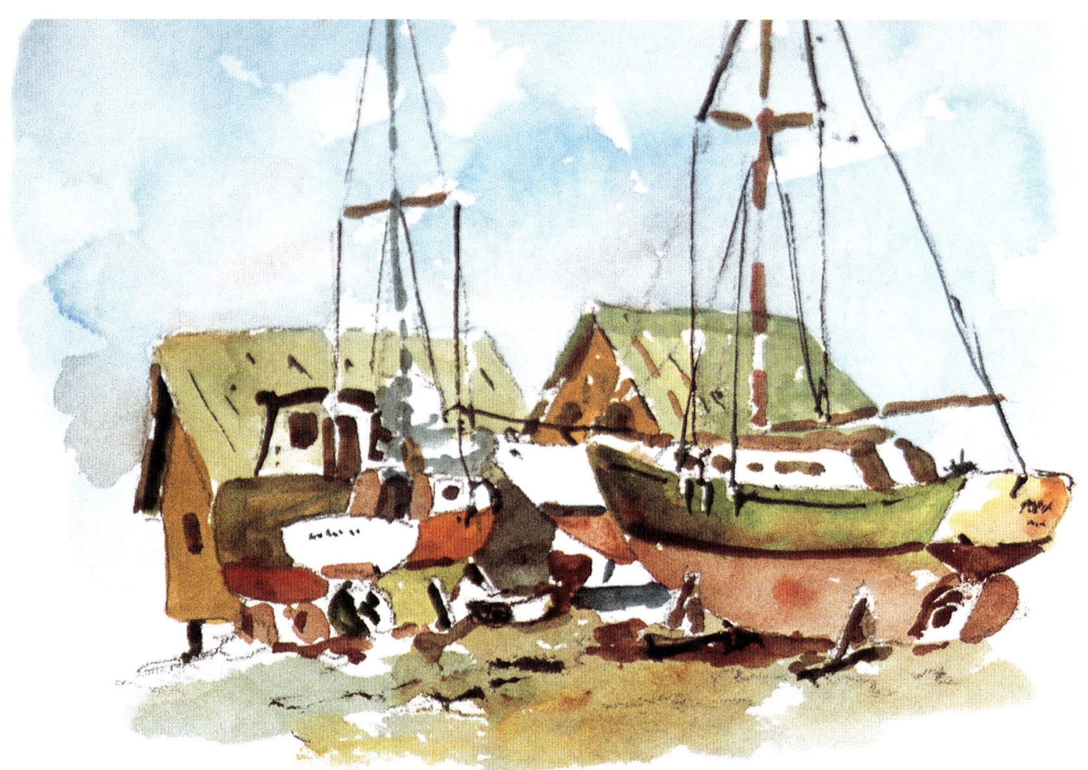

Ambiguous Light.

The California school of watercolorists made good use of this light, saying, "Forget unified light direction and just let light areas play around to emphasize the composition." Somehow, I think using this type of light creates more of a design than realistic art. All in all, I think of it as a fun light.

Reflected Light.

Picture a row of buildings, one side of each in full light and the other side in shadow. The light side of the second building in the row reflects its light (diffused, of course) into the shadow side of the first one. While this reflected light is lighter than the shadowed side upon which it falls, it can never be lighter than the light side of the building that it is reflecting.

Mixed Directional Light.

Even though we try to utilize one source of light, a mixed directional light means that there is more than one light source in the composition. For example, there can be a streetlight with a secondary light from some other source like a sign. The moon can add another light. While this gives an interesting display of various light areas and a crisscross pattern of different values of shadows, use care because the display can get rather complicated.

Feel Free to Edit Your Picture

Ten-Pound Island sits out in Gloucester Harbor just inside its entrance. Gloucester and close-by Rockport dominate the small neck of land in northeast Massachusetts that's known as Cape Ann. It is about forty miles north of Boston, which comforts residents, and visitors as well, because of its proximity to, and, at the same time, distance from, the state capital. Over the years, I've been in that area quite often. On this occasion, I was in Gloucester to attend an artists' breakfast that was sponsored by the International Society of Marine Painters,

an organization that's composed of the finest marine painters in the country. I am proud to say that I am a past president of this prestigious group of artists.

After breakfast, a bunch of us gathered for a painting trip to Ten-Pound Island. According to some accounts, the island got its name in the early settlement days of Gloucester. It appears that ten pounds was the price that was paid for it. By whom to whom seems to be unknown.

The focal point of the island is a stubby little lighthouse, the only structure there. It has guided boats in and out of the harbor for decades upon decades, and still functions in that role. I had seen this lighthouse many times, but only from shore on both sides of the harbor. I had always wanted to capture it in a sketch or a painting. We got to the island by way of a pontoon boat. As soon as I stepped on shore, and went just a short distance, my first sketch was under way. I finished that sketch in short time, and since I would probably never get the opportunity to

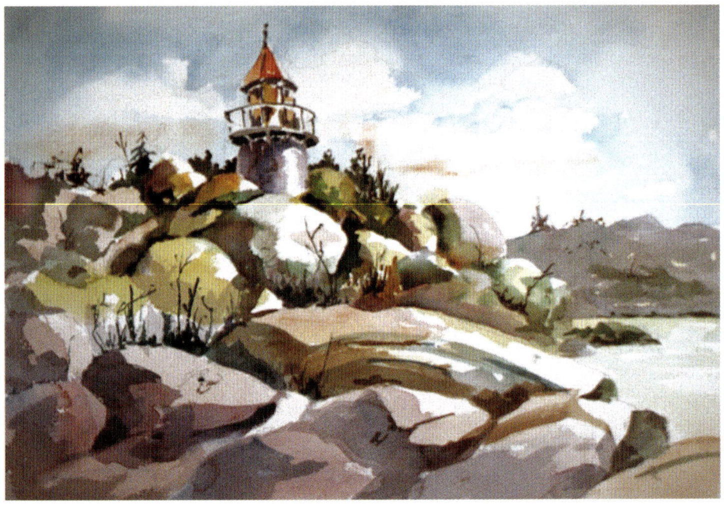

8

A Lighthouse
on Ten-Pound Island

This was my first sketch
of the lighthouse on
Ten-Pound Island.

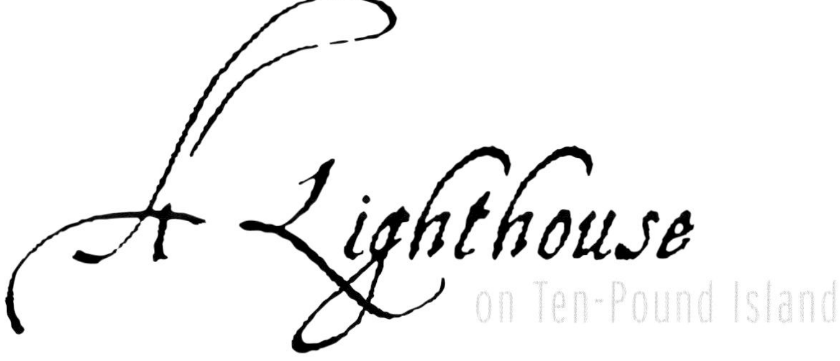

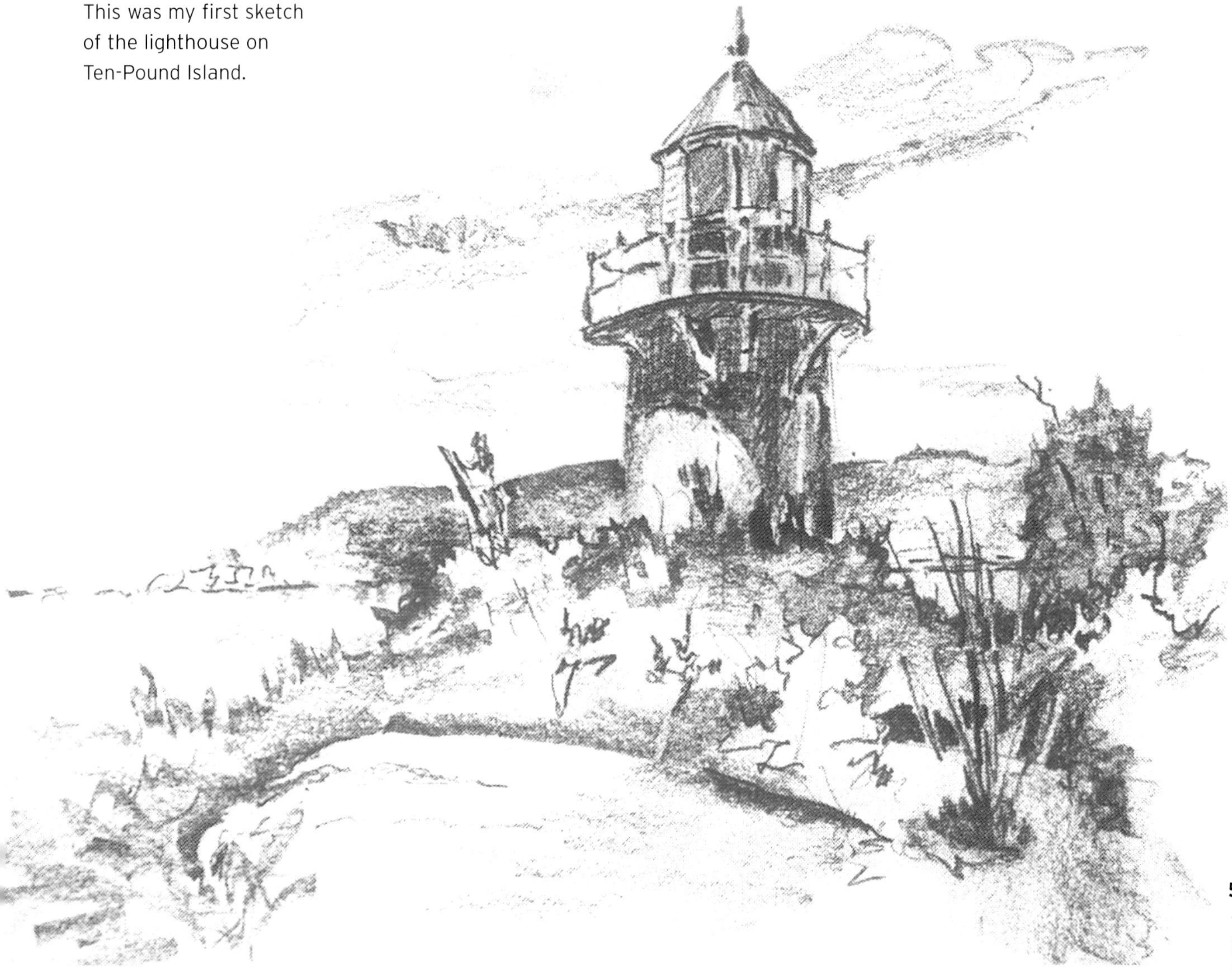

I liked this second
sketch better and
decided to paint it.

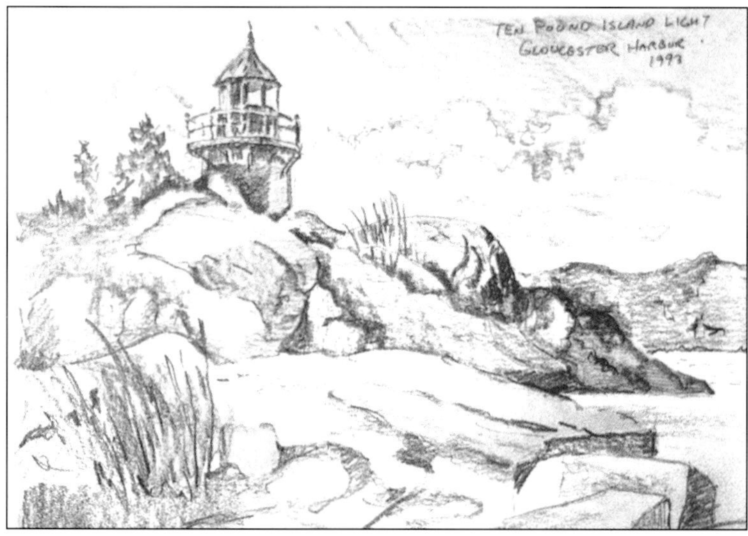

visit the island again, I immediately started a second drawing, this time from a different location. I liked it better; it was a more appealing composition. I hauled out my watercolors and made a little value painting. While the lighthouse is the only structure, the rocky terrain that covers most of the small island dominates it. I used a low horizon view that nuzzled the lighthouse partially in behind some large boulders as I looked up at it. Little patches of vegetation were in and around the rocky crevices. The scene fascinated me.

STEP 1 ▶

When moving the sketch to the watercolor paper, I decided to simplify the composition. The sun was out and the sky was deep blue with puffy white clouds giving a beautiful summer backdrop to the scene. I loosely sketched the white cloud tops. In the foreground, there were massive boulders and there were a few flat surfaced rock formations that slopped down to the water's edge. Those I lightly outlined. You will notice that there are only a few fairly straight lines, most of them are on the lighthouse, the only man-made element on the island. The distant shoreline contained just a couple of nature-made, almost straight lines. When I had finished the drawing, it was a simple sketch that just said: "Boulders with a lighthouse sitting on top."

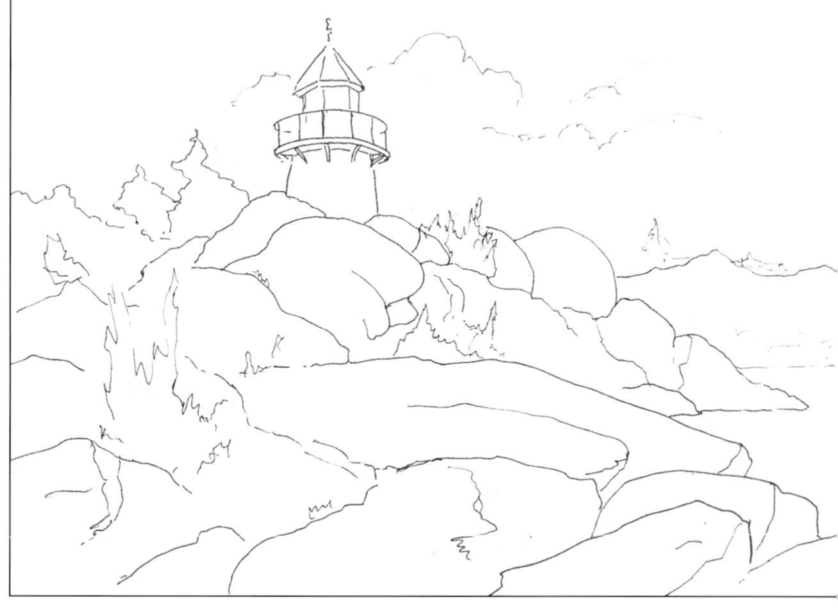

While transferring the drawing to the sheet of watercolor paper, I decided to make some slight changes in the composition.

STEP 2 ▶

I painted the sky first, light blue with filmy white clouds. I wanted to emphasize the lighthouse not the sky. I painted around the clouds and then teased some of the edges so they would not be too glaring. I dropped in touches of Burnt Sienna and/or New Gamboge in some places while the wash was still wet. My light source was almost right side light. I mixed a light lavender made of Alizarin Crimson and Thalo Blue, and placed it on the left shadow side of the lighthouse. I then adjusted the mixture with Burnt Sienna, Thalo Green and New Gamboge and, adding some water, I tinted some of the upper rocks, leaving some white on the right sunlit side. Below that, blue, green, and yellow was used to shape various rocks. Across the bottom, I used some of the lavender and added Burnt Sienna, blue, green and yellow. As the rocks were given a background wash, the color and values seemed to solve themselves.

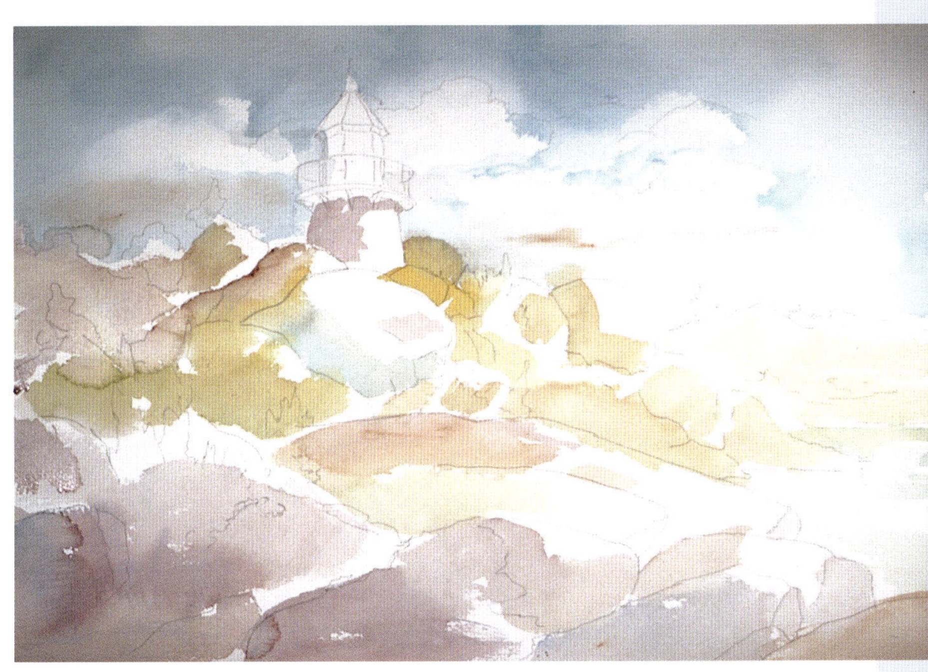

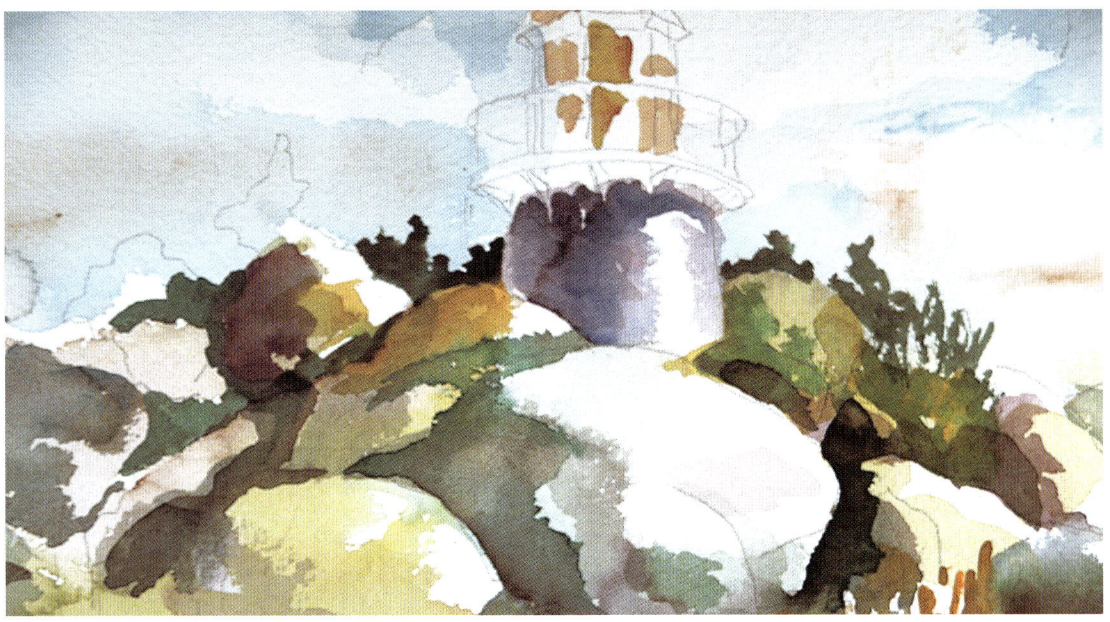

STEP 3 ▲

At this point in the painting it was time to add deep values. I started in the rocky terrain around the base of the lighthouse. I usually use most of the colors in my palette in varying the puddles. I may start a mixture with Thalo Green and Burnt Sienna. Then, as it gets mostly used up and perhaps a little watery, I will add other colors or water to lighten or darken the puddle, or to go from warm to cool or vice versa. Here is where I edit the watercolor. Most of the deeper value colors were in the area around the lighthouse base. The contrast of light against dark was established in this same area. This step shows a close-up of the area.

STEP 4 ▼

The lower foreground rocks have less value change in abutting areas than those nearer the lighthouse—my center of interest. Also, the patterns get larger and have less definition. Red and green were added to some of the puddles to gray them. It's best not to mix the colors too much. Over mixing, especially in opposite colors, can lead to a muddy look. Just keep each puddle small and separate. They will probably be used up before they could mingle with adjacent mixtures. Up to this point, I had largely ignored the lighthouse. With a lavender mixture with red dominance, I painted the shadow on the left side of the tower. Notice that the shadow immediately under the walkway was well defined. As it worked its way around the structure, it got some softened edges. A reddish roof was placed on the roof panels with the deepest red in the middle panel. Some of that red showed up along with yellow patches in the glassed area that held the light mechanism.

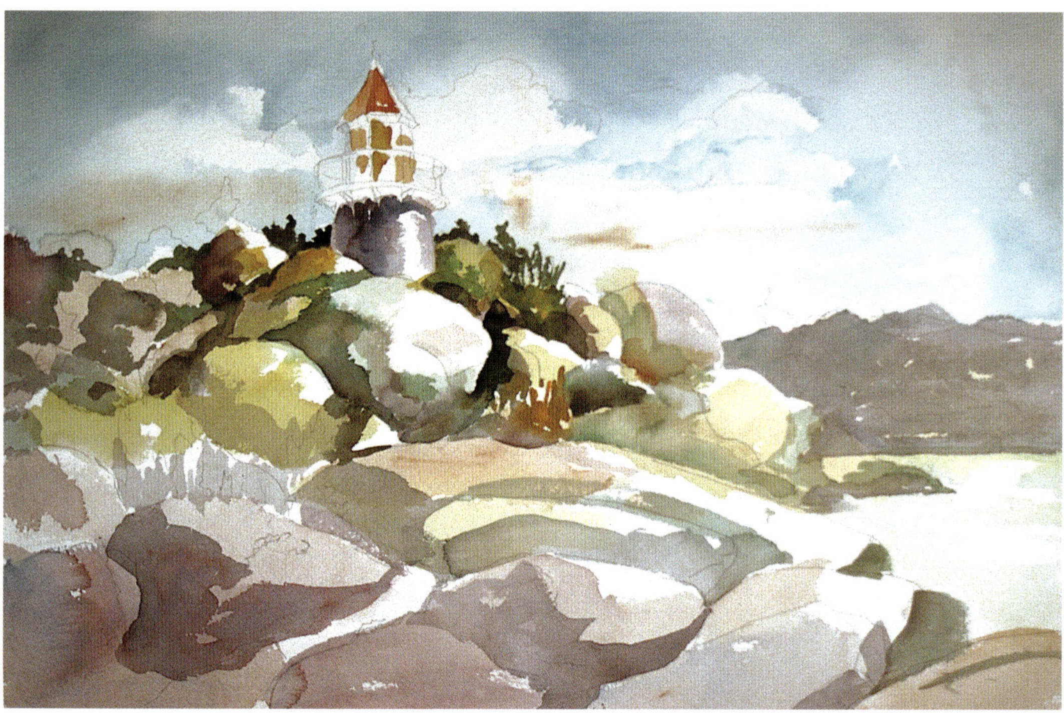

STEP 5 ▶

The real fun of the painting is always that part where little details are added. In this case, it was the sprigs of grass and weeds that were mingled in with the rocks. I chose to show a close-up of this portion of the painting to illustrate this more clearly. You can also see how I adjusted the shadows and the definition throughout. In the jumble of rocks, I used, alternately, a number 4 round red sable and a rigger brush to put in grass and weeds. It is important to vary the height, direction and shape of the vegetation patches.

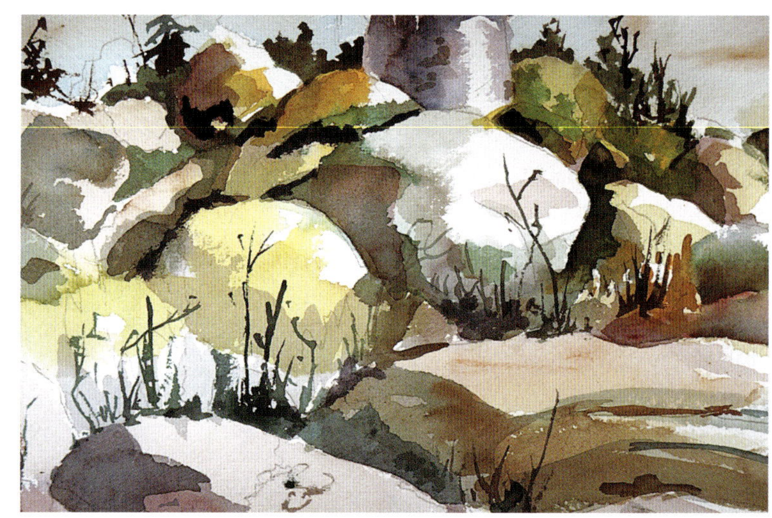

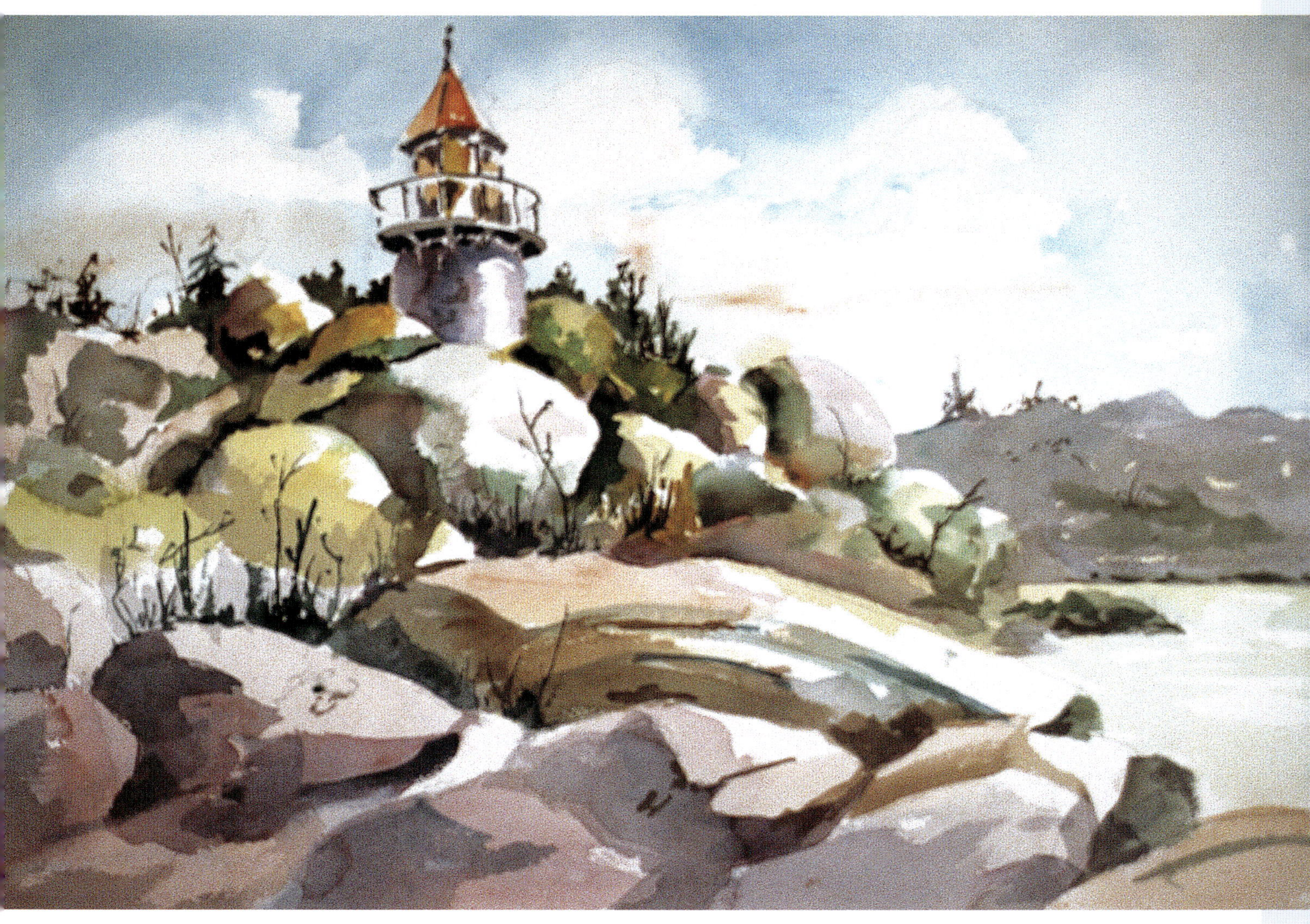

Ten-Pound Island, 15 x 22", 140 lb. Saunder, Waterford

STEP 6 ▲

I finished the painting. I put the picture in a mat, stuck it on an easel and stood back to look. Some of the crevices between the rocks needed a little more definition. That was done. I also indicated some small squiggles on the far hill on the right side. The watercolor now said: "Ten-Pound Island Light."

You Can't Ignore Perspective

n this project—painting a wooded area— a major ingredient, as in all landscapes, is the use of perspective. The important element I want to stress in this painting of a forest is how to inject the feeling of dimension to heighten the perception of reality. The diagram that I prepared for this chapter should make it easier for you to pull this out of context.

I started my drawing by outlining a major tree in the foreground. It was placed in a way that its mass was somewhere near the picture's center of interest in the lower left side of the sheet.

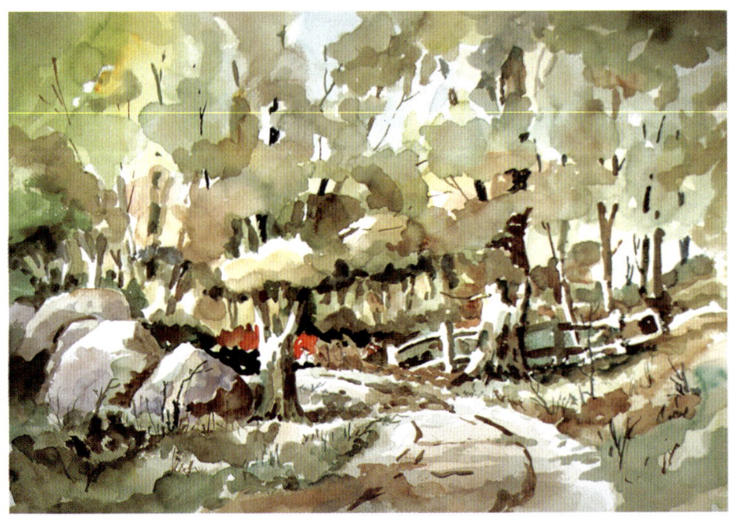

On the right in the foreground, I placed a secondary tree. It is virtually on the same plane but just back a short distance so the base of its root structure is a little higher on the sheet than that of the major tree. This tree balances the first tree, the center of interest. These two trees, even though they are rendered in black and white, have the appearance of being bathed in sunlight. A little farther away, though still on the same plane as the second tree, is a third tree, thus completing the foreground plane of the painting.

In the middle ground, which I rendered with halftone, there is a row of trees that is in a shaded area of the composition, and beyond these trees, we see again trees that are in the sunlight, represented in outline, the same as those in the foreground. Finally, I drew trees in the extreme background that are rendered in black silhouette. This variation of values makes the creation of three dimensions work. And while there are no lines leading to vanishing points, which we all expect to see in any instruction

9

Painting *A Forest*

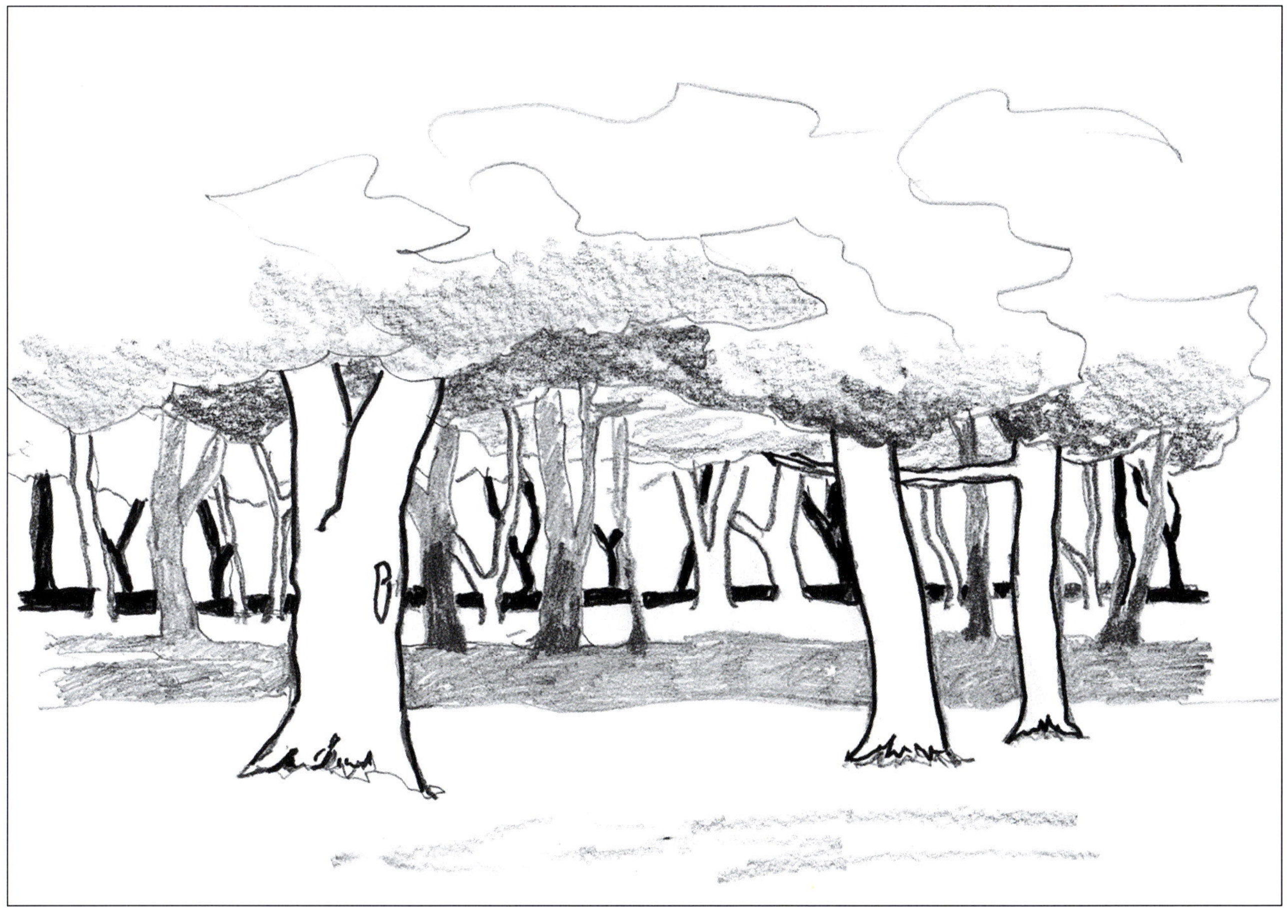

that deals with perspective, we can't deny the existence of perspective in this pencil diagram. The dimension, even in this roughly penciled diagram, is effectively established.

The appearance of depth in a wooded area is plainly seen in this pencil diagram.

With my dimensional sketch established, albeit a rudimentary diagram, I was ready to use it as a guide for my composition. I started to design my painting, from memory, without the benefit of a photo or even an on-location sketch, Why not? I was familiar with what a tree, a bush or an area of foliage looked like, and so, using that knowledge, I proceeded to build this scene. I knew it would be a lot easier if I had had source material from which to work, but calling on my age-old memories of this subject matter, I felt that I could be more spontaneous, consequently looser with my paint applications. I would be able to "plant" trees, "grow" bushes in appropriate spots, plop boulders in wherever I wanted to, and then paint in the foliage poking in and out of the leafy areas to suit me and my composition.

I drew a curving pathway leading back into the woods. I followed this with an area of boulders on the left side and I put in the first tree just to the right of those rocks. The curving lane with much perspective wended its way up, turned to the left and went behind the tree. The perspective may have seemed excessive but it was necessary if the lane was to lay flat and not go uphill. The lane reappeared for a short way in the opening between the rocks and the tree. This little extension made sure that the lane continued on its merry way; it might be called a center of interest.

On the right side, I drew in a middle ground tree, and to break the monotony, a split rail fence was nudged in behind it to suggest a third dimension. The fence dipped down on the left, maybe going downhill. It would be a little boring to continue it further across the scene. A viewer's eye might want to follow the fence rather than focus on the lane area. Rather than laboriously trying to draw the foliage patches, they were only hinted at. Foliage has no definite shapes or boundaries and it can be built up as it is painted. Why draw it twice—once with a pencil and again with a brush? The background trees showing in some areas were just suggested. In a drawing of a tree, if it has leaves, the trunk starts at the ground and goes up, disappearing into the mantle of leaves. It then appears again, maybe several times, as it weaves its way up through the foliage. I drew a few of those openings and showed the bits of limbs. This sketch is only minimal, with just enough detail to paint a woods scene. I was now ready to paint.

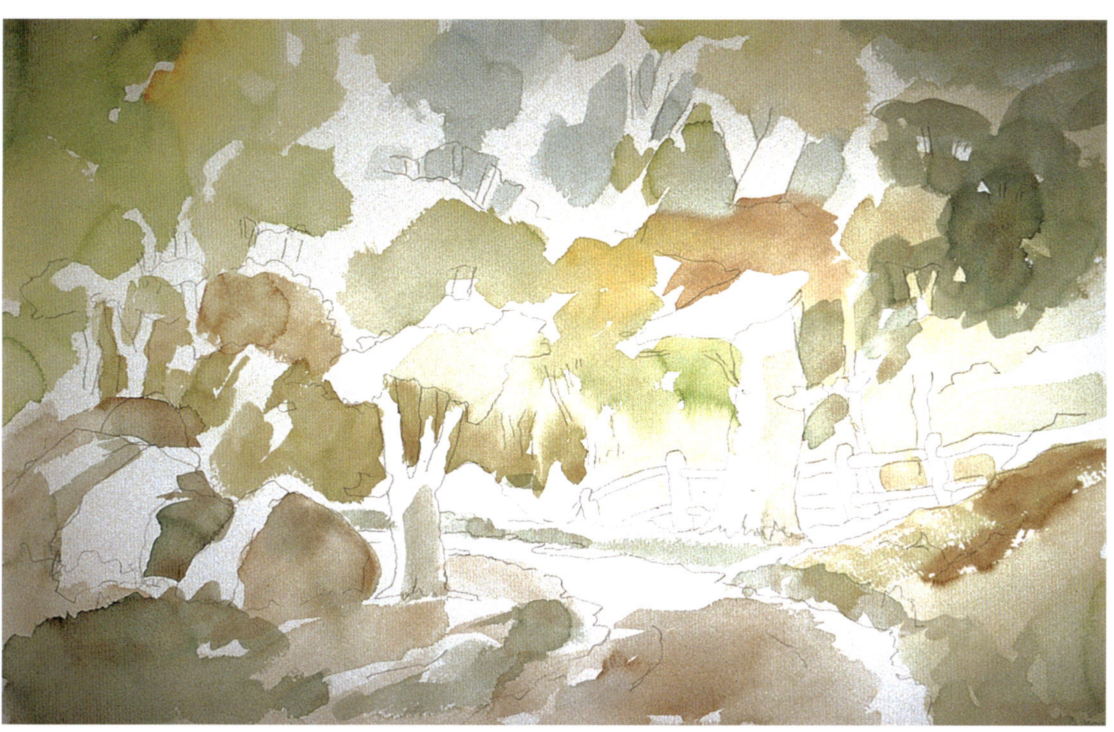

STEP 1 ▲

I made a mixture of Thalo Green, New Gamboge and Burnt Sienna on my palette. This initial puddle will be adjusted in many ways as I paint varied background shapes through the foliage areas. I started in the upper left corner, and used a 3/4-inch flat brush to put in the first color. Working my way across the foliage area left to right, other jumbled areas were painted using different values and slightly different color as I adjusted the first applications of paint. In the upper center, slightly on the left side, two light blue sky areas of different sizes and shapes were inserted. Some of the foliage patches had a little Cadmium Red Light added. I felt here that I needed some warm color to make an interesting composition. The boulders on the lower left side received a light wash when I added a dominant, but very light, Burnt Sienna. I tinted the foreground with green on the left, Burnt Sienna with a touch of blue in the lane in the right center, and, adding a touch of New Gamboge in the puddle, I painted the right lower corner. With a little more pigment added to the puddle, giving it a deeper value, I painted a narrow horizontal row of interesting shapes through the lower center of the picture. In this sequence, there is some negative painting, especially around the fence. Up to now most of the values in these early washes have been very light. They merely formed a background for the painting procedures that would follow. They also got rid of some of the glaring white paper and helped to set the scene. At this moment in the painting, it started to say: "A lane going into a woods."

On the left, behind the first tree and the boulders, I made a dark mixture using Thalo Green and Burnt Sienna and painted various spots. The mixture was so dark that it looked almost black. I lightened the puddle with a little water and areas of the foliage were filled in. Using the same puddle of green-brown, I continually altered it lighter and then darker. Adding Burnt Sienna, or Thalo Green, I painted some spots in the foliage. I mixed up pale lavender, using Thalo Blue and Alizarin Crimson, and molded the rocks. This puddle was constantly adjusted from dark to light and back again by adding touches of Burnt Sienna and Thalo Blue. I gave one plane a light green cast for variation. In the background, I painted miscellaneous trees using negative and positive alternation. Now I was ready to shape the foliage. If you recall, my initial puddle was made of Thalo Green and Burnt Sienna. Mixing up a dusty medium value of green, I did some random washes in the upper left corner. This was the shadow area of foliage and being some distance from the center of interest, it really just passively filled in an area. I was careful to leave some of the light underpainting to show through. Working down towards the center of the picture, I deepened the value in the puddle and wove in a series of half darks. In the left area above the major tree, I added New Gamboge to the mixture and painted random areas. I stroked a little Cadmium Red in the foliage to liven it up. Above the fence on both sides of the tree trunk, deeper Cadmium Red was added to balance the deep red areas to the left. I now felt that the curving lane deserved some work. It was a receding plane and in order to assist the perspective that would make it lay down, it had to change in value, color, or definition. I decided to cool off the foreground area and then warm up slightly the color as it went away. Burnt Sienna with some Thalo Blue added gave a cool foreground wash. I lightened the mixture, putting in a little texture where the lane turned.

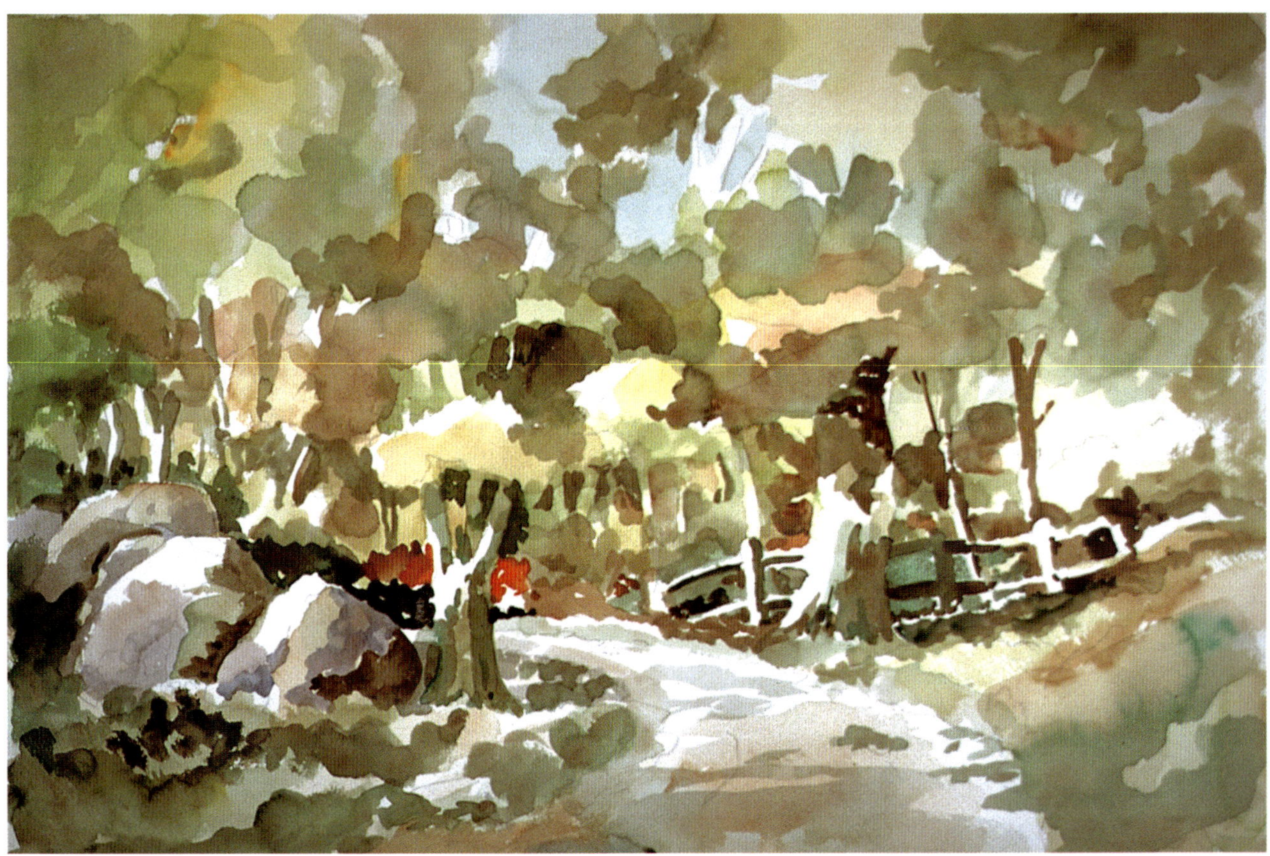

A close-up of the fence area.

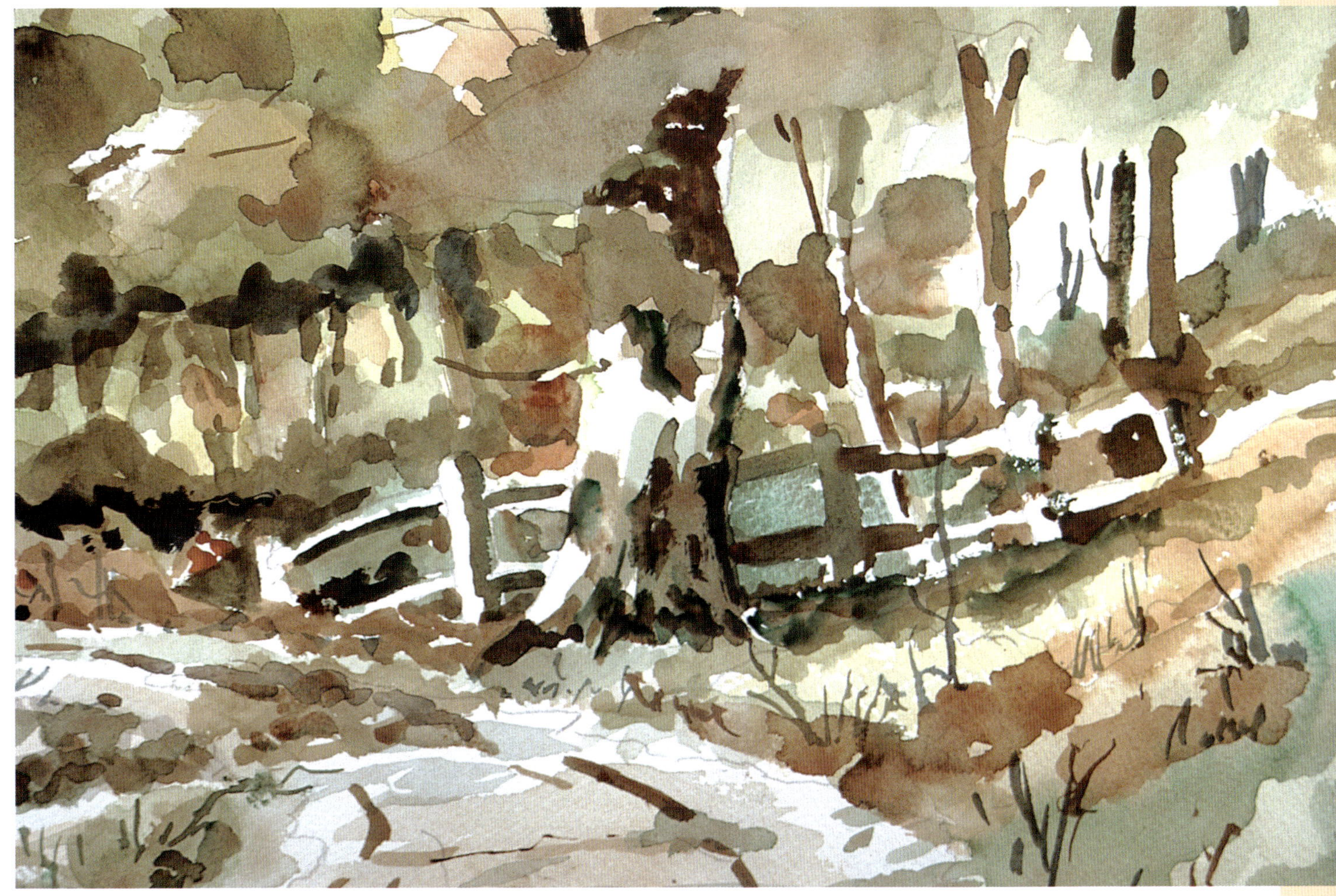

On the right and left side of the lane, a wash of green dominance was painted. The left side had a deeper value than the right side that received more light. I used a number 18 round brush to dab and paint these random areas. In the boulder chain, the left side did not seem to recede, so a dark muted green was dropped into the carpet of forest on the left side. A watered down light wash of the same green was glazed over some shadows on the rocks. I was ready to put some details like branches in the trees and sprigs of grass or weeds in the foreground.

STEP 3 ▲

This is a close-up of the fence area in the center of the picture. It will be the first place where value is added. I painted a small area in between sections of the fence openings. The light was coming in from the left front quarter, which required me to place shadows on the right side of the fence posts and the underside of the rail. On the right side of the tree to the right, a portion of the fence was in shadow; I painted it dark. The rest of the fence on that side was light. This dark against light and light against dark is called alternation.

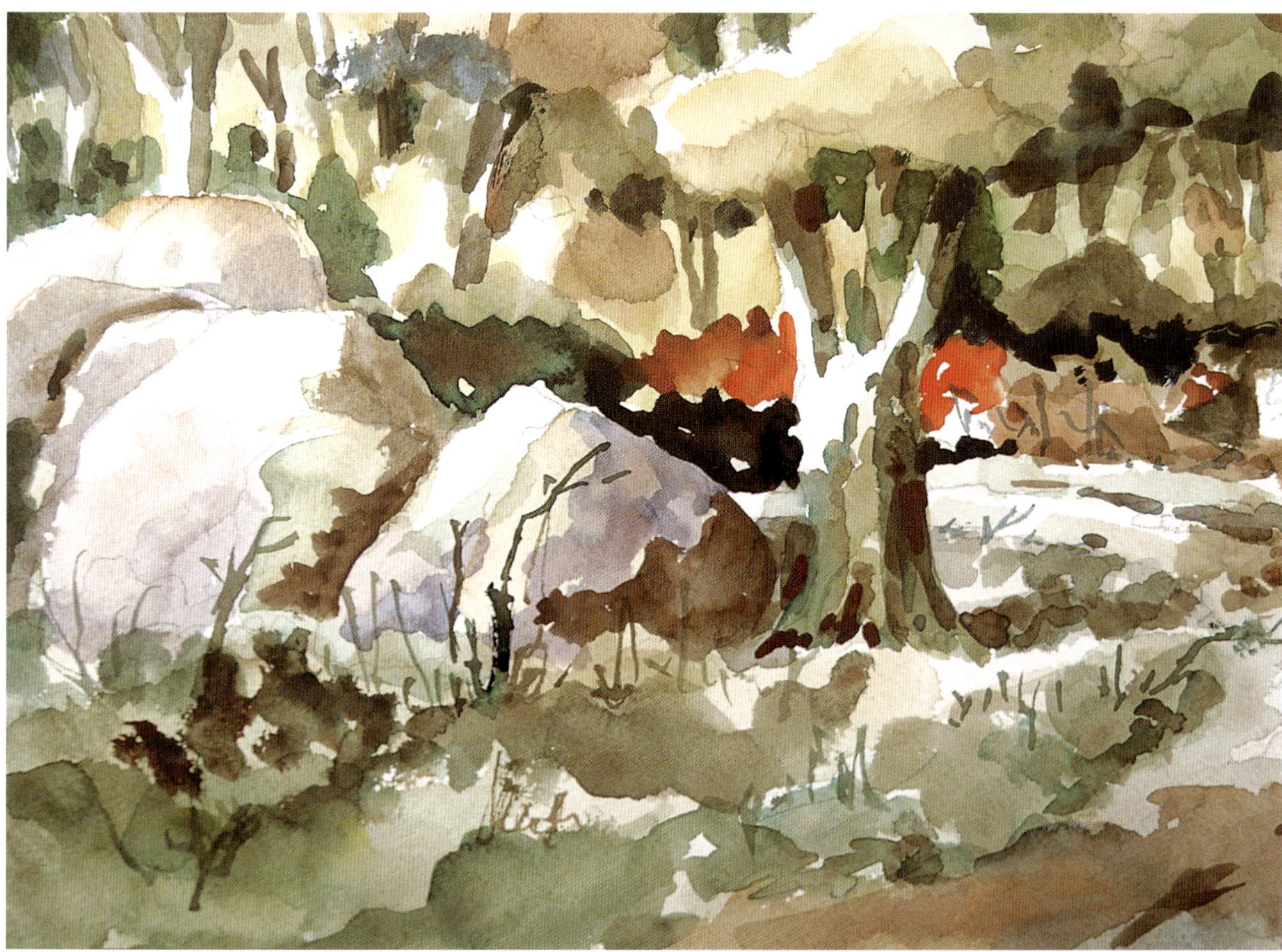

STEP 4 ▲

The brilliant sunlight that came through an opening in the foliage illuminated the trunk on the left foreground tree. Middle ground trees that poked their way up into the foliage were added. Moving over to the left tree trunk, the left side in shadow seemed to be lost. I reinforced the area between the rock and trunk below the lane with a spot of real dark value. It now stood out. Some lightly muted Burnt Sienna was dabbed in on the dirt bank in the lower left corner along the side of the lane. It helped to separate the lane from the little rise in terrain. Further on the left side of the lane, I painted some small areas of cool forest green. The lane was cool on the left and a little warmer from sunlight on the right.

Working my way up into the interior of the forest above the lane, I painted in some tree trunks that came up from the undergrowth, and I made them disappear into the leafy area above. To make the transition between the trees and foliage, I darkened the lower under portion of foliage to put it into shadow. I switched to a small rigger brush, and painted little branches in the various leaf openings. In the foreground, areas of weeds and grass were painted randomly. There were a few larger foreground weeds painted up and over some background areas to give a third dimension. At this point, I realized I could make or break my painting. At the same time I could have some fun. But I knew that I had to be careful not to overdo the embellishments that were so easy to create with the rigger brush. I restrained myself. My painting truly represents a forest scene painted as a loose watercolor.

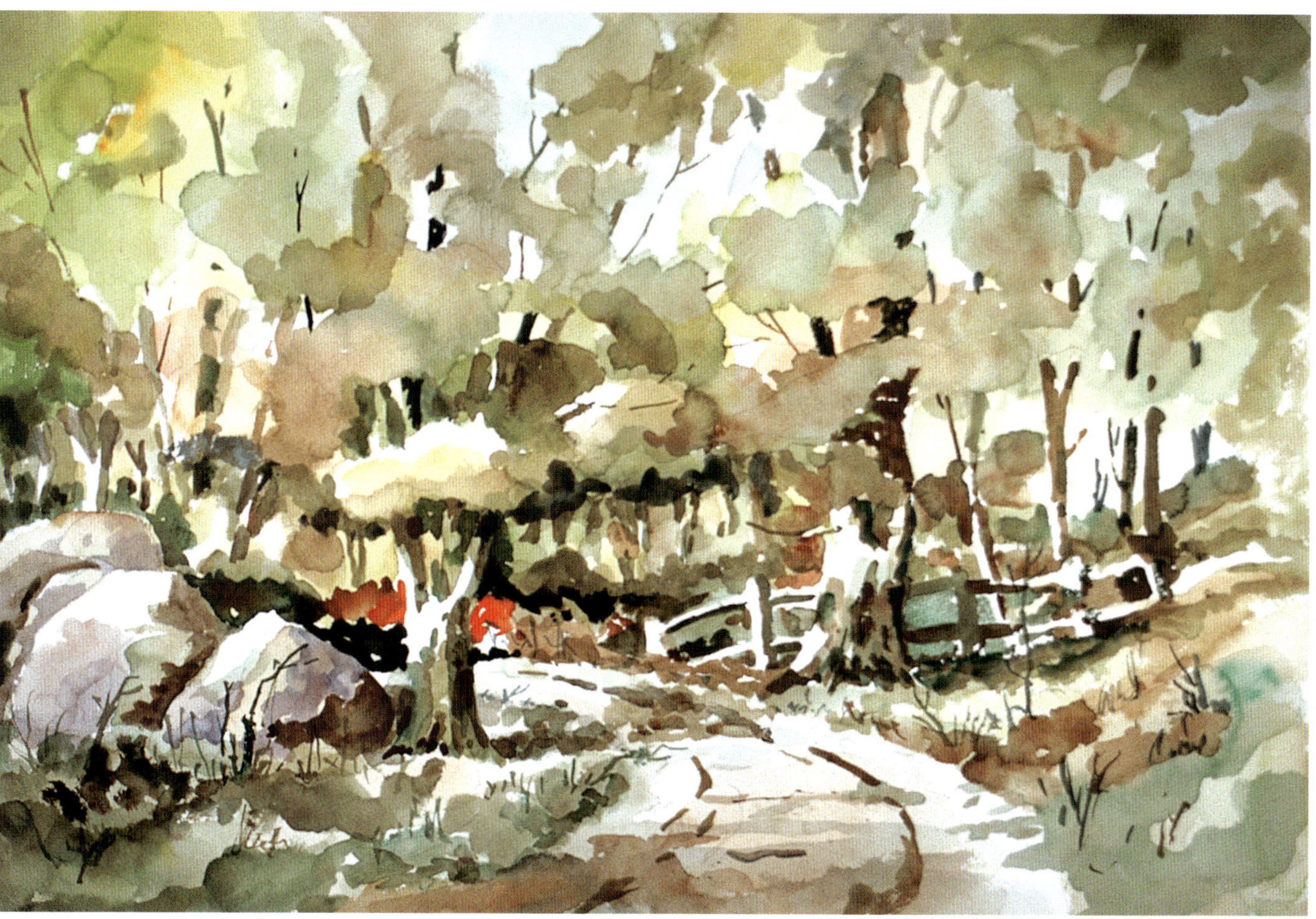

Silent Forest, 15 x 22", 140 lb. Arches

Be Spontaneous
in Your Studio

During a watercolor workshop, while traveling through central Illinois farm country looking for a scene to paint, we happened upon this interesting group of barns. The overgrown lane took a sharp left turn and disappeared between the two barns. This made it an ideal place for a center of interest. I especially liked the barn on the right with the cupola or dormer. It contrasted with the plain red roof of the central barn. The row of sheds also was interesting, though in my sketch I took the liberty of moving a few of the buildings closer together for the sake of a better composition.

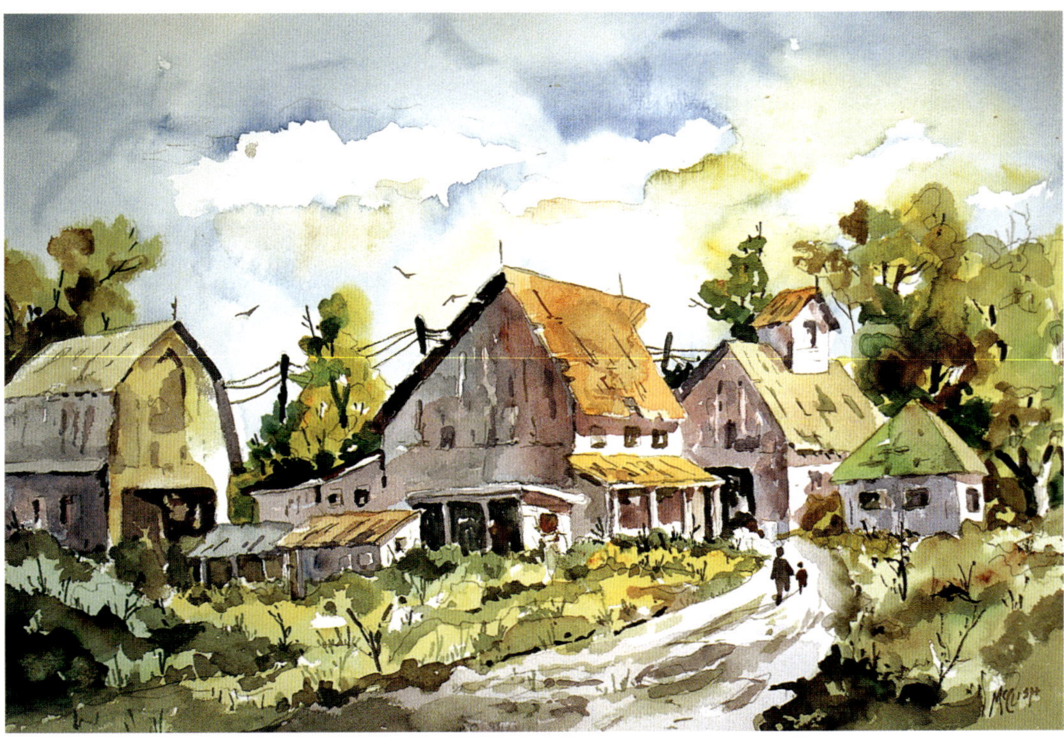

10

A barn
in Illinois

I edited the scene in my sketch
to help the composition.

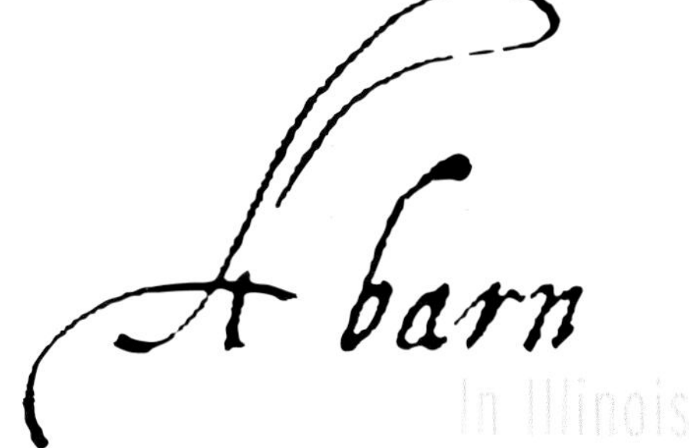

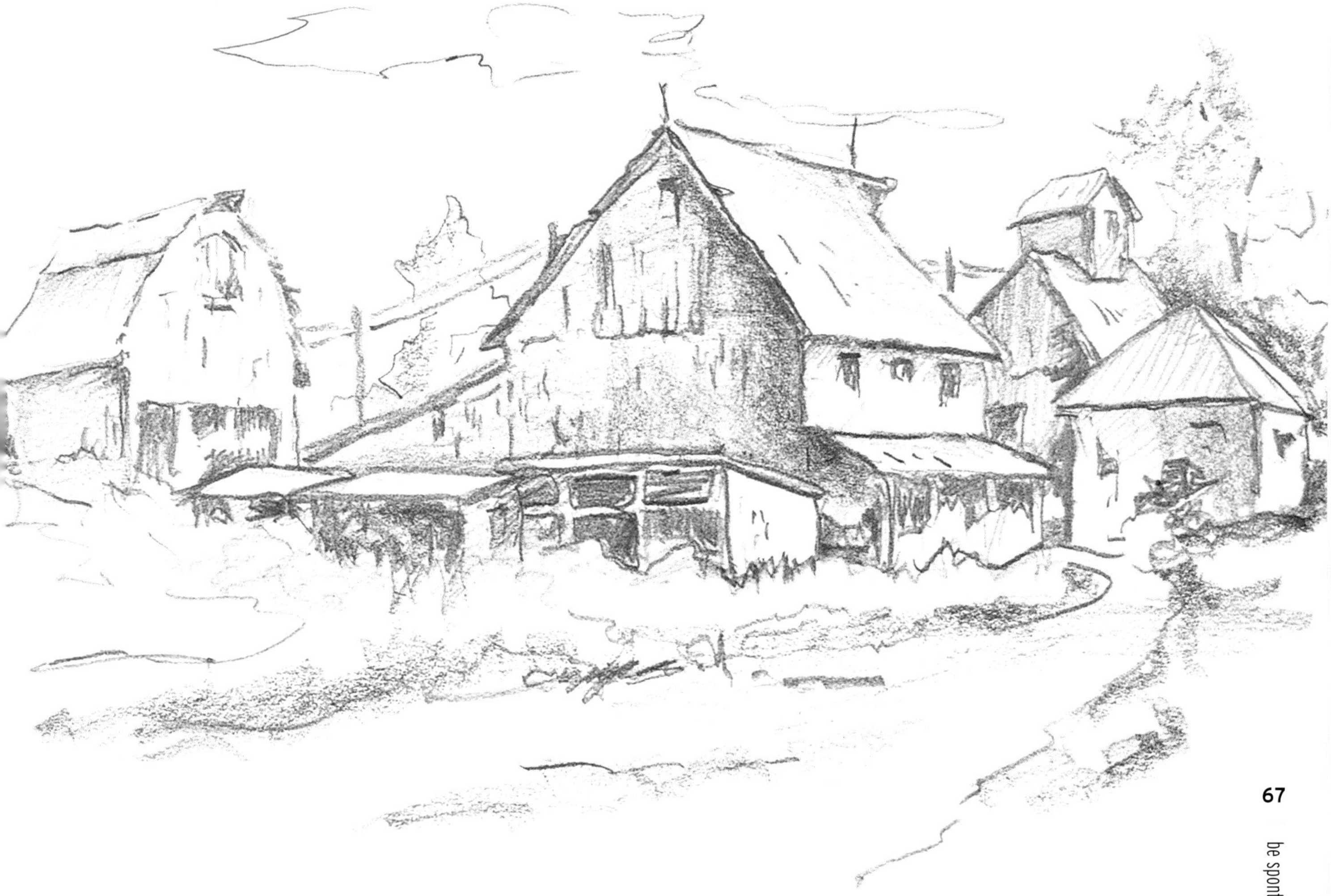

STEP 1 ▶

With my value sketch in hand, I made a limited sketch on a half sheet of watercolor paper. In the pencil drawing, as you can see, all details were kept to a minimum.

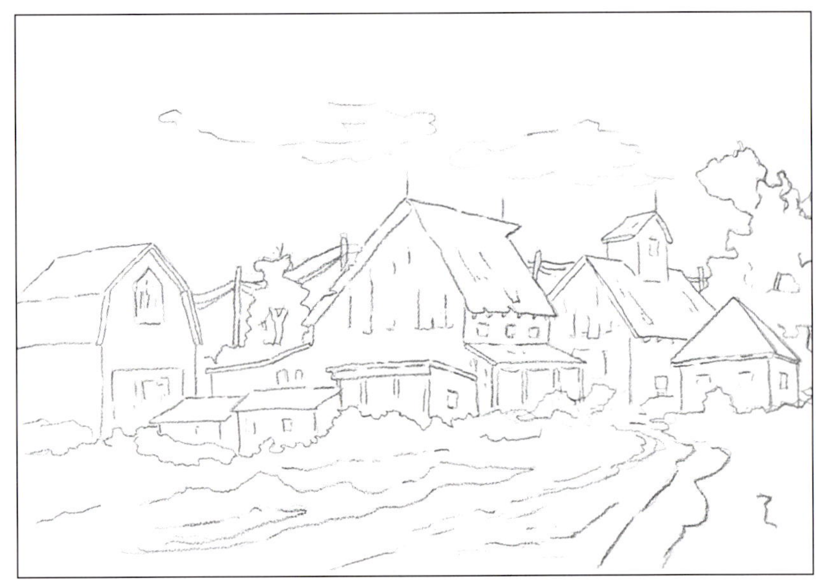

STEP 2 ▼

I painted the sky first. Starting on the left side with a number 12 round brush, I dampened the sky area with the exception of the clouds. Using a wash of Thalo Blue, I painted all the way across the sheet. The upper left corner of the sky was a little deeper value of blue than the right side. I painted around various cloud shapes. The tops of the clouds were mainly well defined and the bottom edges were partially softened. While still wet, I spotted in a little Burnt Sienna under the clouds. Then, I added some New Gamboge in various areas of the sky to lighten it and to vary the Thalo Blue. I painted around the tree foliage shapes but did not follow the drawing exactly. Once the tree foliage will be painted, it will overlap the sky areas in some places giving a color and value change. The sky should not predominate. It should just say "Sky." In the lower foreground, I mixed up Thalo Blue and New Gamboge to get a nice light yellow-green. It made an under painting for areas of foliage and ground cover. The puddle of yellow-green was alternated many times by additions of some Burnt Sienna, New Gamboge, or Thalo Blue. These varied mixtures were added in various places to add interest. I added a touch of Thalo Green to cool off some areas mainly in the two lower corners. These washes were all from the one puddle of yellow-green that was alternated several times.

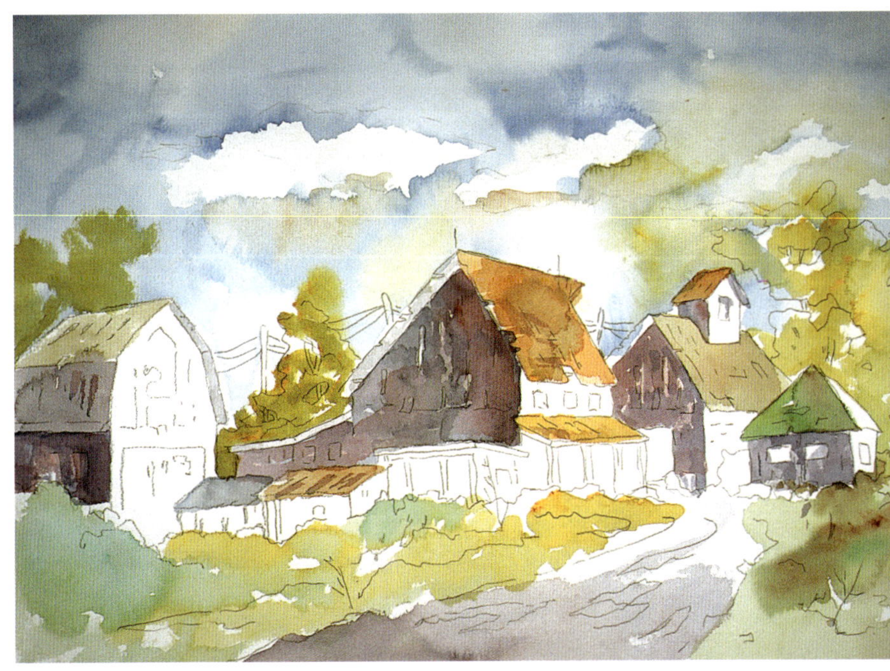

STEP 3

It was now time to work on the roof area. I made a puddle of Cadmium Red Light mixed with New Gamboge. Since it was a little on the bright side, I added a touch of Burnt Sienna to quiet it down. Although it was still warm it seemed about right. I used this mixture to paint the central barn roof. I added some Thalo Blue to cool it down and painted the roof of the barn on the right. The barn with the double gabled roof on the far left was not one of the principle buildings in this picture but it was necessary in the composition. Its roof didn't get much direct sunlight but got some light from the sky. I mixed a small amount of light lavender using Thalo Blue and Alizarin Crimson. The top roof panel got more light than the lower section so I added a little New Gamboge and water to its wash. I painted one small shed roof with grayed lavender. The middle-shed roof got a little of the warm orange that was left over

in a paint puddle. I painted the interior of the sheds with a dull lavender made from blue, red, and Burnt Sienna. The road was a receding plane and varied in value, size, and color as it went back. I reinforced the puddle of lavender and, starting at the bottom of the page, I laid in a wash that got lighter because I added water as the plane receded. To alternate the color a little, I dropped in a little New Gamboge in the far areas. Using the same lavender puddle, I mixed a little more Alizarin Crimson in to warm it up and used it to paint the shadow side of the buildings. They were all a little different in value and the mixture was varied with Alizarin, Thalo Blue and Burnt Sienna. On the two barns to the right, I darkened the wash where it met the sunlit side. On the shadow side, some of the vertical plank edges were left as narrow white streaks. I put some dark green areas as random places in the foreground foliage.

STEP 4

Green is one of the most difficult colors for most artists to handle. Full strength Thalo Green is a cold color that is seldom used alone but is a good basic color to use in a mix. Mixed with New Gamboge, it results in a nice warm yellow-green. Using small and large amounts of Burnt Sienna, you can get many different colors of green that range from a light warm brown-green all the way to where it is almost black. By adding New Gamboge, Alizarin Crimson or Thalo Blue you can further expand the range of dominant green colors. You will also get a good variety of greens by mixing Thalo Blue and New Gamboge. I put all this into use when I added more detail in the different foliage areas by putting into play various mixtures of green. Where the tree foliage met the building roofs, sections were painted with a dark, almost black-looking green. This dropped the foliage back and brought the barns forward, helping to create a third dimension. Using a light value of Thalo Blue and Burnt Sienna, I put some background lines in the roofs following the slope to indicate rows of shingles. These would be varied and reinforced in the final painting.

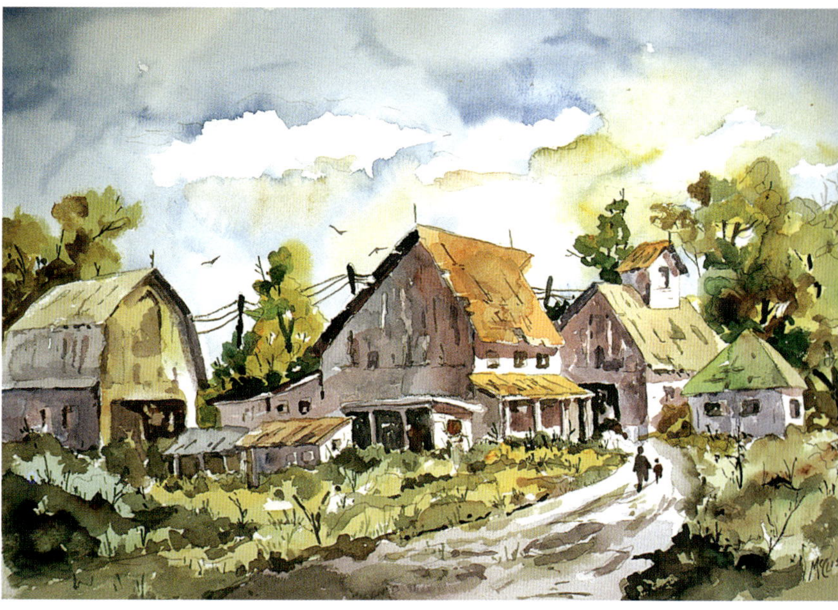

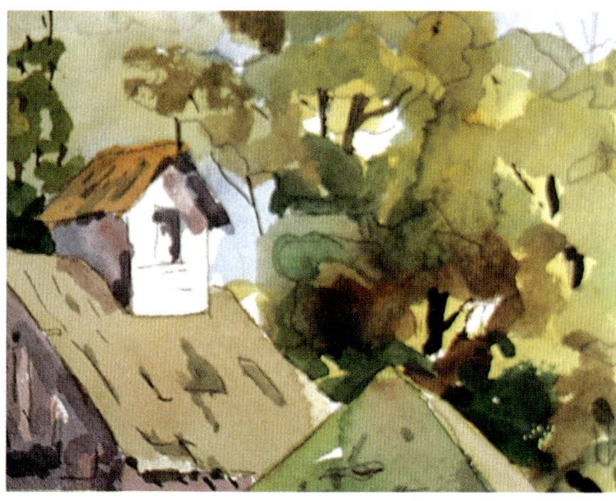

DETAIL. This is a close-up of the shed area. I used grayed colors to paint the interiors. The interior of the larger shed on the right received a deeper value of paint because it was closer to the center of interest.

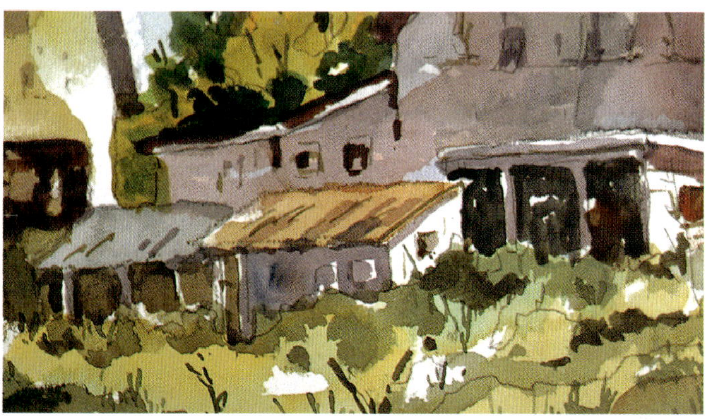

MORE DETAIL. I was intrigued with the cupola on the right barn. The tree foliage on its left side was darkened dropping in behind. On the right side of the cupola, there was light blue sky. This variation separated it and the rest of the barn from the background foliage and sky. Tree foliage was further darkened to the right where it abutted the barn roof and where it met the peaked roof of the building on the right. I added some warm color in the upper right area of the trees indicating distant foliage.

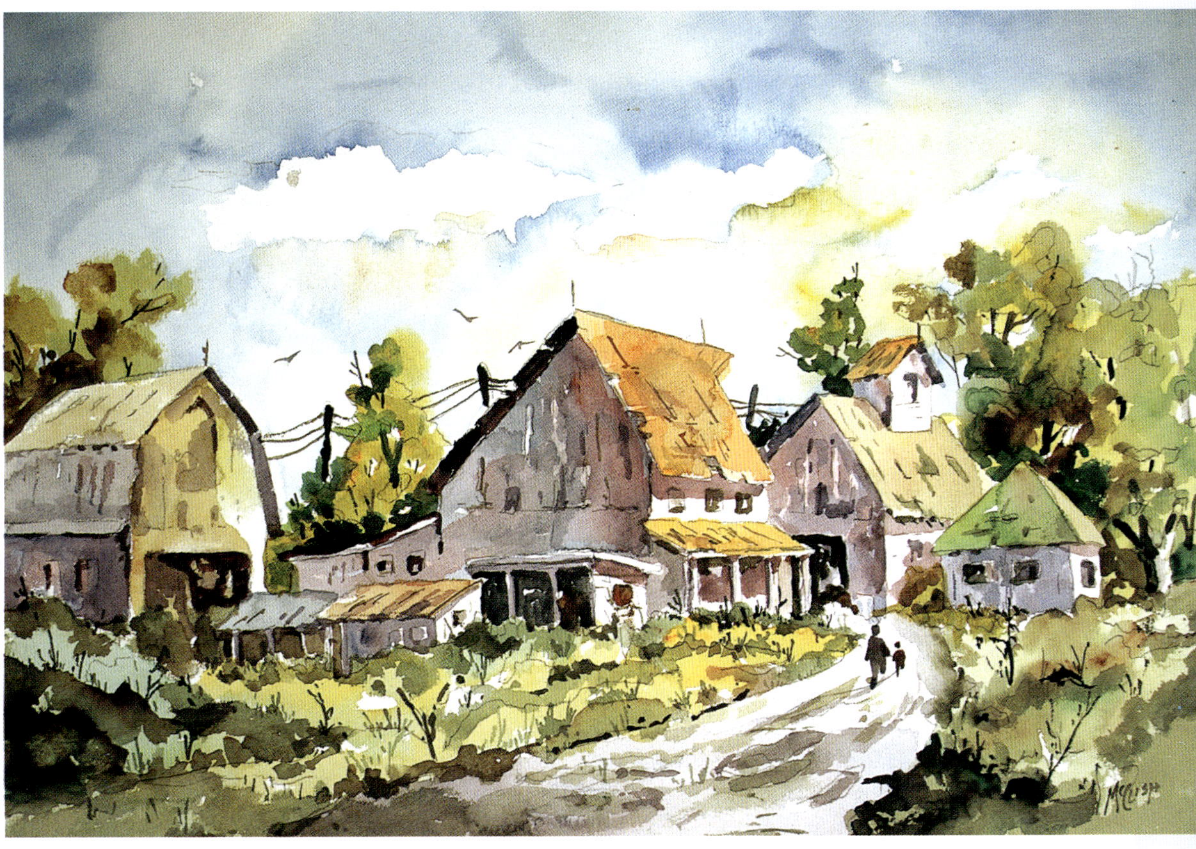

Illinois Barns, 15 x 22", 140 lb. Arches

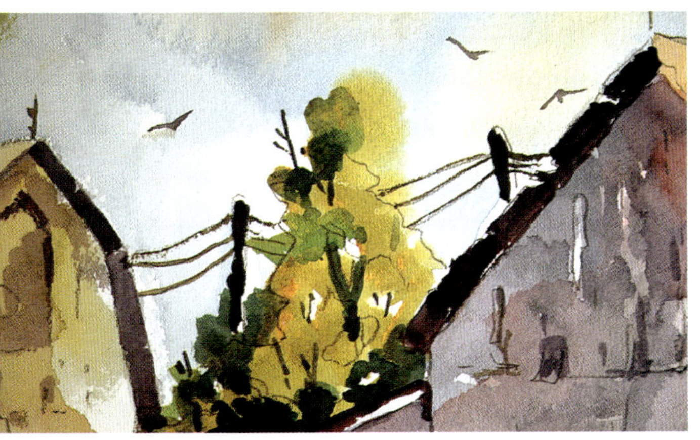

AND MORE DETAIL. In this close-up of the area between the two left barns, I want to point out the tree with electric poles and wires going across behind it. I created the third dimension with the tree behind the barns and the poles and wires behind the tree. The poles are leaning and the wires are splayed out to not follow the same pattern. The shadow side of the central barn is cooled off with an addition of Thalo Blue as it recedes. There are always pigeons or other birds around a barn so I put in three birds. I placed two birds on the right side and one on the left. The left bird balances the other two.

STEP 5

The fun part in any painting is always adding details. Using a mixture of Thalo Blue and Burnt Sienna, I made a warm dark to be used under the eaves of all the barns. I then used variations of this mixture in the shadow areas under the two sheds. Next, I lightened the mixture and used it to put cast shadows under the eaves on the sunlit walls under the roof eaves of the barns. Some of the foliage areas were darkened. Some had a wash of yellow green in some areas for variation. I had fun with the foliage but did not get it overly complicated. Some of the foreground weeds and grasses were given a touch of warm yellow green. With a rigger that was loaded with a very dark green mixture, I put weeds or tall grass sprigs in scattered areas of the ground foliage. In the tree foliage, I painted just a few indications of tree trunks and branches. They appeared in openings of the foliage mantle and then disappeared back into it. I painted a couple of renegade leafless branches coming out of the tops of the trees. Some details were added in the roof planes to just say "shingles." I modified lavender with Burnt Sienna and glazed over some sections of the foreground area of the lane. I added little details to the lane indicating ruts and other textures in the roadway. Finally, I painted a farmer and his son walking up the lane just to inject some human interest into the piece.

The All-Important Sketch

n my teaching experiences, I have found that one of the areas where many students are woefully weak is in not making a detailed pencil sketch before going to a brush to paint. The reason, some have said, is that they did not want to draw; they only want to paint. Without a reasonably correct sketch, I would tell them, it would be difficult for them to come up with a successful painting. Sketches have always solved for me the important problems of composition, value and perspective. In fact, my sketches work out all the problems, except color, before I make even one stroke of the brush. Of course, not all painters do this. I know artists who, seeking to produce loose watercolors, will choose to sketch directly with a brush onto their watercolor paper. Their paintings are very good, and they are loose and sparkling. But their success with this procedure does not mean that this is the only way to paint a loose watercolor. Doing a detailed pencil sketch has never stopped me from getting a loose look in my watercolor paintings. The reproductions throughout this book are evidence of the success of my approach to painting loose watercolors.

One of the fringe benefits of my sketchbook is that it reminds me of the exciting places I've been to. The important asset, however, are the sketches that furnish me with material for studio paintings. As far as color is concerned, I sometimes use a reference photograph taken at the site. Actually, correct color is not that important unless you are making an engineering drawing. There are artists who place their photographs in an overhead projector and then superimpose the colored image directly onto the painting surface. They switch the projector on and off during the painting process, managing to paint the picture entirely from the image; this gives them a faithful rendition, but also one that is extremely mechanical. This process produces what is called "photo realism" and I consider it a serious hindrance to an artist's pursuit of a loose watercolor.

I make two kinds of sketches. The first one I draw is a value sketch that includes the major elements of a scene. In it, I eliminate unimportant things and concentrate on the more relevant items that contribute to the aestheticness of the picture. I move things around; I make sure the perspective is valid and I get all of my values as accurate as I can. Keep in mind that the sketch serves as a pattern for a painting, a kind of blueprint. Admittedly, the sketch has not solved the use of color.

The second type of a sketch that I draw is simply an unadorned line drawing that is lightly sketched on the sheet of paper in preparation for the painting. I use the value sketch as my guide for all of the proper values.

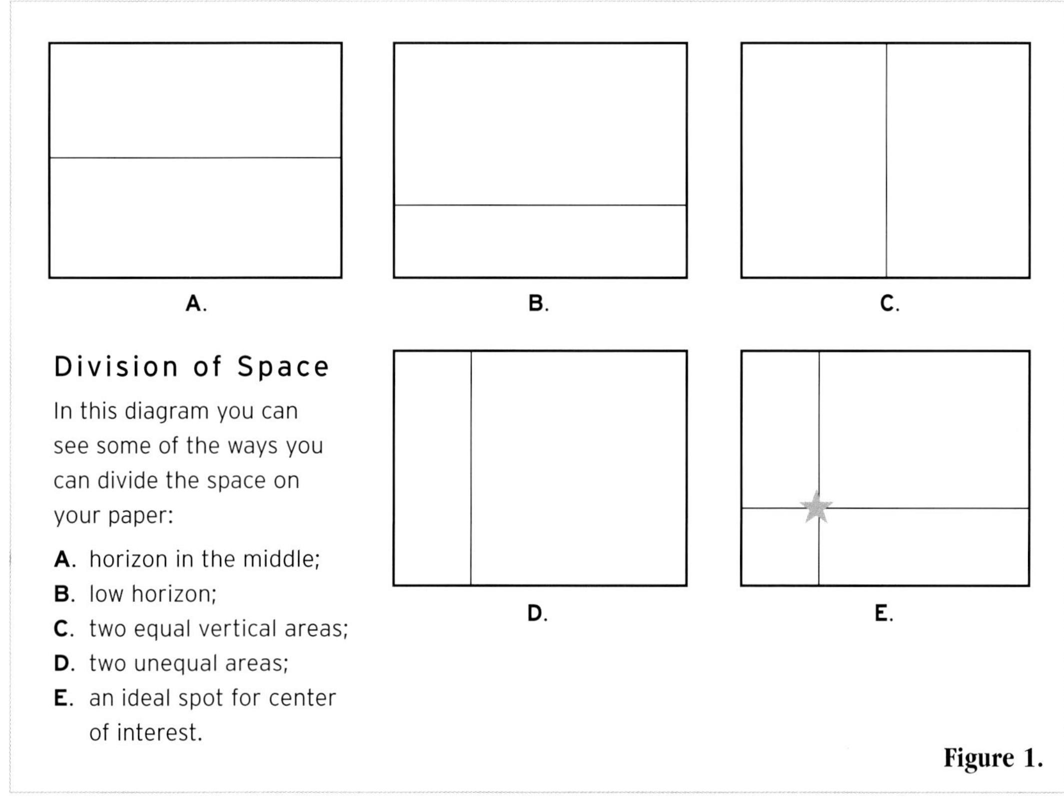

A.

B.

C.

Division of Space

In this diagram you can see some of the ways you can divide the space on your paper:

A. horizon in the middle;
B. low horizon;
C. two equal vertical areas;
D. two unequal areas;
E. an ideal spot for center of interest.

D.

E.

Figure 1.

Elements of a Sketch

When I plan a sketch, the first thing I establish is the picture area. What am I going to have in my picture and what am I going to say? If it's a farm scene, for example, am I going to emphasize the beautiful cloudy sky with a low horizon thus relegating the barns to a secondary role? Or should I focus on the barns with a high horizon, making the sky secondary? Or is the focus to be the field in front of the barn structures that will make barn and sky secondary? All of this compositional planning is a matter of division of space as well as center of interest.

Division of space

In Figure 1, example **A**, we see a horizontal division of space with the horizon and eye level in the middle. The two equal areas will compete for viewer attention, which makes for a difficult composition. In example **B**, I have lowered the horizon. This is a much better division of space with the two unequal areas. A lot of landscape compositions are designed to use this division of space. If you were to turn this design over, you would get a high horizon, also a good division. Example **C** is a central vertical division of space that again has two equal areas—right and left—that competes for your attention. I have corrected that error in example **D**, having moved the division to the left, thus creating two unequal areas. This is a much more interesting division of space. Even if a low or high horizon is decided on for a composition, as the drawing proceeds, that horizon will somehow start creeping toward the middle of the sheet. In **E**, I have used examples **B** and **D** in one composition. The lines intersect and that gives me a good area for a center of interest. If you move the horizontal to the top and the vertical to the right you will get other intersections that are all safe places for centers of interest.

Center of interest

The center of interest is, oddly enough, never in the center. This is the area—also referred to as the focal point—that is designed to direct the viewer's eye to the salient points of the painting. The centers of interest are usually situated in the upper third on the left, the upper third on the right, the lower third on the left and the lower third on the right. Again, never in the center. There are other kinds of centers of interest: It can be a divided center, in which objects that create the center usually are close together; in a split center, like the divided, where objects creating the center usually are close together, but in a split center, they

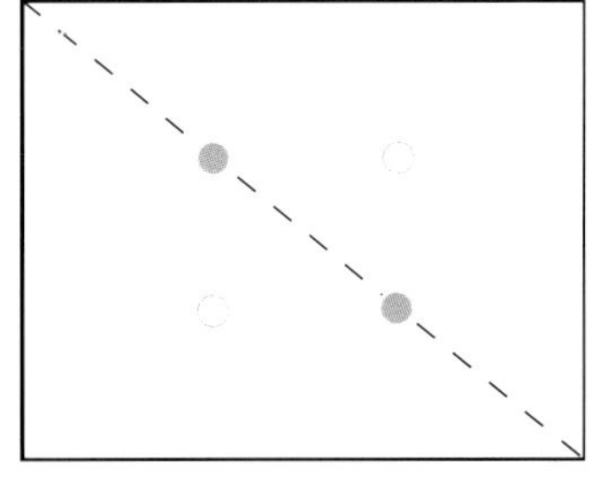

Center of Interest

The four spots you see in this diagram are located one-third in from the top and bottom and left and right of the sheet of paper. They represent the ideal establishments of centers of interest in most paintings.

Figure 2.

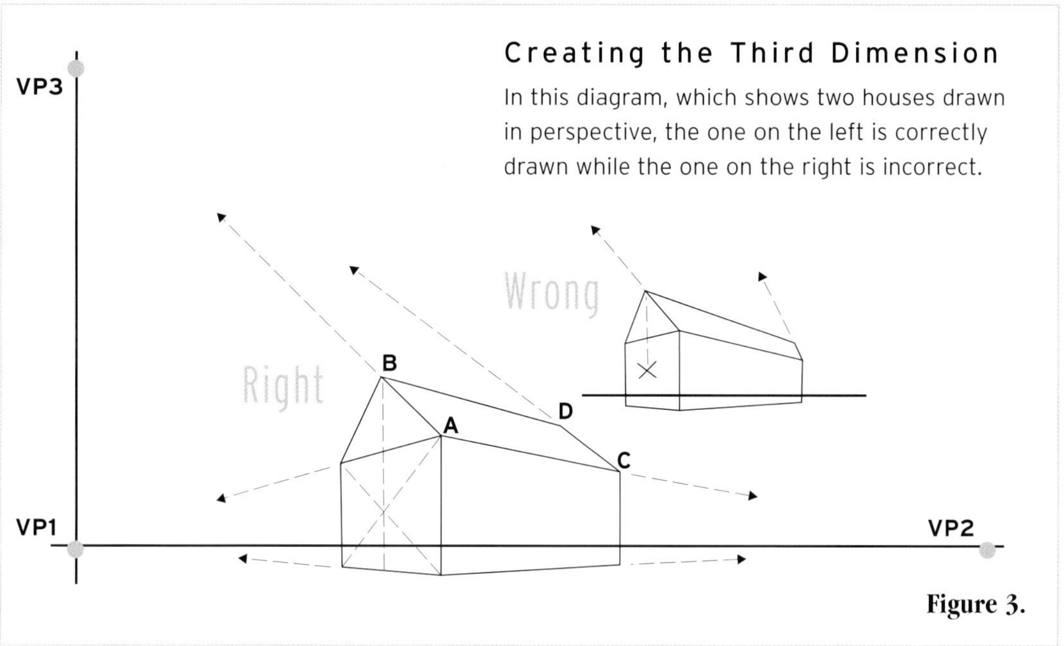

In this diagram, which shows two houses drawn in perspective, the one on the left is correctly drawn while the one on the right is incorrect.

Figure 3.

can be almost anywhere in the composition; and there's a scattered center, much like a wallpaper pattern, which is used in a lot of folk art, with little interesting areas all over the composition.

In Figure 2, we see the traditional way to locate safe, interesting areas. I've drawn a diagonal from one corner of the composition to another. It is divided into thirds and either of the two junctures would be a safe center of interest.

Creating the third dimension

A painting surface has two dimensions: length and width. In order for the artist to interpret reality, he has to create a third dimension. Let's call this depth, which is the appearance of an object coming out from the surface of the painting surface— the watercolor paper, in our case— toward the viewer. There are several ways for the representational painter to get this illusion of a third dimension:

- Perspective
- Change in size, color, texture or definition
- Overlap of objects
- Change in value

Perspective

I did this diagram of a simple building using two vanishing points. In many cases, there is a third vanishing point, either up or down, but in this instance it would be such a long distance away that we can consider the vertical lines to be parallel. To locate the center of the gable end, I drew two diagonal lines across the end of the building and where they crossed was the perspective center of the square. If you draw a vertical line up from this point, the peak of the roof will lay at some arbitrary place on that line to be decided by the artist. The vanishing trace might be compared to a special case of a vertical horizon. It is a vertical

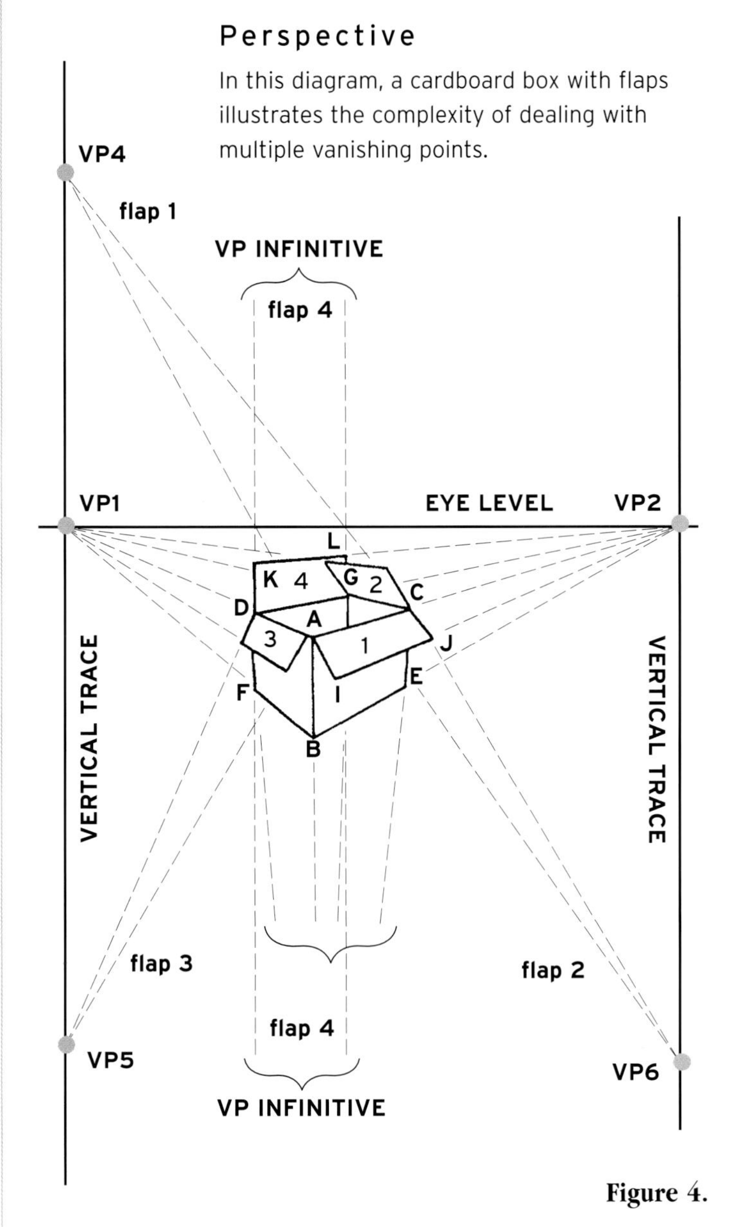

Figure 4.

So far I have dealt with horizontal or perpendicular lines, but how about the angled roof of a house, or a flap on a box that may be at any angle? When a plane departs from a vertical or horizontal position and becomes oblique, the vanishing point moves up or down from eye level on a "trace," or a vertical horizon.

I've redrawn the box of the house (Figure 3) and put flaps on it along the sides of the box. How do we know which way a line is receding to a vanishing point? It is easy. Just look at the two ends of the line and figure which end is closest to you. The line is then receding the other way from that point. Each flap has its own vanishing point, as follows:

- The front line (**I-J**) is parallel to the rear of the flap (**A-C**). They both recede to the same **VP2**.

- The sides of this same flap, **I-A** and **J-C**, are parallel to them and recede in their own plane toward the upper left to **VP4**.

- The left and right flaps will recede in their own plane. The left flap (**3**) to **VP5**; the right flap (**2**) to **VP6**.

- The back flap (**4**) is a special case. The top and bottom appear equidistant from the eye, so the vertical ends could recede either way. In this case, it would be proper to make lines **K-D** and **L-G** parallel, which would put two vanishing points, **VP7** and **VP8**, at an infinite distance, one above, the other below the planes of the flap.

You can see that by looking at the angle of the flaps of an actual box, you will be able to locate the vertical vanishing point.

line that goes up or down from the reference vanishing point on the horizon. In this case, it goes up. Draw a line from point **A** through **B** crossing the vanishing trace to local vanishing point three. A line from point **C** to this **VP3** will have the correct angle on the other end of the roof. Then a line **BD** to **VP2** will finish the roof. In the house shown in the inset at the right, there's a common error in perspective that happens when the vanishing trace is not used.

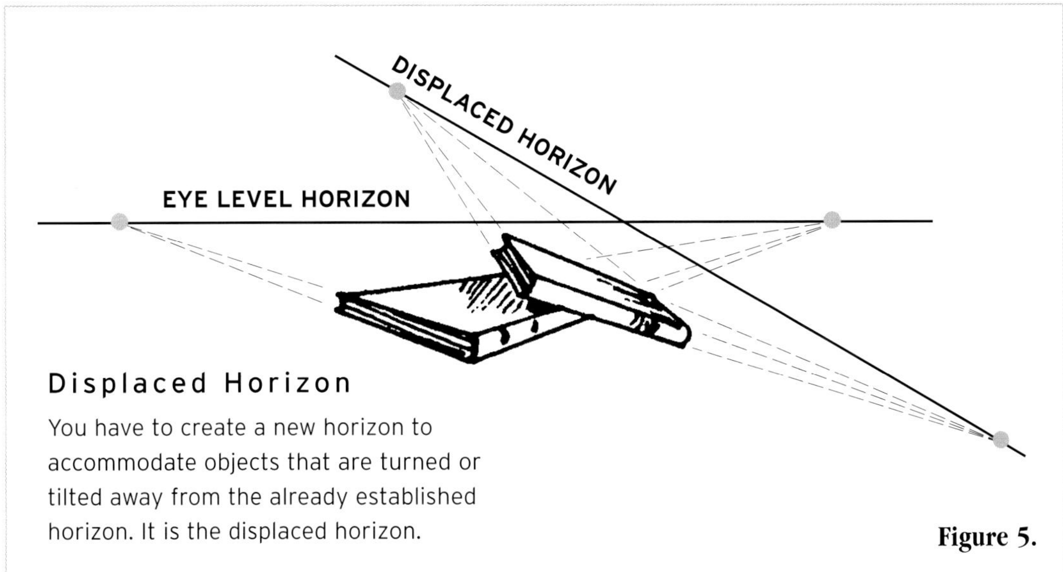

Displaced Horizon

You have to create a new horizon to accommodate objects that are turned or tilted away from the already established horizon. It is the displaced horizon.

Figure 5.

Eye level is always directly in front of you and level with your eyes. This is true if you are standing on a mountain, in a valley or even in a coalmine. The horizon does not, in all instances, coincide with eye level; it may be tilted or displaced, thereby needing to have its own horizon.

All vanishing points do not have to lie on a special line like an eye level or vanishing trace line. In Figure 6, there are three drawings that show more wandering vanishing points. Each point has its own horizon line due to the change of plane when the road goes up or down hill.

In example **A**, the road goes from level to up hill, then down and finally back up and over a hill. Example **B** has the road turning. In the final example **C**, the road disappears over a hill and reappears again going in a different direction.

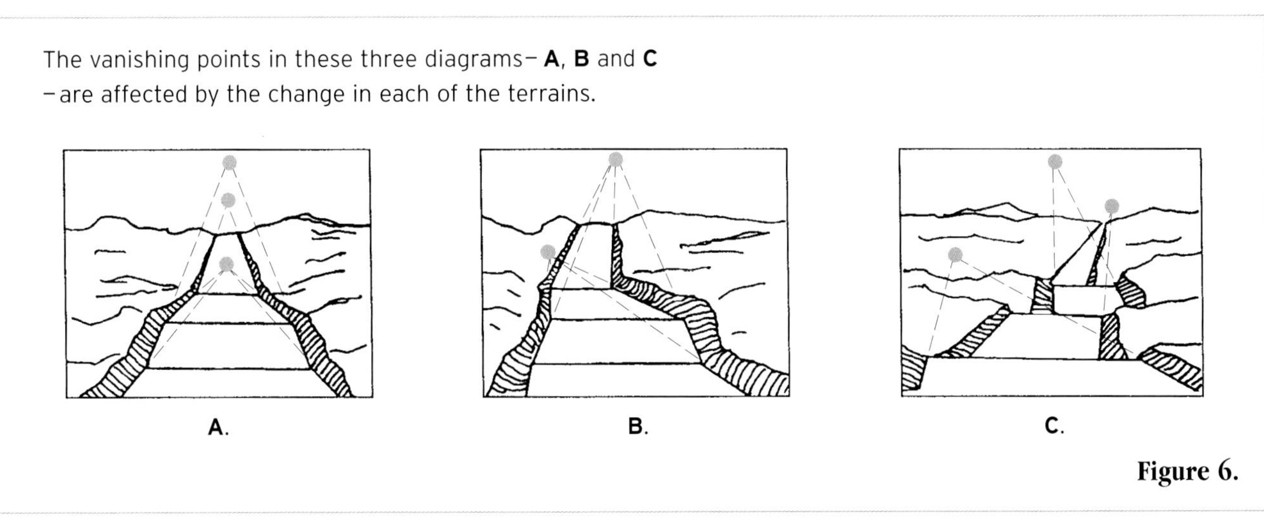

Figure 6.

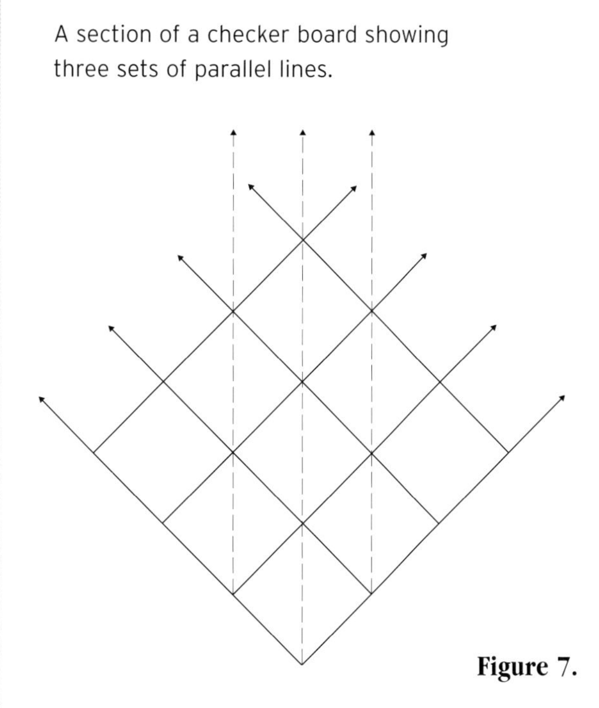

A section of a checker board showing three sets of parallel lines.

Figure 7.

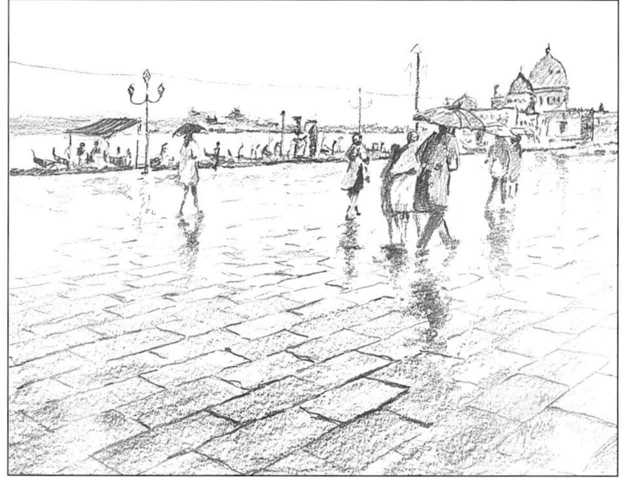

In this sketch, the paving blocks of St. Mark's Square in Venice, Italy, are treated the same way as a checkerboard in perspective. Only the foreground blocks are well defined. They lose definition as they recede into the background.

How to make a patio lay down flat

You can use a portion of a checkerboard to analyze how to make the square blocks of a patio look like they are laying flat instead of going up or down hill. The top view of a checkerboard (Figure 7) has parallel lines running in two directions to vanishing points on eye level. Since any two points form a line, there is a third group of parallel lines running diagonally through the board going to a third vanishing point that lies between the other two points on eye level. This elusive point is the one that makes the board lay flat. It is established by drawing (Figure 8) an arbitrary first square— **A B C D**—of the patio. A line from **D** to the center vanishing point establishes point **E**. It is easy to see how the system can continue to build the patio. This first square then controls all others that follow. Using a little artistic ingenuity, you can overlap blocks and change their shapes.

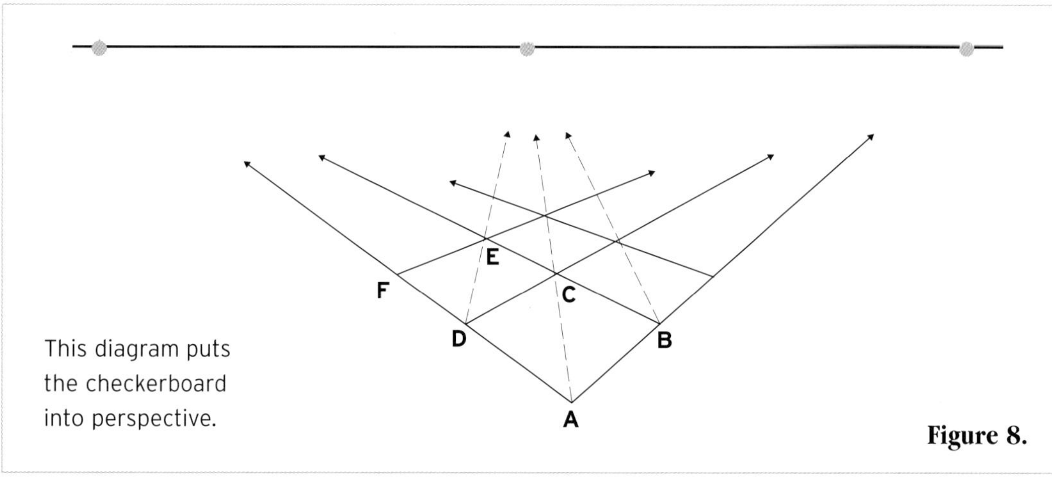

This diagram puts the checkerboard into perspective.

Figure 8.

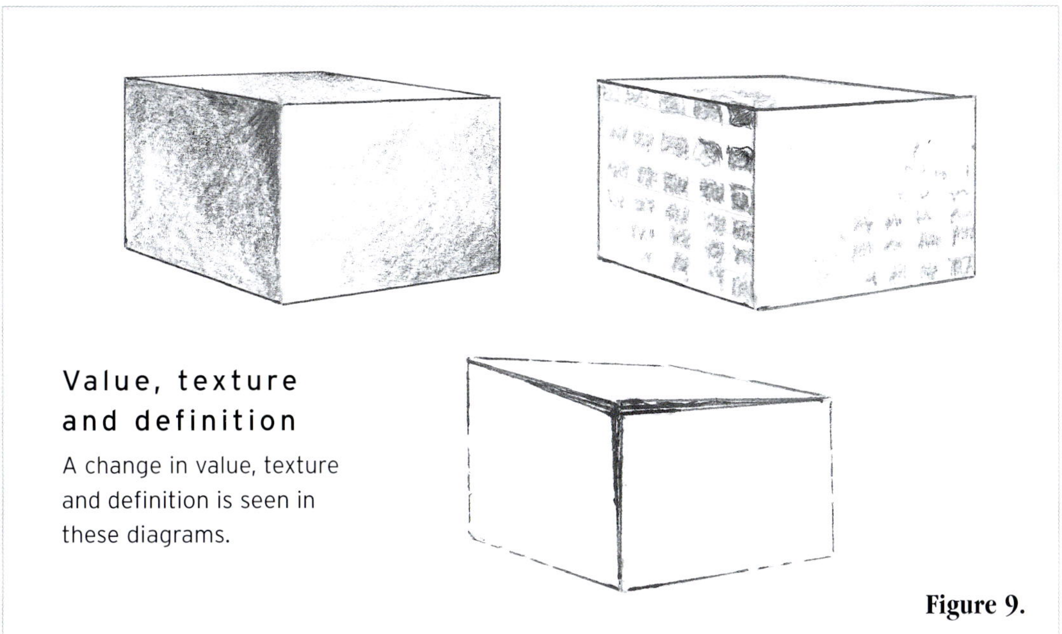

Value, texture and definition

A change in value, texture and definition is seen in these diagrams.

Figure 9.

Value, texture and definition in a sketch

To create the illusion of a third dimension, any receding plane should vary in value, size, texture and definition. It can vary in only one or any of these. From an artistic viewpoint, the rate of change can be speeded up. In the distance, objects may become dim, smaller and may disappear entirely. In a color sketch or the final picture, color also changes with distance. It can be grayed, lightened, darkened or changed from warm to cool. In some rare instances, it can also go from cool to warm. The point is that it has to change.

Overlap of objects

Overlapping one object with another definitely says distance. Multiple overlapping may be used. If the object that is overlapped is some distance away, its size also has decreased along with definition, texture and value. Just remember that distant objects may say, "I am here but a little harder to see."

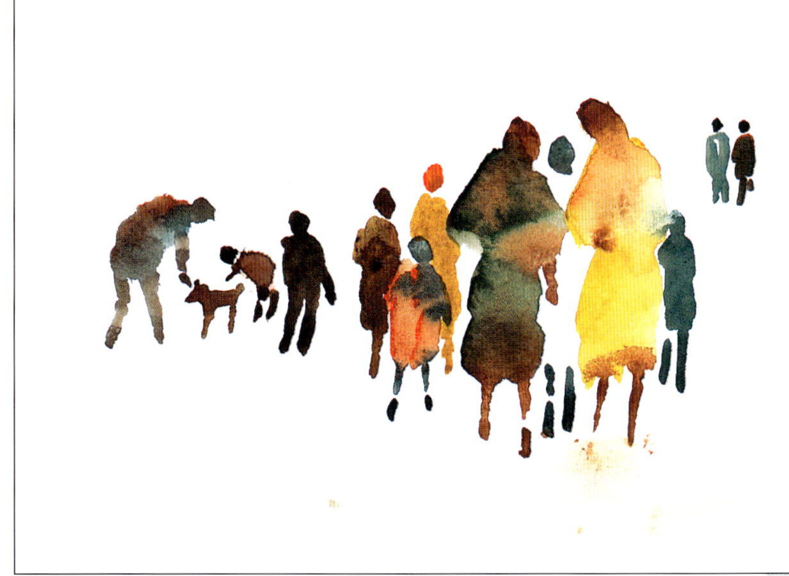

A painting of people shows the value of overlap and insertion.

Dramatize with Darks

sketched this scene at the beautiful Lake Piediluco in Italy's Umbria Province, and, knowing that I'd want to do a more finished painting later on, I also painted a full-color sketch. Since the town was a long distance away across a finger of the lake, I had to make an adjustment in the perspective. It made me move the vanishing points in to bring the scene closer to me. At the same time, I eliminated a few of the buildings because there were just too many of them, which would confuse the composition. Another decision I made was to keep the horizon low in order to focus on the town, the main subject. It's apparent that neither the foreground nor the lake deserves this distinction. It was important, however, that some of the water had to be shown in the composition to indicate that the town was located on a lake. As for the sketch itself, I drew it in lightly and made sure that I was reasonably accurate with the perspective.

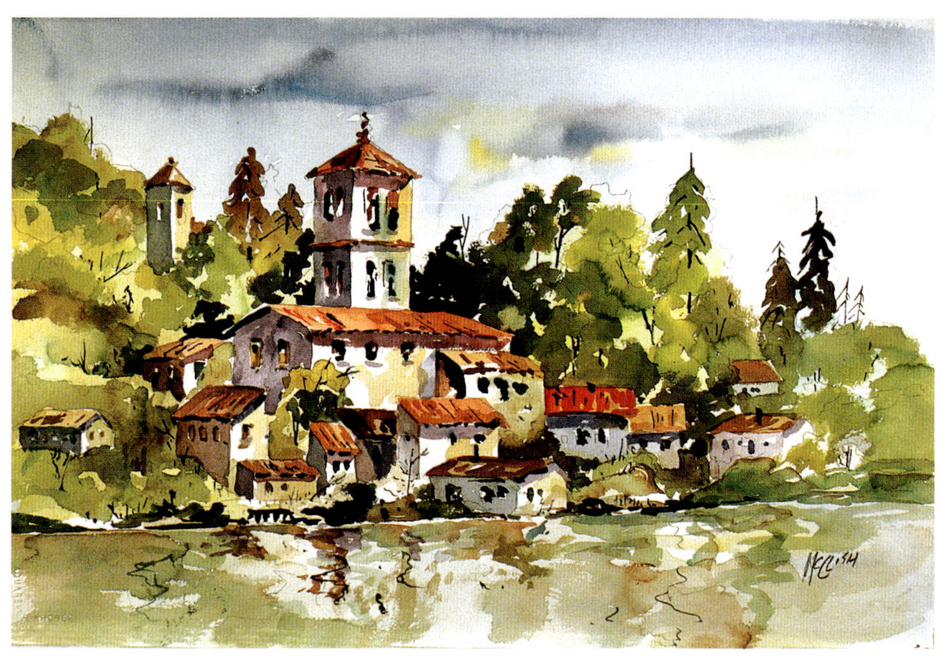

Lake Piediluco
in Italy

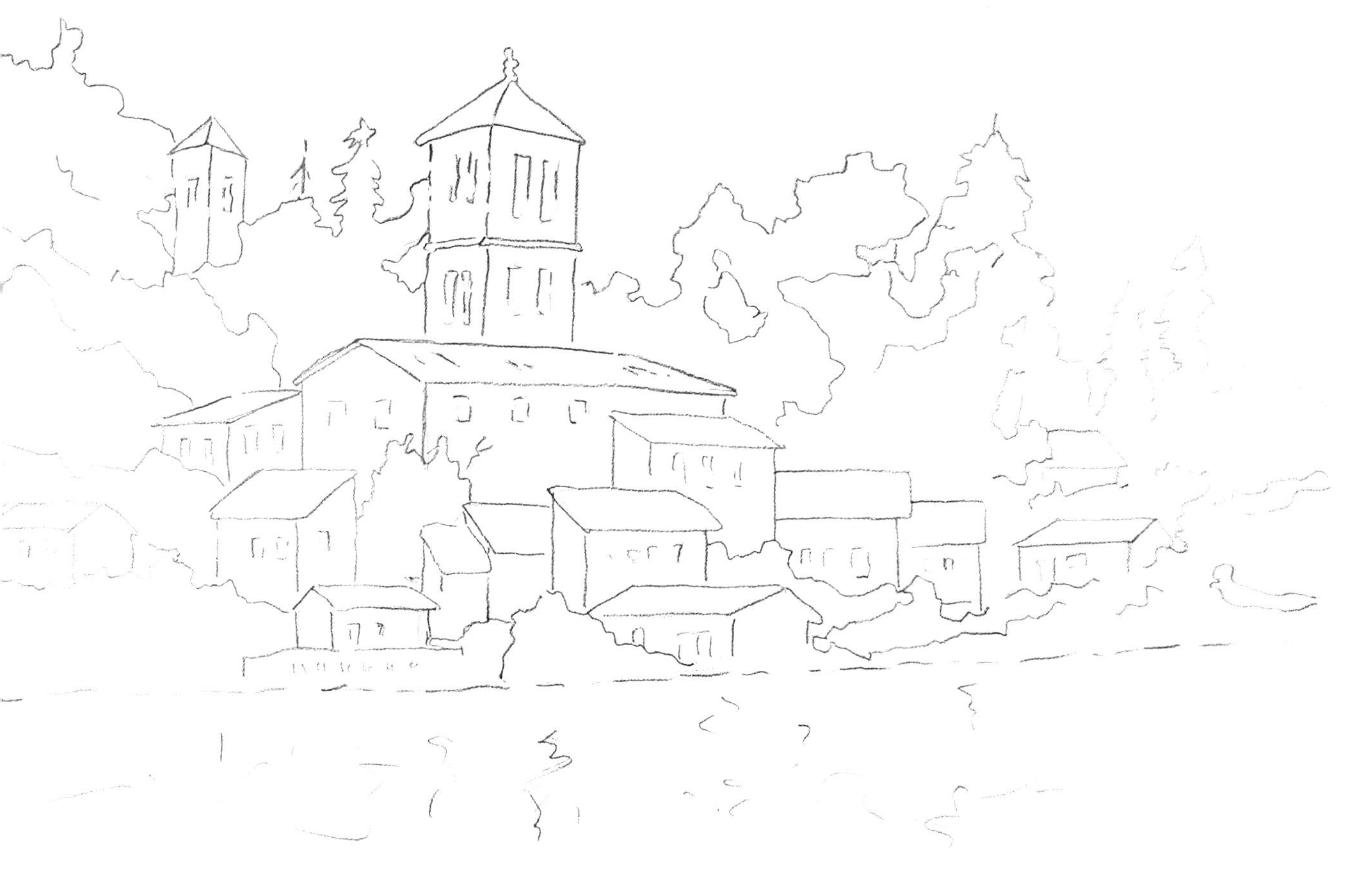

While at the lake, I fortified my penciled
value sketch with one in full-color.

Back in my studio, I began the painting process. Starting with a 1½-inch flat brush, I painted a fairly light wash of Thalo Blue across the top of the paper. With additional water, I brought that wash down to the foliage and building line. While the area was still wet, I stroked on some New Gamboge. I then indicated a couple of clouds by wiping out sections of the blue wash, using a partly dried brush. To get the brush dried out to do the wipeout, I swished it through the upper water in the pail and then raked it across the forward lip of the bucket a few times. Wiping the brush on a rag or paper toweling may deform the hair. As the paint started to dry, I teased in a bit of Thalo Blue with a touch of Burnt Sienna above the clouds. In some places the sky wash overlapped the line of foliage and it also wandered over into the shadow side of the central tower. When glazed over later in the painting those areas will be interesting. Adding New Gamboge to the same puddle, I mixed different light greens. Using these varied greens, foliage patches were dabbled in. There was also some Burnt Sienna in some of those washes. I added a little Thalo Blue to the mixture to paint the surface of the water in the foreground. Since the water was a receding plane, going back and to the right, I gave the left side more graying pigment than the right side. On the right, more yellow was added. I varied the original Thalo Blue puddle and used it in this step. All washes were light; I merely put in a background to separate different areas. Some were meant to tone down some of the white areas that I knew would not be needed.

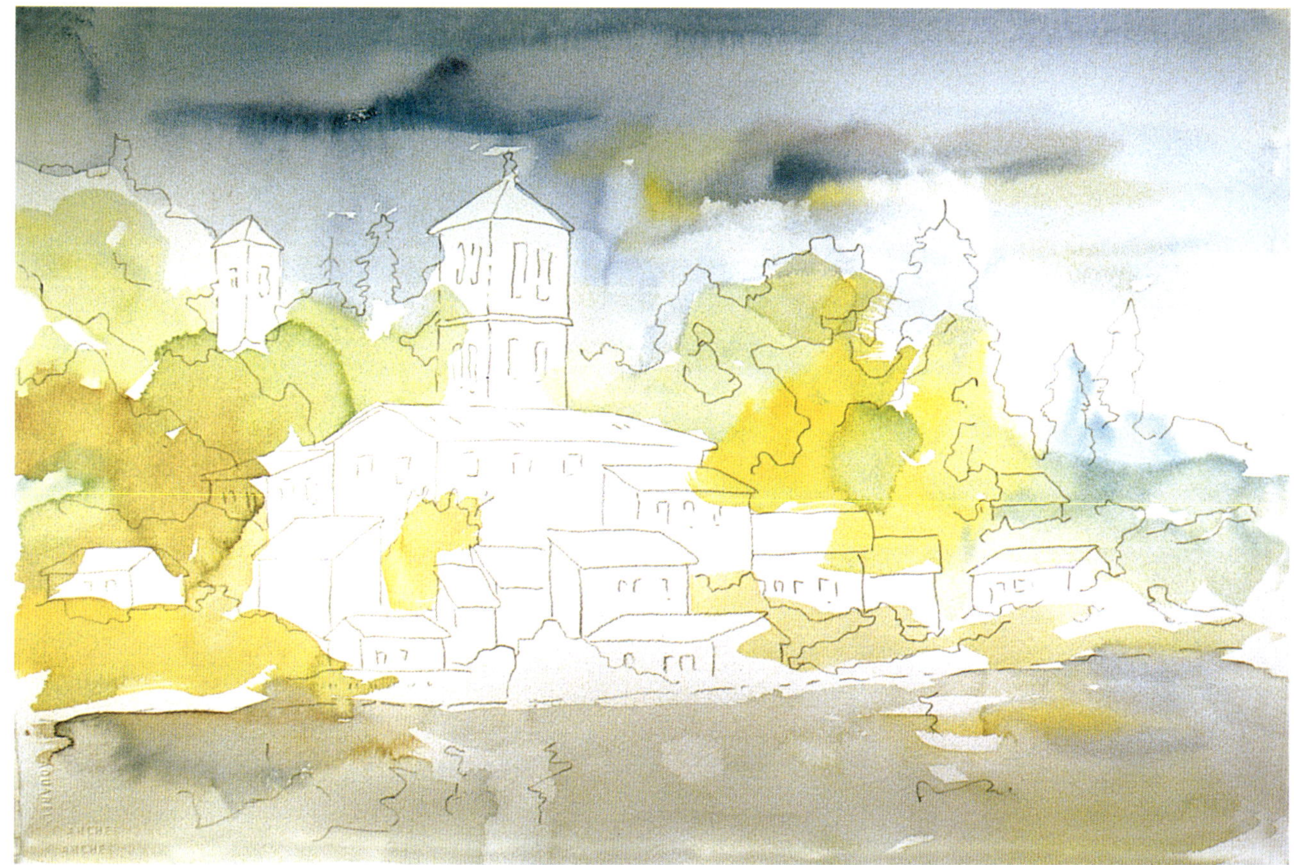

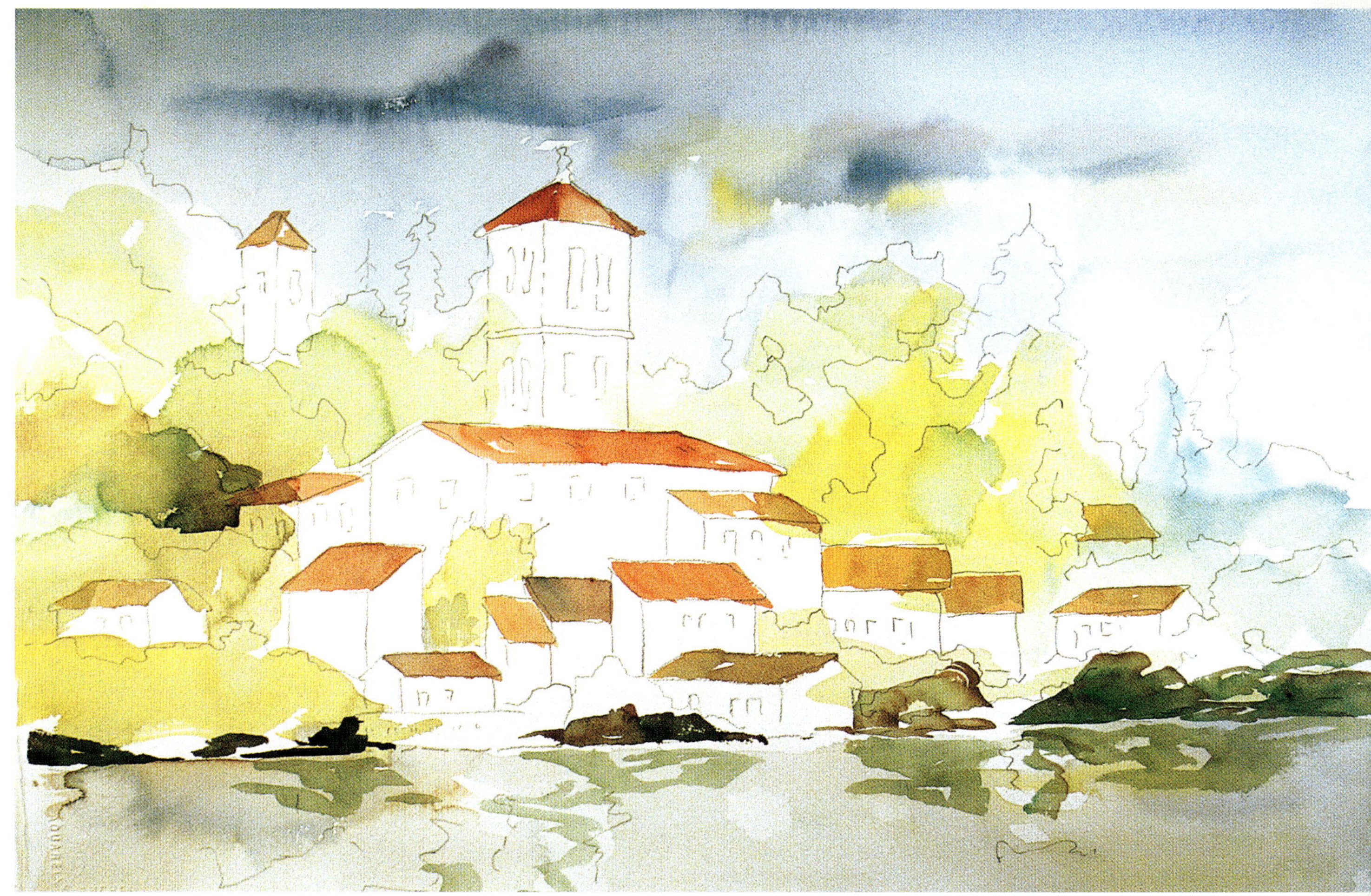

STEP 2

Light is the painter's friend. I chose to have it enter the scene from the right front quarter. The left side of the buildings, therefore, will be in shadow and the right side in sunlight. A beneficiary of this picture's lighting will be the varied shaped tile roofs. Most of them, dull red or a dirty yellow-red combination will cause a pattern of unity through the composition. I approached this area at this time. Using a $^3/_4$-inch flat brush, I mixed a light wash of Cadmium Red Light as a basic color for most of the roofs. While red is the predominant color, it was not used in full strength but as a much lighter value. Some of the roofs on the shadow side have had the Cadmium Red Light dulled when I added both Burnt Sienna and Thalo Green. Then, a mixture of the complement, green, was dulled with Burnt Sienna and placed across some of the shoreline. It looked so good that a brush full was watered down and painted in on the left side of the slope about halfway up. Still using the watered down dirty green, I introduced some random brush strokes in the water area. Finally, I left a few lighter patterns for those sparkling reflections that said "water."

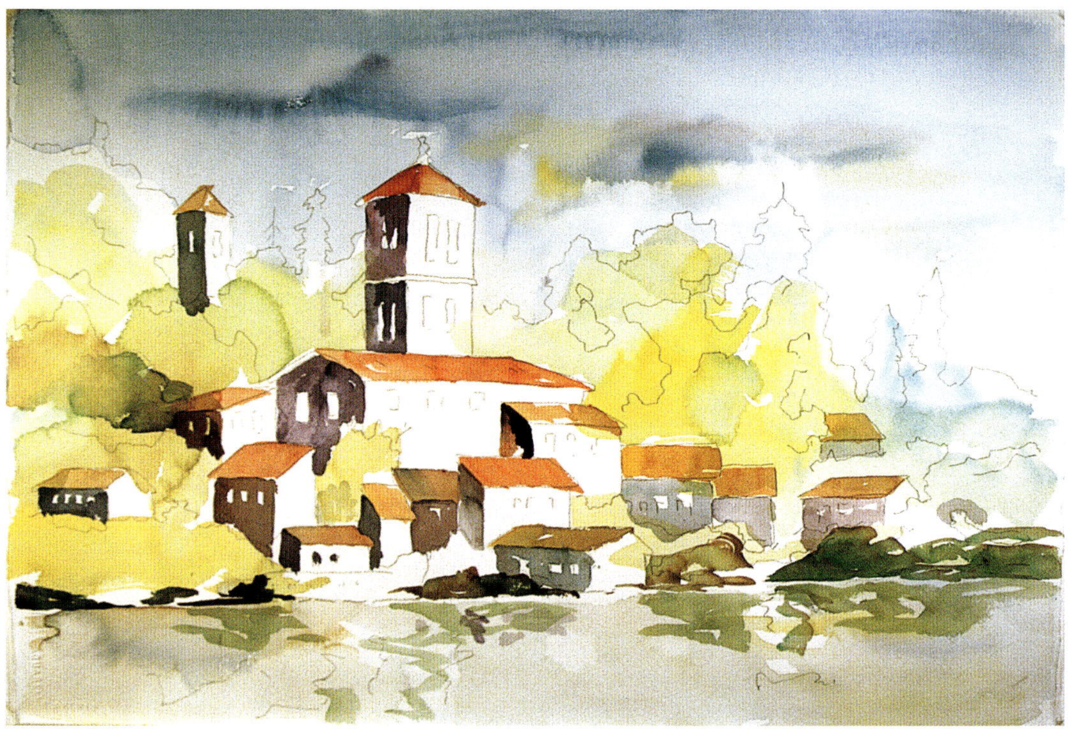

STEP 3

It was time to establish the direction of light. I mixed up lavender on the warm side with a little excess of Alizarin Crimson. Then, varying it alternatively with Burnt Sienna, New Gamboge, Thalo Green and Alizarin Crimson, I painted in the left side of the buildings. I also lightened its value and painted a few of the front views that were not receiving full-strength light.

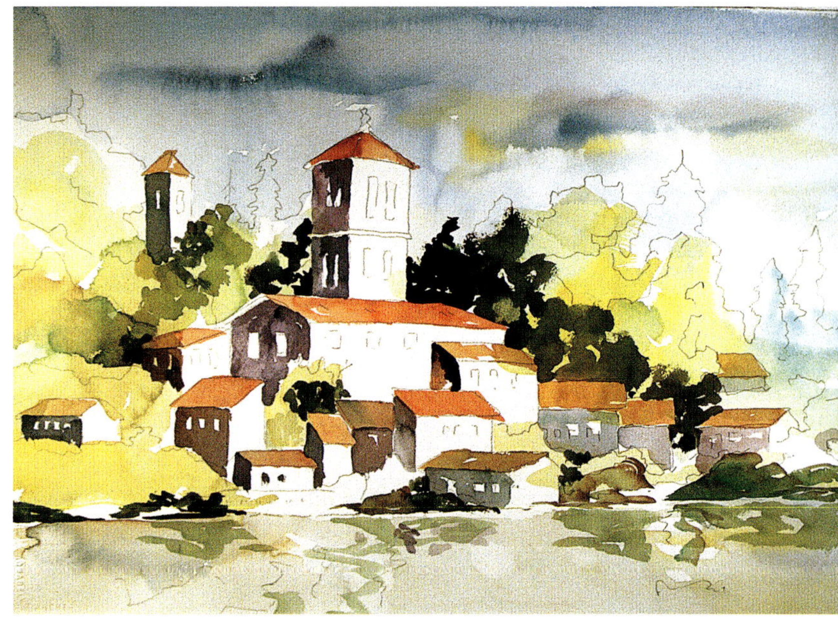

STEP 4

At this point, I noticed that the painting had a rather pale look. A dark pattern of color was what it needed. The center of interest in this picture was spread out at the base of the tower and the long building below it. A Thalo Green and Burnt Sienna area of foliage was painted next to the right side of the tower. I repeated that on the left side of the tower above the roof of the building just below. There was a difference in texture and shape between these two areas. Adding some water, I continued the left-hand wash on down to the lower left going around the buildings. I followed that by painting in a few half darks in various other shadow places. I added a little New Gamboge in some areas to vary the color. The addition of dark values had punched some life into the composition.

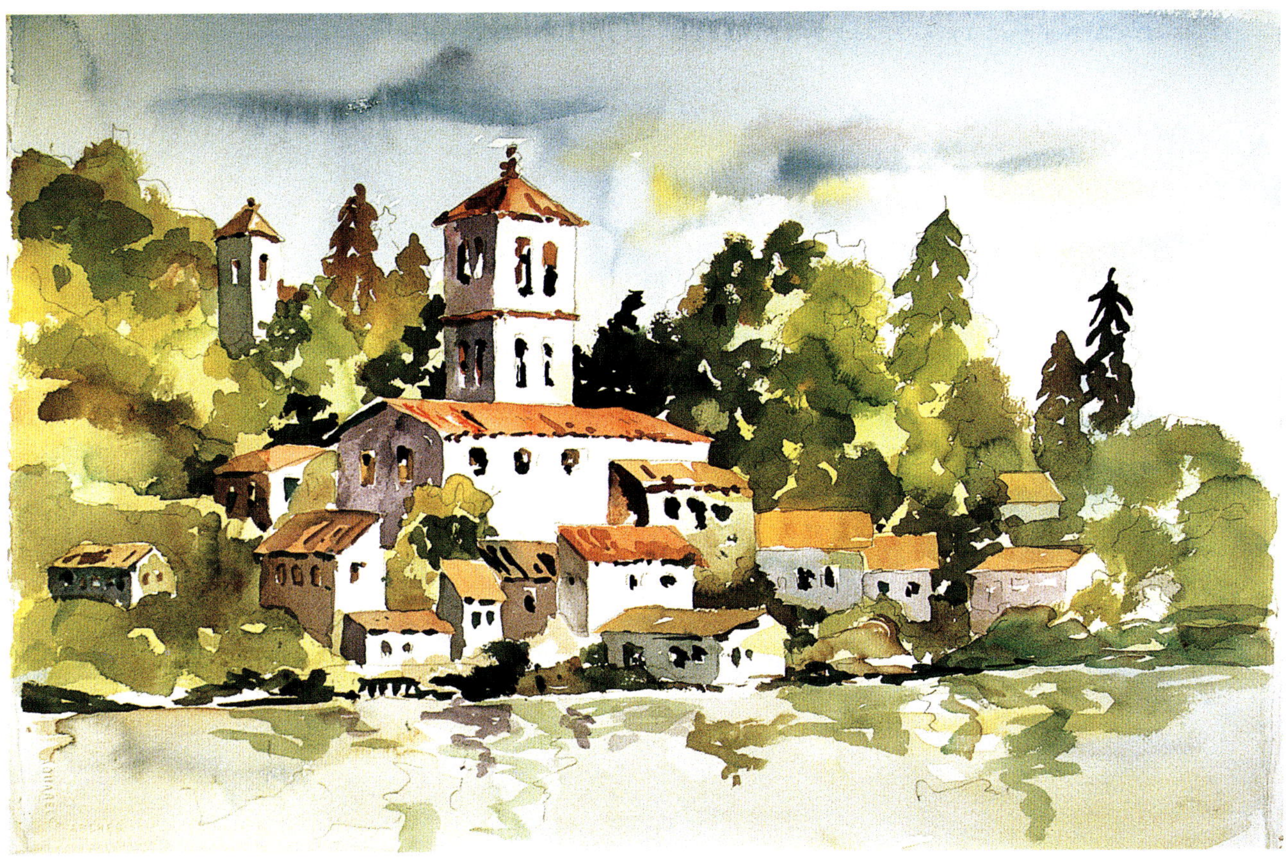

STEP 5

Using different values and colors of green I reinforced the dark and light areas of foliage. On the right side, I painted the fir trees with their branches characteristically angled down. I painted the different foliage areas, created by the variety of the greens, by alternately adding Burnt Sienna, New Gamboge, Thalo Blue, and even a little touch of Cadmium Red Light. Down at the water's edge I strengthened some of the darks to create a definite break from land to water. Using a number 12 round brush, I painted in some windows. I guess a better term than "paint" the windows would be that I "suggested" windows. I didn't want a portrait of windows, but merely an indication of them that would be in character with the rest of the painting. To heighten this treatment, I tried to make every window a little different even though they were in a line of identical windows. I moved to the roof area to add a bit of color. Some of the red roofs received full strength Cadmium Red Light, featured by random brush strokes running in the direction of the tiles.

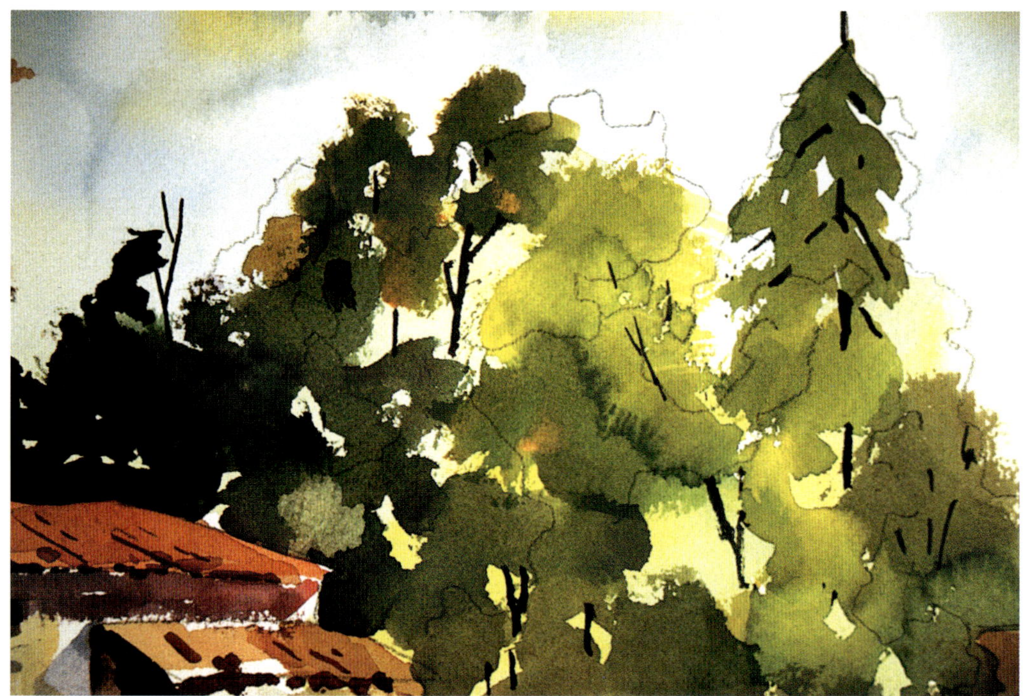

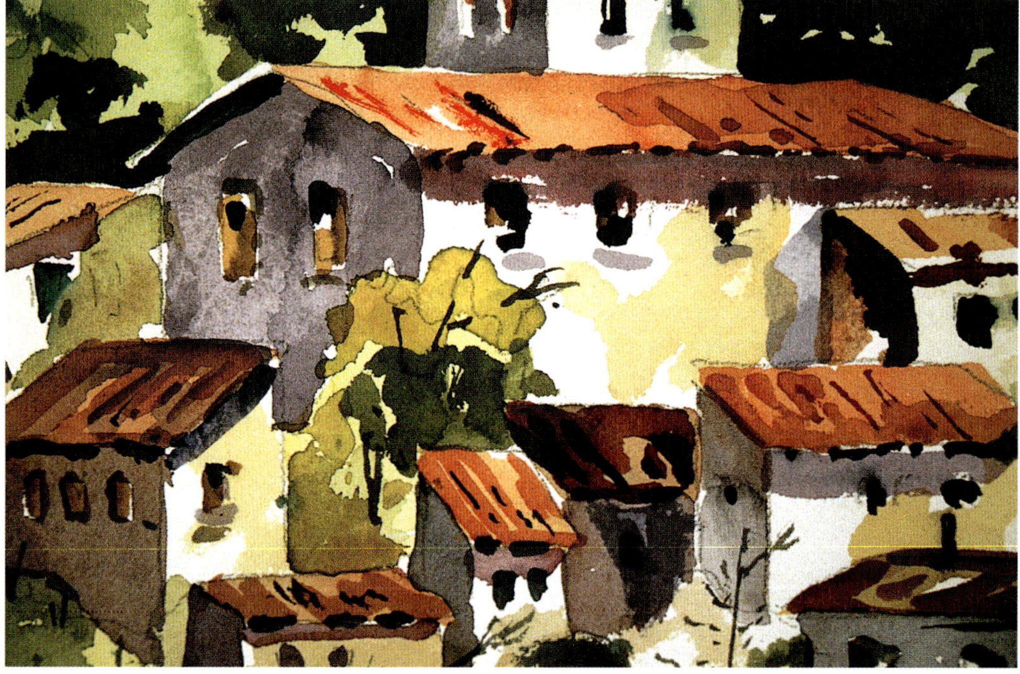

STEP 6

Details are always the last things to be added to a picture. I painted shadows under the eaves on the sunlit sides of the buildings; I used a number four round brush for this. Since the scene was in brilliant sunlight, the base color for the shadows was warm lavender, yellow's complement. When painting these shadows, keep in mind that the angle of the sun casting the shadows is the same on all buildings. A dark mixture of Thalo Blue and Burnt Sienna was used for the calligraphy of the tree trunks and branches. As the script brush moved around to insert those details, it hesitated around some of the windows to just suggest a frame or a sill.

STEP 7

I looked the picture over to see what else had to be done before I could call it finished. I dropped the brush down to the surface of the lake and put in some indications of reflections. Using a number 12 round, I darkened the water up almost to the shore leaving a broken light line to separate the two planes. The water on the left side of the picture was reflecting the hill so I cooled it off with some blue added in the wash. On the other side, the water was reflecting the open sky so it was much lighter in value. There were some competing white areas that I toned down with a little pigment from some of the puddles in the palette. On the sunlit planes, the lightest of the light was nearest the viewer and the darkest of the light was on the receding portion of that plane. I gave the right side of most of the light planes a graded tint to interpret this condition. I gave the painting a final look and decided that my watercolor version of Lake Piediluco, Italy, was ready for a mat.

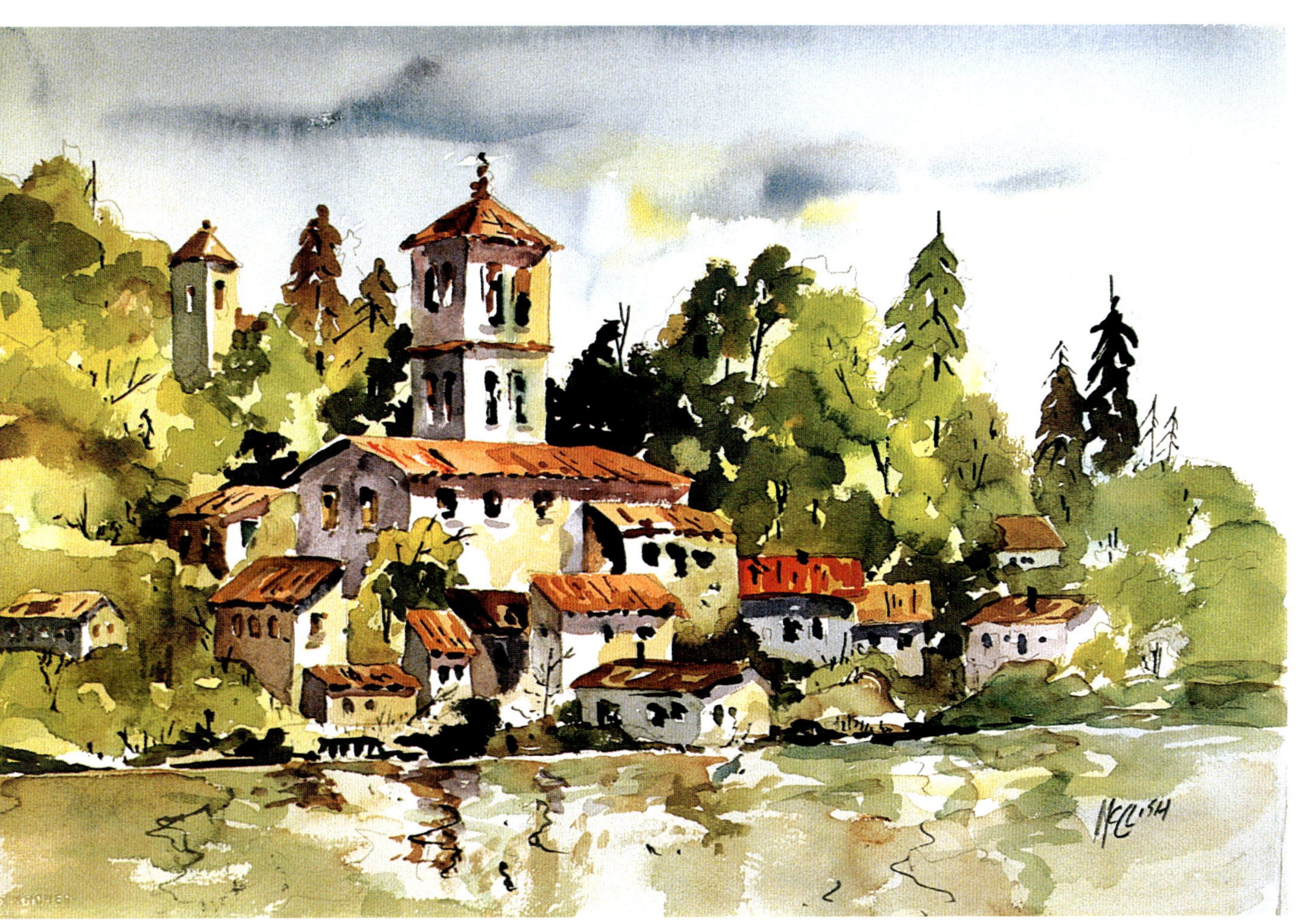

Lake Piediluco, Italy, 15 x 22", 140 lb. Arches

Putting People in Your Paintings

Maany of the Italian hill towns are situated in places that are hard for residents to leave for their major food shopping and so, every Saturday morning, the merchants come to the shoppers. They arrive in huge vans that convert, with the twist of a few hands, to loaded pushcarts. Displayed for all to see is a delectable assortment of meats, cheeses, fish, oils and produce, which townspeople are somewhat free to also feel and smell. The shopping, accompanied by a cacophony of voices, runs wild. By noon, the trucks are gone; the central square has been swept clean and the beautiful *piazza* has been returned to the pristine state it was in before the market that morning had started.

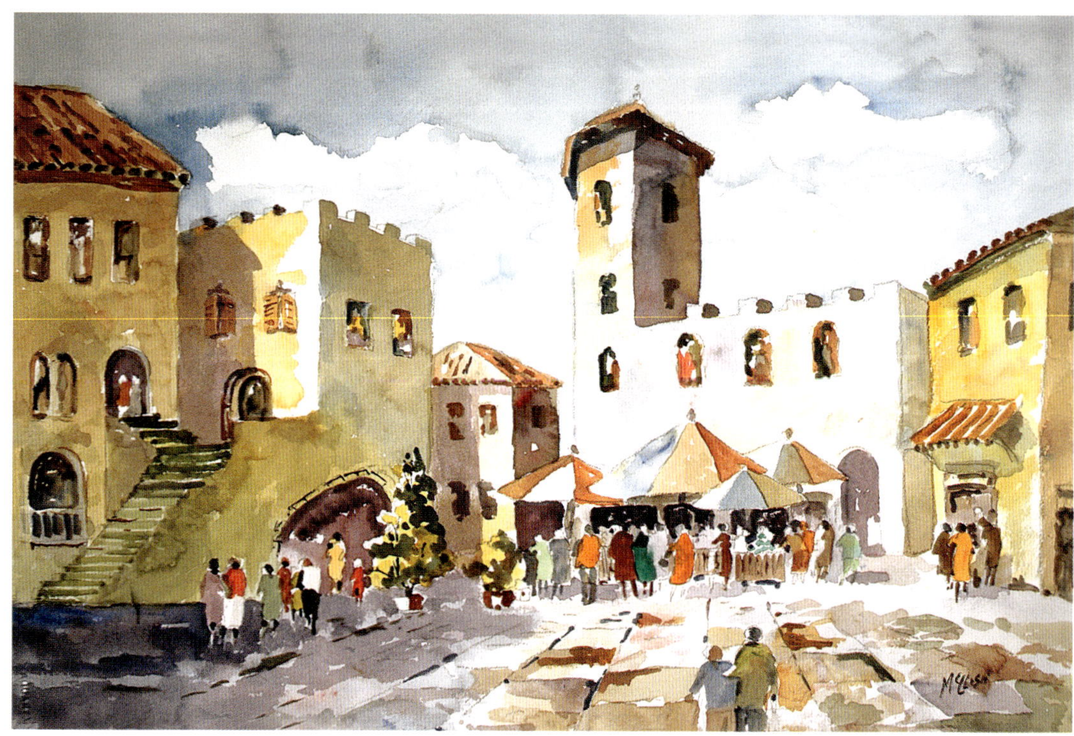

A Market
in Todi, Italy

Since the major feature of a market scene is the crowd of people–buyers as well as sellers–I first tried a composition with only those elements.

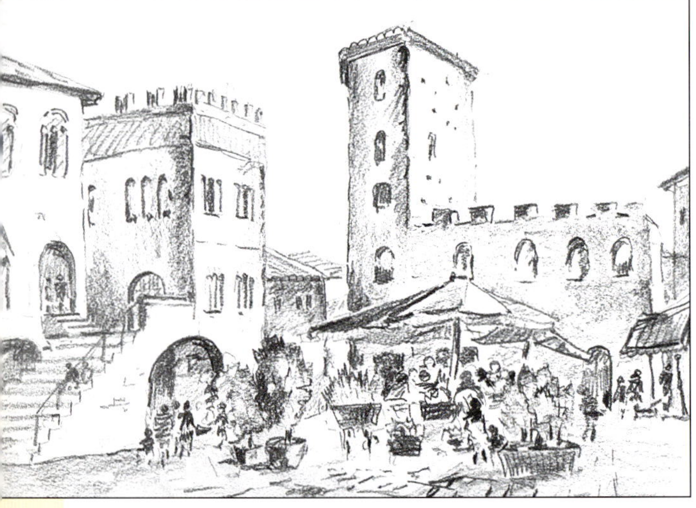

I followed this up with a value sketch that included the buildings around the town square. I liked it better and it became my composition.

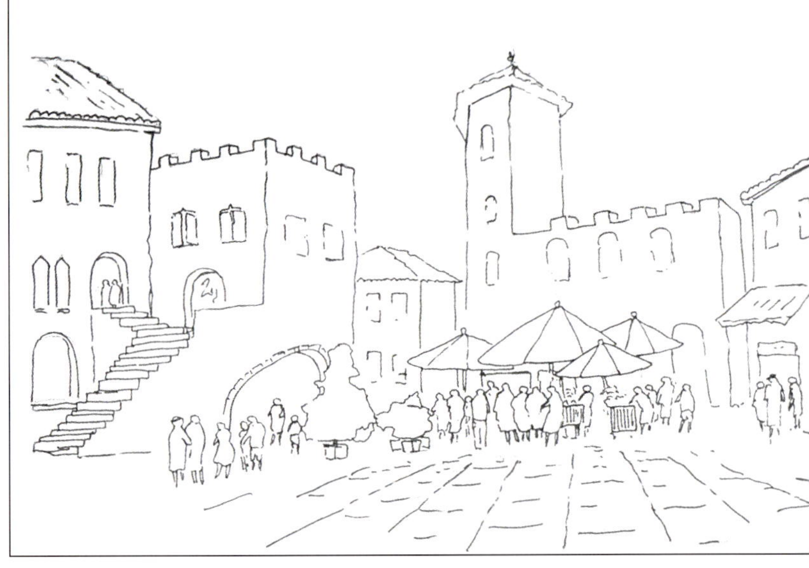

STEP 1 ▲

This is the farmers' market in Todi, an Italian hill town in Umbria. The jumble of many different buildings, the umbrellas and the crowds of people shopping inspired me to paint the scene. I made two value sketches. The first pencil sketch was of the market that focused only on the people and the umbrellas. It seemed to be missing the flavor of the market without the jumble of buildings. I made a second sketch putting in buildings, the square itself and all the people. It seemed to say, "Italian market." I repeated the drawing onto the watercolor paper as a simplified guide to direct my watercolor paints.

I first painted the planes that were in shadow.

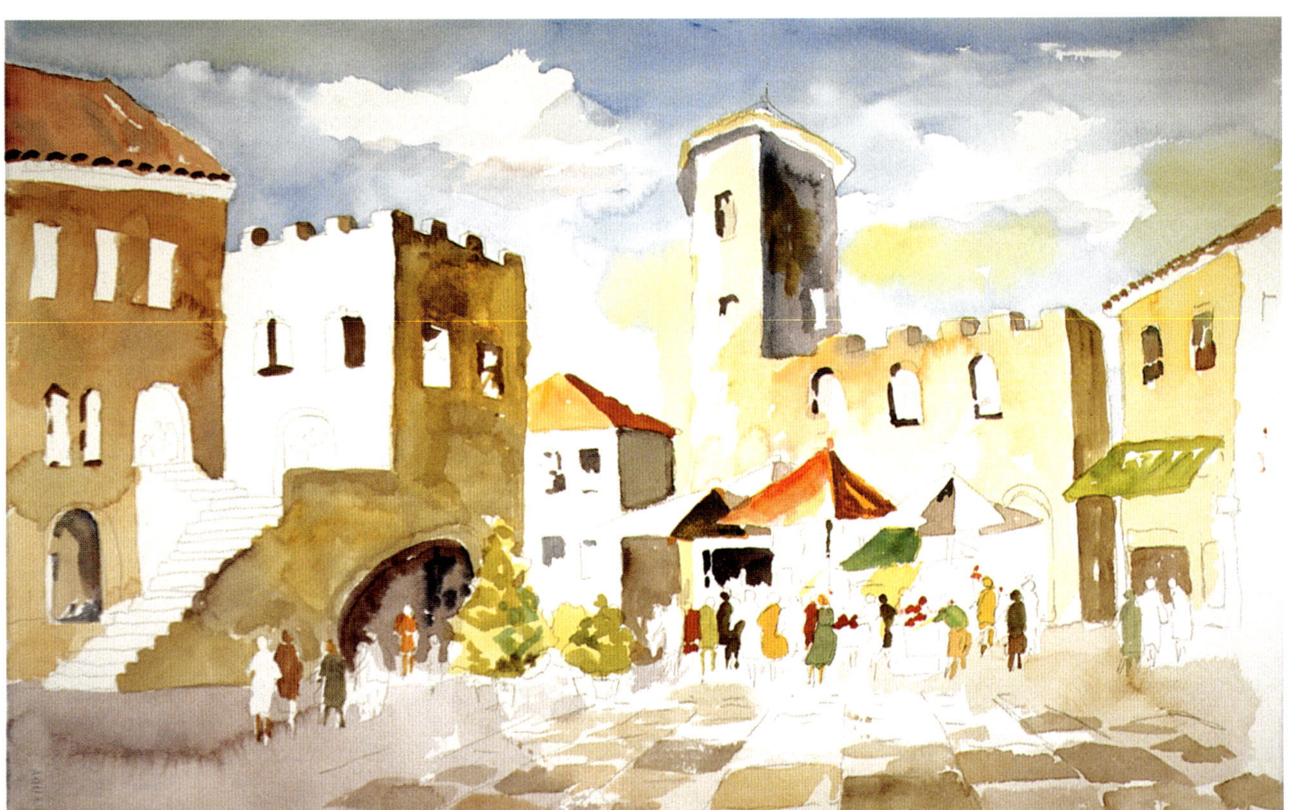

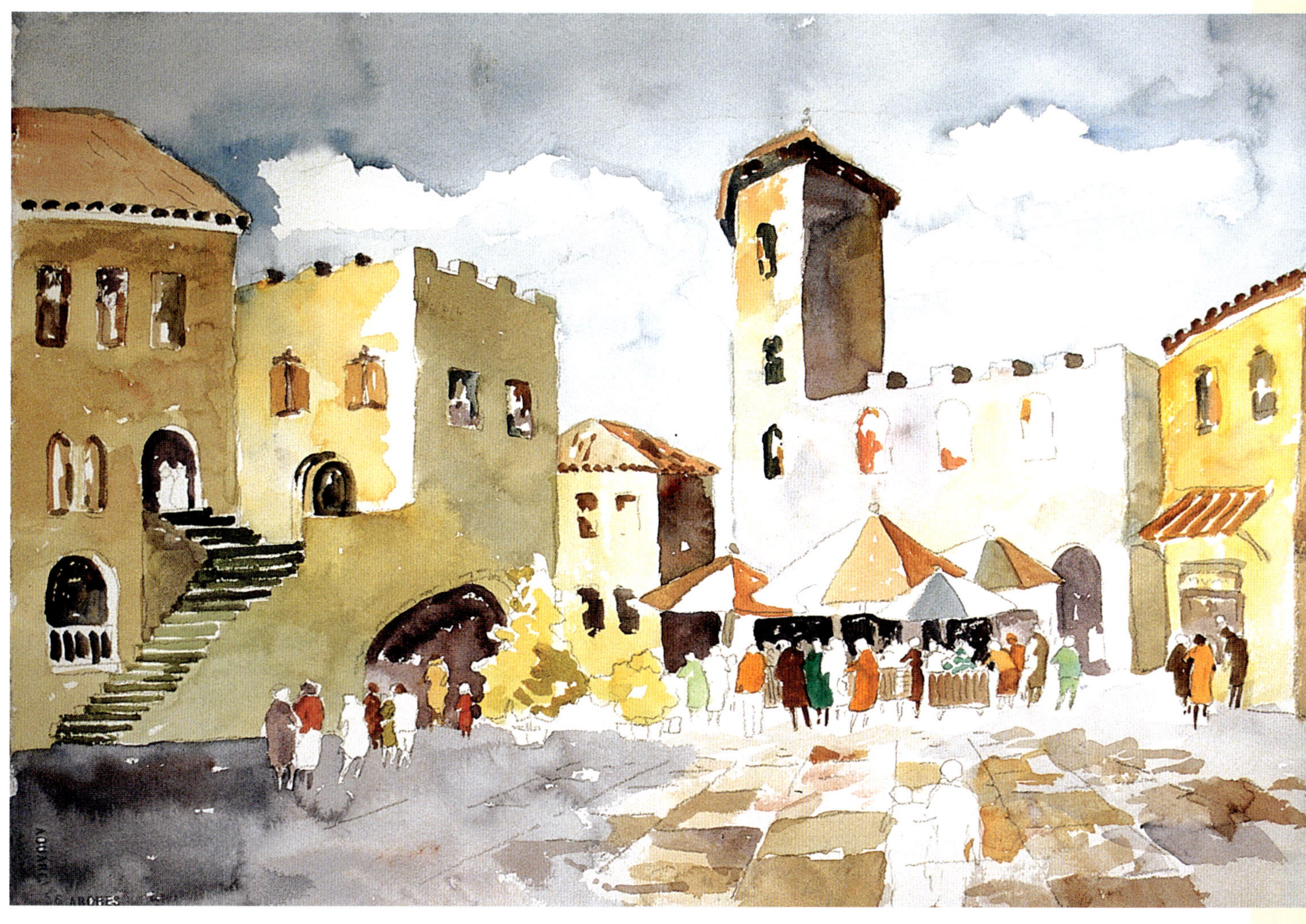

STEP 2 ◄

     With the involvement of people and buildings, I knew that this would be a very busy water-color. The many buildings and small details meant that I could not put large under painting washes on. The major loose painting in this picture will be in the crowds of people on which I would use a positive and negative technique. I pattern painted the shadow sides of the buildings, varying the colors. The darkest areas were the shadow planes of the tower and the building below it to the left. All the rest of the shadows were much lighter in value. This helped to focus on the center of interest, the crowd of people. I painted the sky using Thalo Blue, Burnt Sienna and New Gamboge. With a scrubbing motion rather than a smooth flow, I painted the sky using Thalo Blue with a tinge of New Gamboge or Burnt Sienna in places. I painted a cast shadow on the square in front of the left buildings. The white paper of the colorful umbrel-las looked a little lonesome so it got a mixture of colors in some areas.

STEP 3 ▲

     This scene was just filled with details; it was fun to paint them. I spotted in a few of the shoppers and then just painted details all over. The windows started out with a dark accent that I would follow with color. No two windows were alike when they were finished. Using varied values and light neutral colors, I painted some of the paving blocks in the foreground. I put a first green wash on the two potted trees that were just a little to the left of center. There were doors, or wide openings, in the building behind the umbrellas. I painted these with a dark value around the people to bring them forward. The structure on the left, apparently a municipal type building, was open underneath. I placed some people in this open area. I put some pale textured washes on the sunlit sides of many of the buildings to ease off the competing whites. In this picture with its many busy details, it all had to be brought along together by painting left and right, up and down.

Market Place in Todi, Italy, 15 x 22", 140 Strathmore Imperial

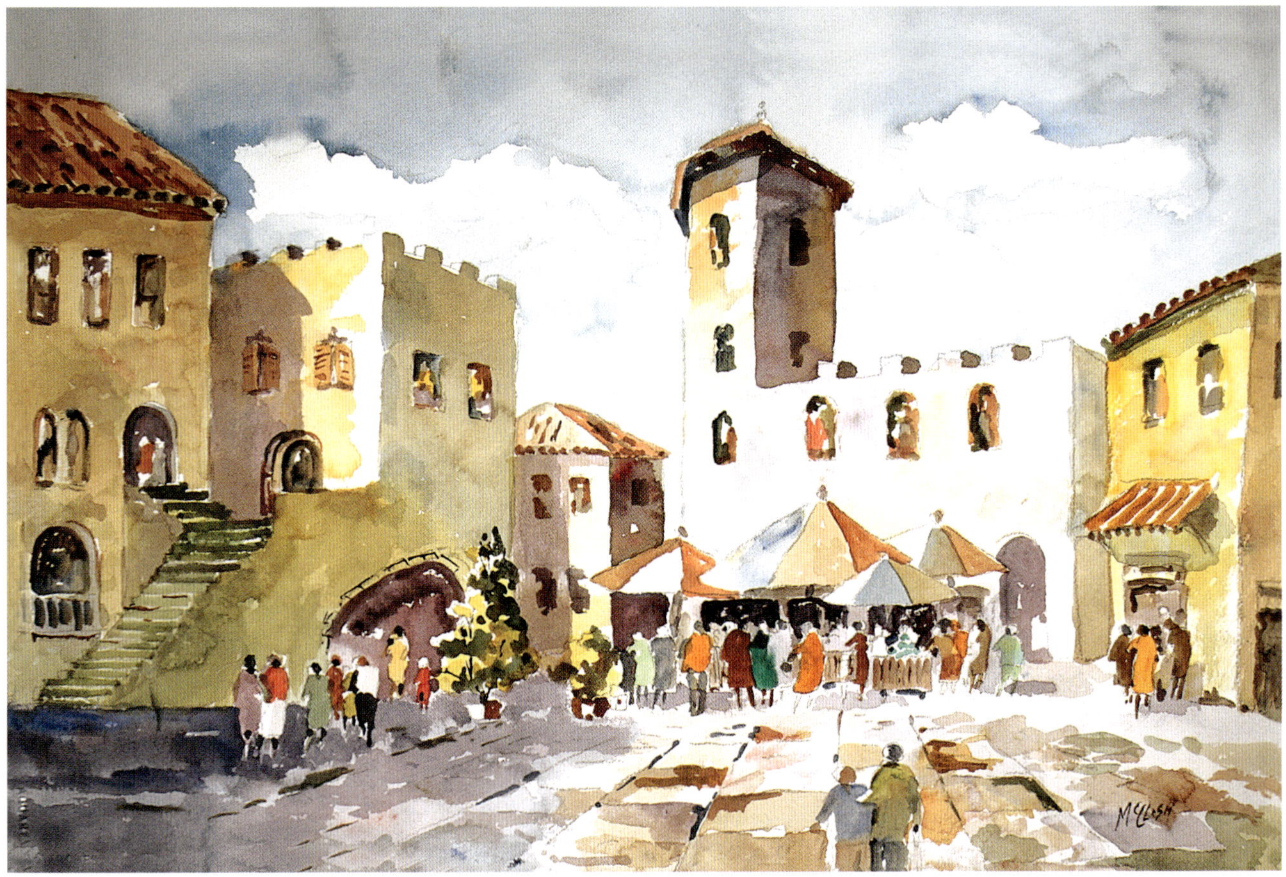

STEP 4

My main job at this point was to bring the whole painting together. Starting at the top of the long flight of steps on the left, I painted each riser on the way down. When dry, I glazed over the whole group of steps since it was all in shadow and while it said "steps" it could not stand out. I modeled the people, starting with the small group on the left. Using several colors to liven them up, I was careful not to use too many glaring colors that might make it look like an Easter egg basket. Using a positive-negative painting technique, it was fun to see the crowd of people come alive. In the lower right foreground, I added the two fellows walking toward the market. I accented the paving stones with warm colors in the sunlight and cool in the shadow areas. The stones made up a receding plane that had to change in color, texture or value as it receded. The foreground blocks were grayed just a little. The ones on the left in the building's shadow area were glazed over with a neutral color. The windows were fun to paint. I used some dark value paint made with Thalo Blue and Burnt Sienna as a basic color to accent the windows. Then I modified it with Thalo Green, New Gamboge and Cadmium Red Light, alternately, and used it randomly to paint designs and shapes in the windows. I painted most sections of the umbrellas to make a pattern of color overlapping and tucking one umbrella behind another. Underneath the canopy, I extended the darks in the openings of the building behind up to the bottom of the umbrellas. It seemed to work better that way. I mixed up a little dusty lavender, using Thalo Blue, Alizarin Crimson and a little New Gamboge. With that color, I painted cast shadows on the buildings. The people in the foreground just under the umbrellas also received the indications of a cast shadow. I am satisfied that the picture now seems to say "Todi market."

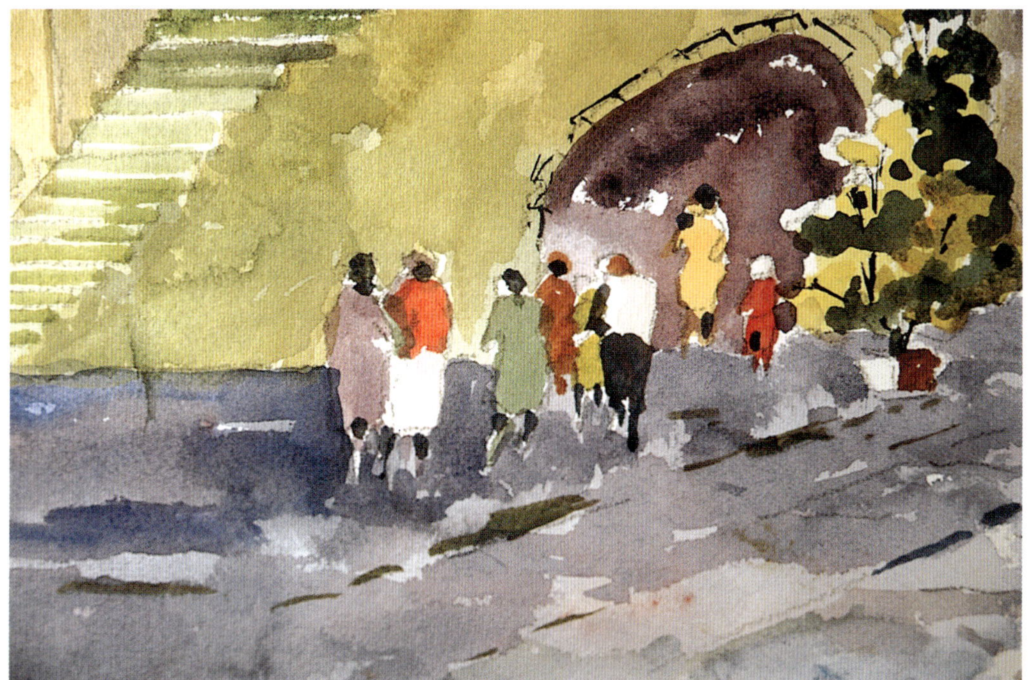

This shows just part of the crowd of people shopping at the market.

In this detail of my painting you can see that it is close in composition to the first sketch that I made. While I am happy at the way this turned out, I am still glad that I chose to include the buildings into my composition.

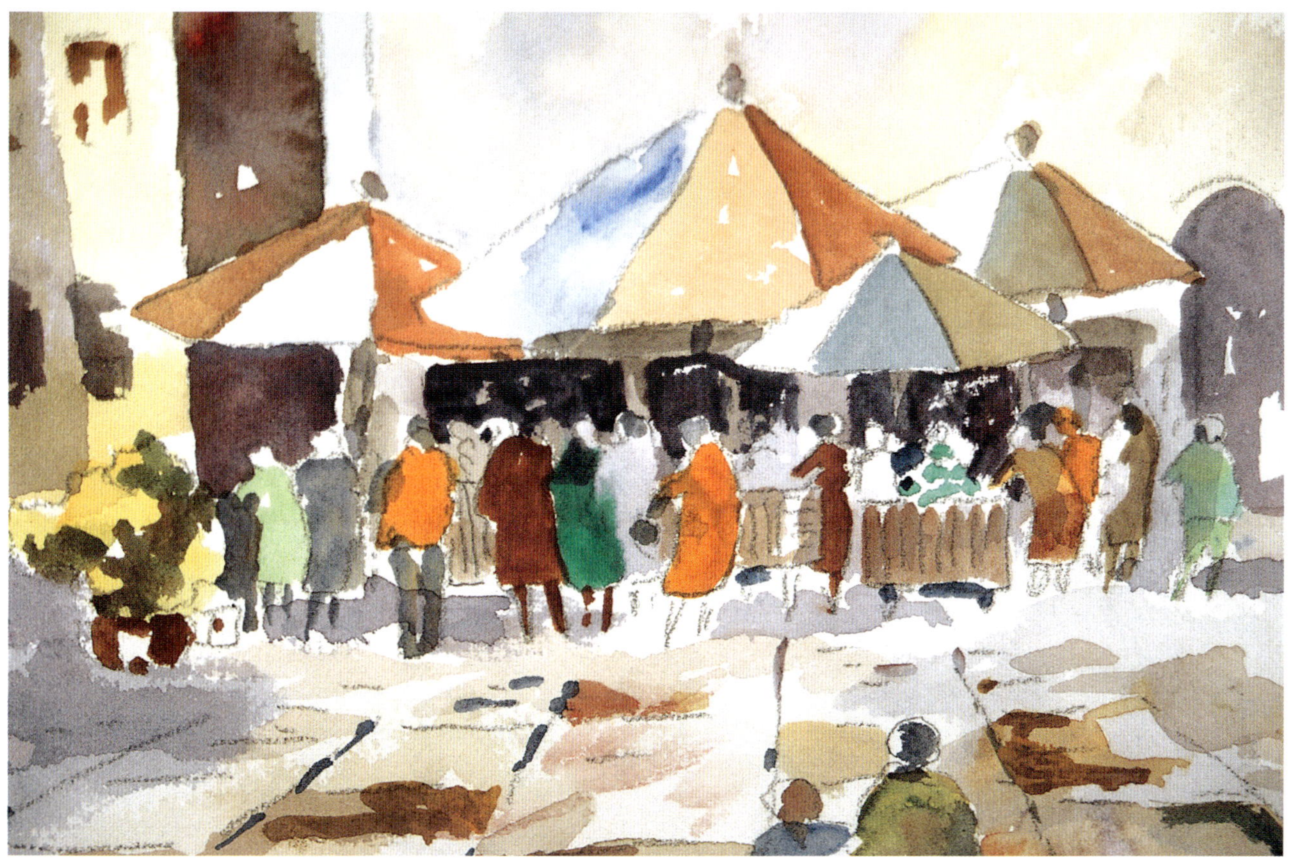

My Six Colors

As watercolorists, we are guided by one major premise: *We buy our white by the sheet.* With this in mind, we choose our colors carefully and wisely. Consequently, we want colors that are brilliant in mass tone but still retaining interesting coloration when reduced with the addition of water. We also want colors that intermix well, that use interesting and fresh admixtures and above all, do not lean to producing mud.

Many people wonder how I can paint pictures of every subject matter with the very limited palette that I use. After experimenting with many different colors, I came up with a palette that has carried me for a long time. It is a short list but it gives me a full range of basic colors including variations in between. These colors are arranged clockwise in the palette, stain colors on the left varying to earth on the right.

The diagram on the next page shows my complete palette of six colors. In the first row, you can see my three cold colors in their mass tones (full strength): **Thalo Blue, Thalo Green, Alizarin Crimson.** In the row below them, I have lightened these three with water to give you a better idea of what they look like. Since it is difficult to identify a color in its mass tone, adding a bit of water to lighten it will show off the true color more successfully. The third row of this diagram comprises the three warm colors of my palette, also shown in their mass tones: **Cadmium Red Light, New Gamboge** and **Burnt Sienna.** I've added water to these colors to create row four, the wash of these colors. Incidentally, of the three popular Cadmium Red colors—light, medium and dark—I only use Cadmium Red Light. With additions of water, it holds faithfully to its red hue, while the others—medium and dark–tend to drift towards blue hues. Another color I prefer is New Gamboge, a yellow. Some manufacturers' lines of watercolor have more than one Gamboge, but I use only New Gamboge, which I feel is the one that mixes best with other colors.

Students have asked me how much water I have in a mixture or on my brush. It is impossible to answer that question.

14

My Palette

I clean my brush by swishing it in the upper surface water, never touching the bottom because that's where the dirty pigment ends up. Then I draw the brush two or three times across the forward lip on the pail leaving enough water to use. Some artists hold a rag to dry the brush in it. Then they have to dip the brush back in the water because it has become dry and disheveled. The scenario starts over again with a too-wet brush. In mixing paint, it is also impossible to say how much paint is used in a mixture. When lifting paint out of a color well, there is just no way to tell how much is on the brush. You have to place it in a mixture and observe the color as you proceed.

You will find that you may have to make continual adjustments in a mixture to get the right color. When the color looks about right, you should put a short brush stroke on the paper to test it. The color of paint that you leave behind a brush as you draw it through a mixed puddle in the palette is approximately what it will be when

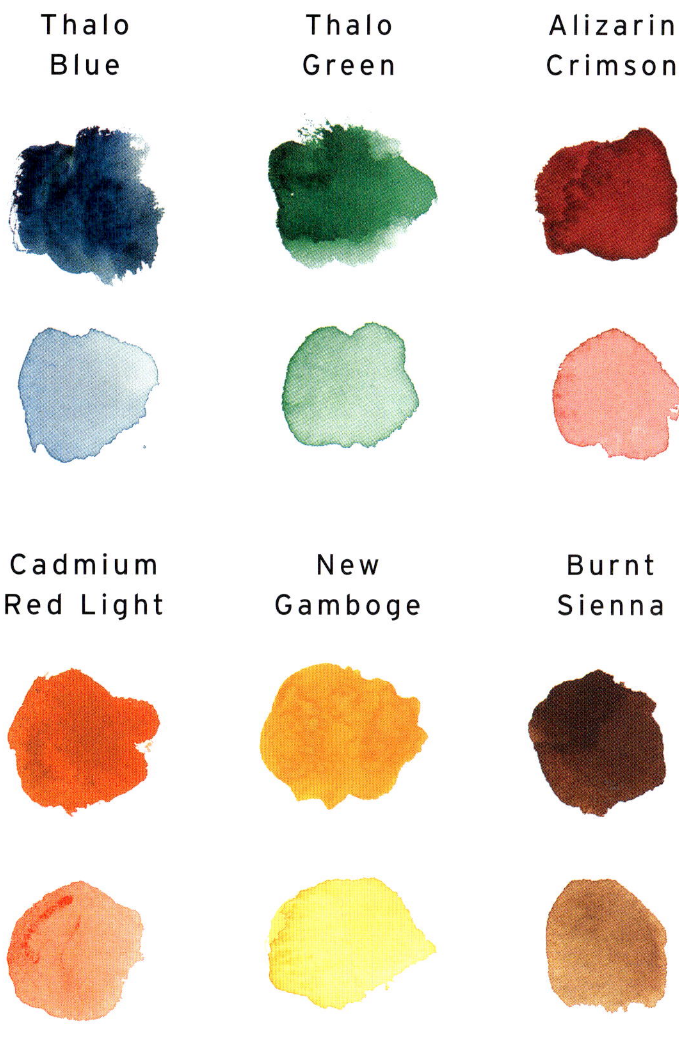

placed on the paper. If it needs further adjustment, go back to the palette and add some paint or maybe just water. Then go back and paint right over the test color and it will blend in with the new mixture. When the paint puddle is used up, take more of the various pigments and add it to the original puddle. It is amazing how close to the color of the first mixture the second one is. If there is a slight difference, it will add to the painting by the subtle variation in color. To liven up a mixed wash, sometimes drop in a touch of another color. Do not mix this dab very well but just let it mingle. The newly added color will add interest to the wash. Many artists claim that you paint your painting on your palette; I tend to agree with them.

Thalo Blue

thalo blue

All manufacturers have this phthalo-cyanine color with some choosing a name that will lock in their proprietor-ship of the color. This is a modern replacement for Prussian Blue and is more reliable than that color. Thalo Blue is a very dark, intense blue that makes clean washes with the addition of water. Adding Burnt Sienna, its complement, can make other blues. This mixture can be tempered with other colors. Mixed with New Gamboge, it can produce many varieties of greens. Adding other colors can alter these greens.

Thalo Green

thalo green

Thalo Green, like Thalo Blue, is a very powerful but almost garish stain color. By itself, it is a very cool color but when mixed, it makes many values and variations of green. When mixed with Burnt Sienna, it can read as a very dark value approaching black and on down through the spectrum of warm greens. Again, it can be mixed with other colors in the palette like New Gamboge and end up either warm or cool. Its complement is Cadmium Red Light

Alizarin Crimson

alizarin crimson

This is a stain color. Mixed with Cadmium Red Light, it makes a very credible brilliant red color. Used alone, with water or with Thalo Blue, you can produce a beautiful range of reds, violets and lavenders. A touch of New Gamboge dropped in a wet lavender wash produces a beautiful warm gold-en color if it is not mixed too well.

Cadmium Red Light

cadmium red light

This is a bright, clean red that doesn't muddy up with the addition of water as the darker cadmium reds—medium and dark (or deep)—do. Cadmium Red Light's hue tends towards a bright orange. This red is very good where brilliant red accents are needed and it mixes rather well with the other colors for a variety of warm combinations. Sometimes when it is mixed too well, it tends to approach that dreaded mud color. Its complement is Thalo Green, another of my six colors.

New Gamboge

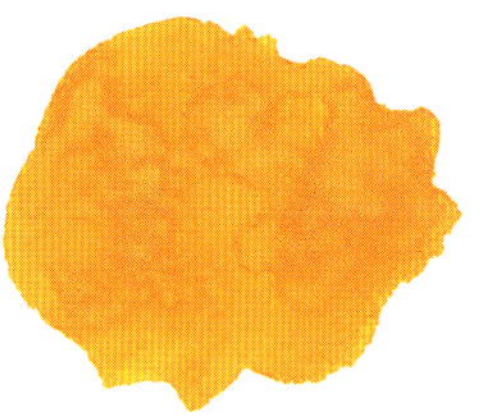

new gamboge

This is a yellow that is light and bright but warmer than Cadmium Yellow Light. It is pleasantly, warm, transparent, and lacks the raw overtone of its cadmium counterpart. Because of this quality, New Gamboge mixes well with the other colors on my palette. I have found it to be the most versatile of the light, bright yellows. Used alone, its brilliance is a delight.

Burnt Sienna

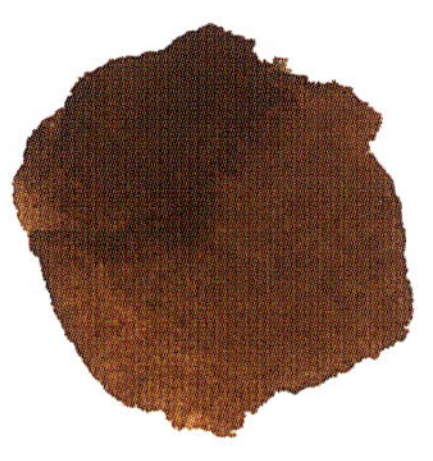

burnt sienna

This is the only real earth color that I use. When used alone, it is a dark, rich orange and mixes well with Thalo Blue for a variety of darks. Mixed with Thalo Green, it makes many greens, warm and cool. With the addition of other colors in my palette especially New Gamboge, it makes other greens. Diluted with varying amounts of water, it retains its orange hue and is invaluable for the rust colors of Autumn, and, generally, of nature itself.

The above six colors are my palette and here is basically how they are used. I do not have a pre-mixed color chart that I go to each time I want a specific color. I go to the palette and mix. To get color out of a color well, do not rake it across the top and then across the little color dam, instead pull it out from underneath. This leaves the top color full strength and unadulterated from a dirty brush in case pure color is needed. The color is placed in the palette in a *small* puddle to mix. In my palette, there are many small but separate puddles containing different colors. Adjust the color and rake a brush through the puddle. What is immediately behind the bristles is the approximate color that will be on the paper. Then try a dab in the area where it is needed. If it requires further adjustment, change the mix. When correct, paint. When you run out of paint, add to the puddle. Yes, it may or may not change the color slightly by doing this but a minor change of color in a wash adds to its appearance. The first trial dab has mixed in with the new wash and it disappears. Try to keep all puddles reasonably separate. If too many puddles enlarge and mix together, stop. With a sponge, clean the palette and replenish colors as needed. When too many puddles get together, you may get mud. When dipping your brush into the water pail, do not go to the bottom. That is where all the pigment is just waiting to contaminate your brush. Just use the surface water. How do I control the amount of water left in the brush without wiping it on a cloth or piece of toweling? Swish the brush through the surface water and then up the far side of the pail. When clean water runs out, the brush is clean. Then wipe it across the top edge of the water pail a couple of times and it retains just the right amount of water to paint and it leaves the bristles in good shape. Try it, it works.

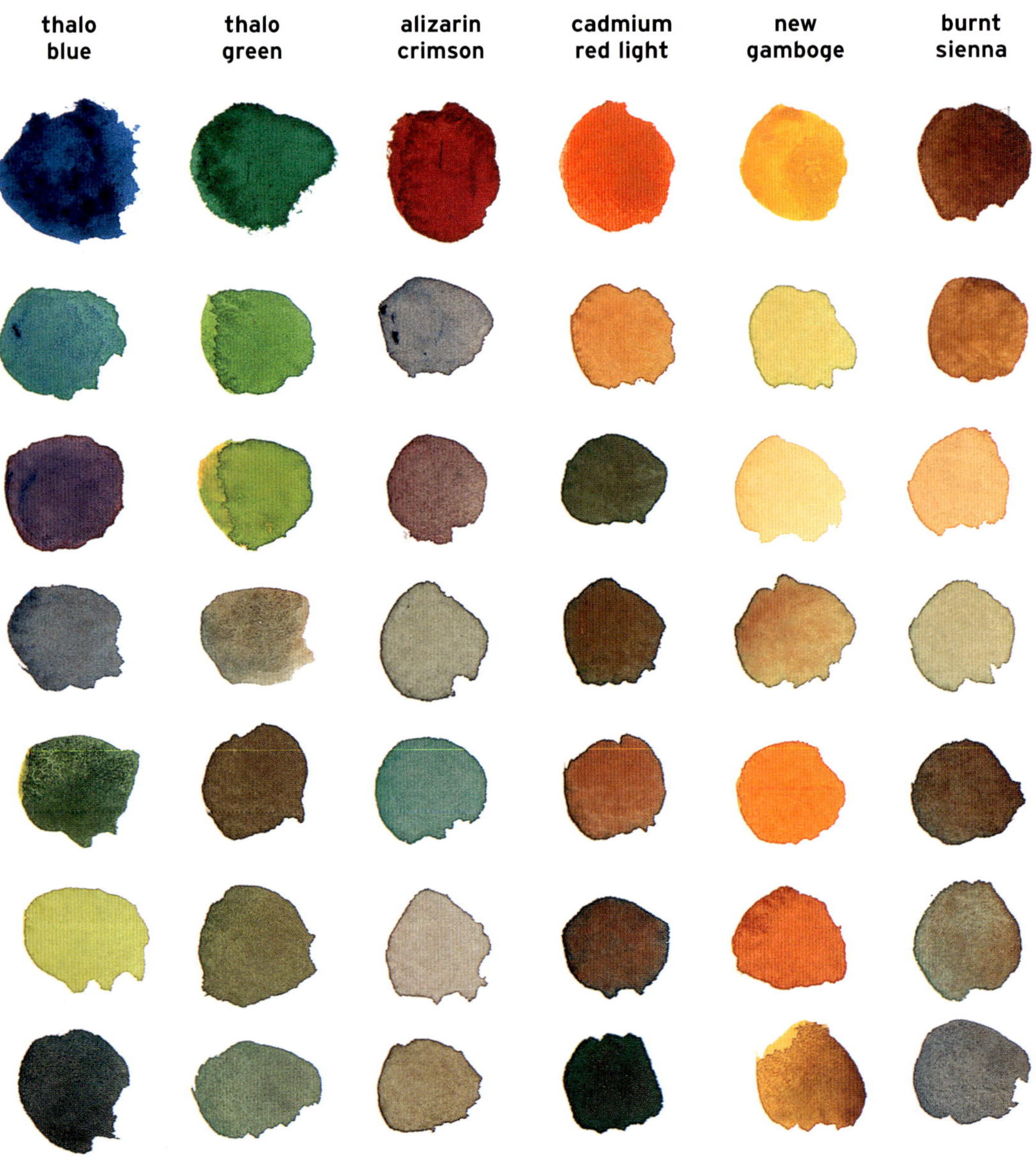

Figure 1.

FIGURE 1 ◄

Shown here are some mixtures that I have made with the use of only the six colors of my palette. You can see the wild array of colors that I created. Have fun in experimenting with paint mixing. It adds excitement to a scene. It is a good thought to have one color dominant in a composition. Some artists make use of a sheet of color patches that they use to pick a new color from and then they try to mix it. I feel that this is time consuming, and takes you away from your painting. I guess you know that it's very difficult to duplicate colors in a watercolor wash. Why not just take a few brushfuls of paint, mix them and then add the colors that you'll need?

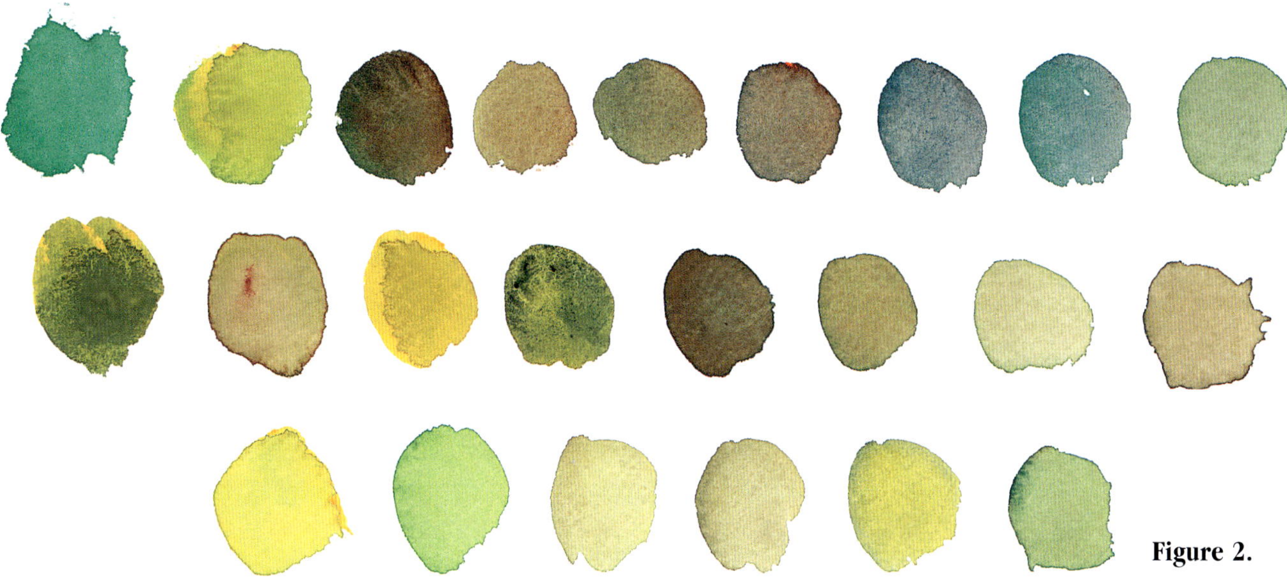

Figure 2.

FIGURE 2 ▲

One of the most difficult colors for an artist to use is green. You can start a green mixture with either Thalo Green or a mixture of Thalo Blue and New Gamboge. The blue-yellow mixture is the classic way to get a warmer green. Thalo Green by itself is a very cool color. Adding Burnt Sienna, Cadmium Red Light, New Gamboge, Thalo Green, or Thalo Blue (my other five colors) will give you many variations in a green mixture. This diagram illustrates the different green mixtures that you may use:

On the left—line one—is Thalo Green. To the right in that line are different mixtures of Thalo Green with the addition of other colors. In line two, I started with a green made from Thalo Blue and New Gamboge. Following that are many mixtures of greens that were made by adding other pigments. Line three shows random mixtures of green using varied colors. One puddle in the palette can be mixed, placed on the paper, and then added to with different colors. You can change the same puddle back to a beautiful green by adding full strength New Gamboge. The same puddle can be changed many times. Try adding different amounts of color and water. That small innocent puddle can change from light to dark and back again. It can change from brilliant color to a dull one and then be coaxed back into beautiful green.

I have left out the amounts of colors to use in each mixture; there is just no feasible way to do that. You will have to experiment and find out for yourself.

99

Editing the Elements of Your Landscape

We were driving through Umbria, Italy, on our watercolor workshop, when our bus finally reached the top of a seemingly never-ending hill to reveal a quite simple, serene building. This was Cassa di Abbazia, a monastery. The structure was unadorned except for the icon in a center front alcove behind a wrought iron fence. Bathed in full sunlight, the setbacks did give some cast shadows, but it was not enough for one student. She remarked that the scene, being so plain, didn't inspire her to paint it.

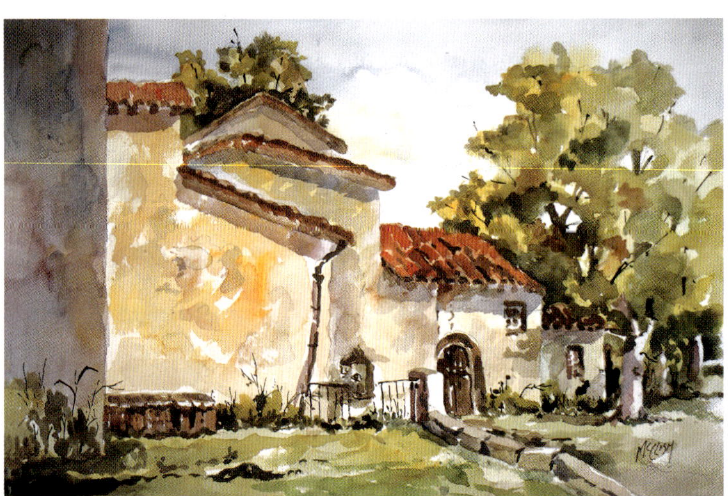

I looked at the building and decided what it needed was some help with color and texture details. I explained to my students that few artists paint exactly what they see. I went on to tell them that artists were known to move things around, to discard and to add things to suit their compositions, even, perhaps, to put in color and texture that were not really there.

Suddenly, what had been a dull, unexciting scene to them became an interesting challenge, one to capture with watercolor. I looked at the monastery again, this time with a deep intent to paint it, and I saw that the tile roofs of the buildings *did* add color and the grass in front was green. The walls exuded a feeling of old time plaster. But there were no shadow planes outside of the cast shadows from the eaves and the building offsets. I felt challenged. I brought out my sketchbook and made a value sketch of the scene. It looked interesting. I then made a plain line drawing on a sheet of watercolor paper, and started painting.

15

A Monastery
in Umbria

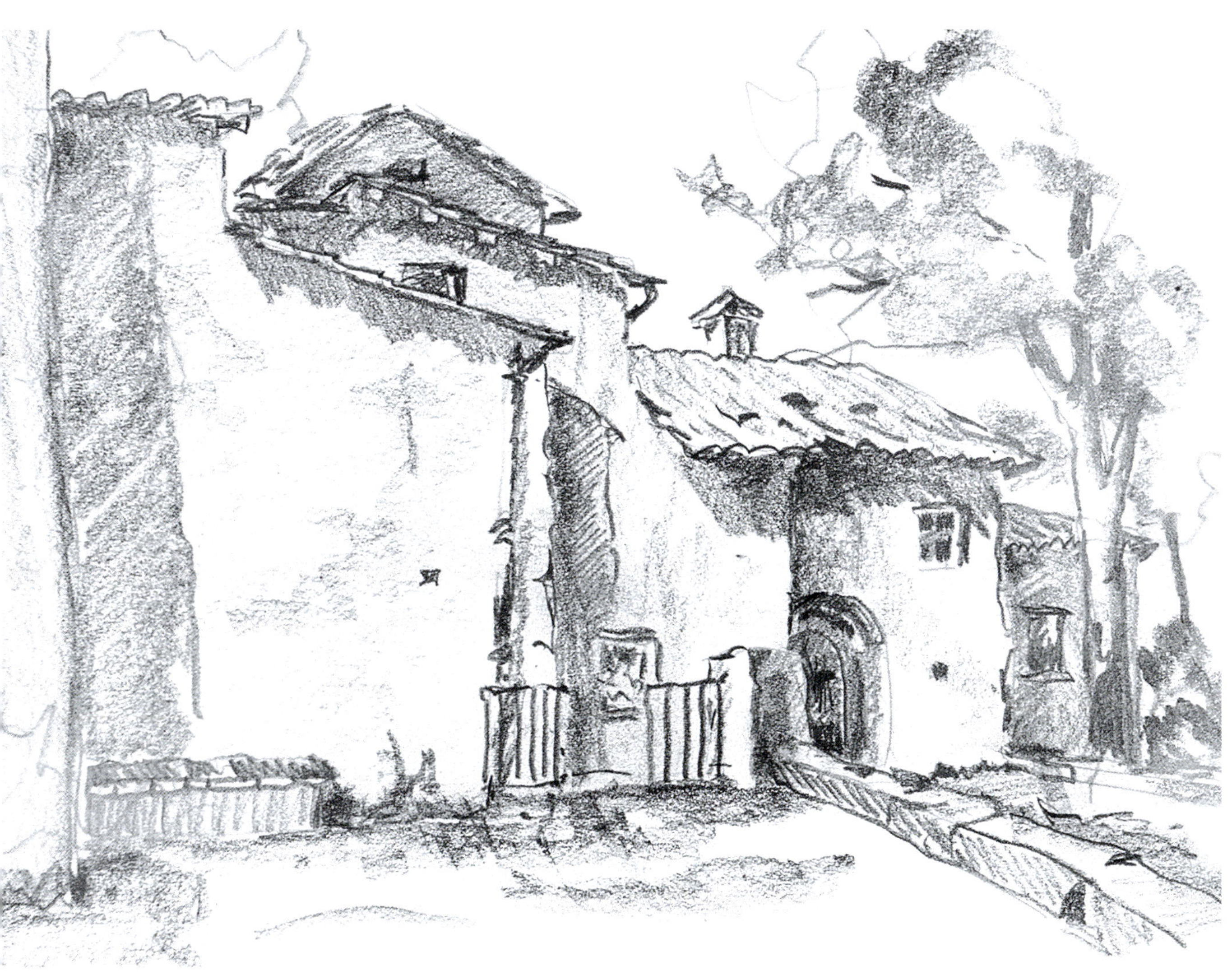

In this page from my sketchbook, you can see the value drawing that I did of the Cassa di Abbazia in Umbria, Italy.

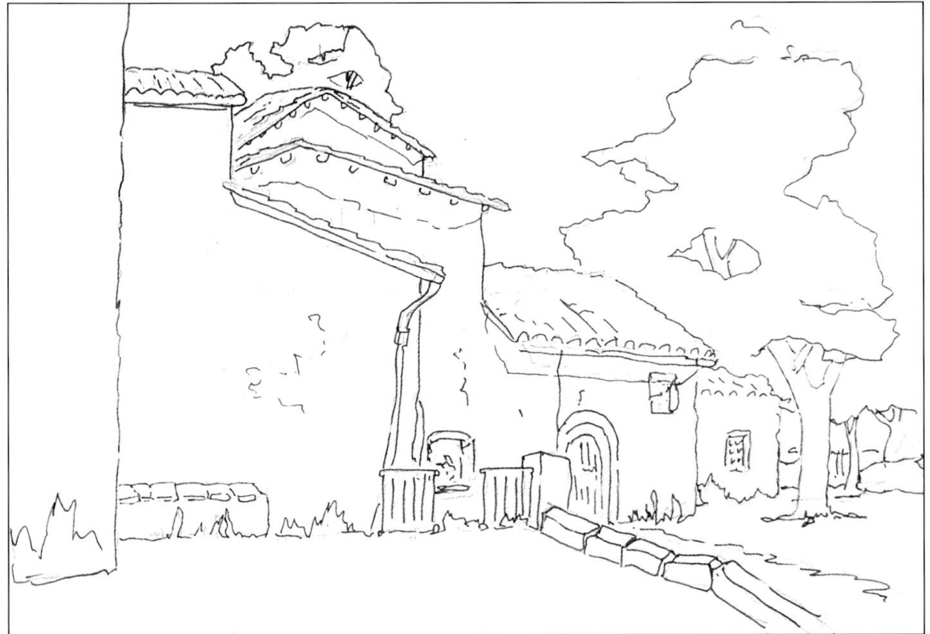

Putting in only the barest of details, I transferred my sketch onto the sheet of watercolor paper.

STEP 1 ▶

I laid the sky in first. I dampened most of the sky before I placed any of the blue wash. This gave me time to paint without getting hard-edged brush strokes. I sharply defined the top of the center cloud but softened the rest of the edges. I mixed a soft yellow-green, using Thalo Blue and New Gamboge for the mixture, and put the first wash on the tree foliage. I varied the value and also the green color in this wash, and then made the puddle a little more vivid by the addition of a small amount of Thalo Green. With this color, I painted the grass area in the foreground. I then painted a light wash of warm yellow, accented with a touch of Cadmium Red Light, in the building fronts to tone down the white paper. Around the doorway and in the area of the wrought iron fence, I did leave a few white areas that might be useful later on in the painting to emphasize the center of interest area. I used a Burnt Sienna and Cadmium Red Light mixture to put a basic coat on the tile roofs. This had to be kept fairly light so deep value details could later be laid in on top.

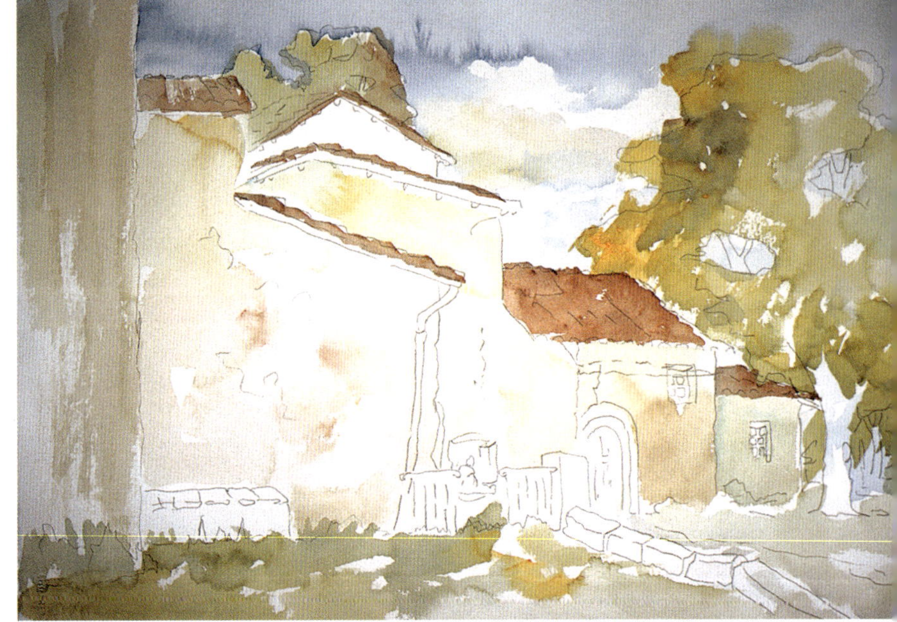

The painting progresses.

STEP 2 ▲

I added value to the foliage areas. The darker values were where the foliage abutted the building. This set the foliage back and brought the buildings forward, giving the area a third-dimensional appearance. I also made the distant undergrowth on the right deep in value to make it recede. I painted along the base of the building where the grass and perhaps a few weeds snuggled up to the vertical wall. The eave of the tile roofs were given a Burnt Sienna and Thalo Blue mixture. Two of the roof areas had the ends of the tile showing while others had a side view of the tile. I darkened the puddle to where it was nearly black and used it to paint the shadow ends of the tiles. The puddle was darkened with more Thalo Blue and I painted the prominent drainpipe in a lost-and-found technique leaving little areas for reflections. I glazed a warm gray paint over the recessed area of the doorway while I used a more colorful Burnt Sienna to paint the door.

I textured and glazed in random patterns over all the walls. I used more color in the nearest wall. The other walls were painted with grayed lavender that I sometimes mixed with a little New Gamboge to set them back. I gave the vertical wall on the left a varied mixture of lavender with a blue dominance. I dropped in some red and yellow in some areas. It formed a cool area that served as a buffer to keep the viewer's eye focused on the right center of the picture. Varied sprigs of grass were added along the front.

Now, with Burnt Sienna and just
a little Thalo Blue, I reinforced some of the
tiles in the roof over the door. I looked the
picture over and decided that, rather than
picking the picture to pieces with too many
additional details, I should consider it done.

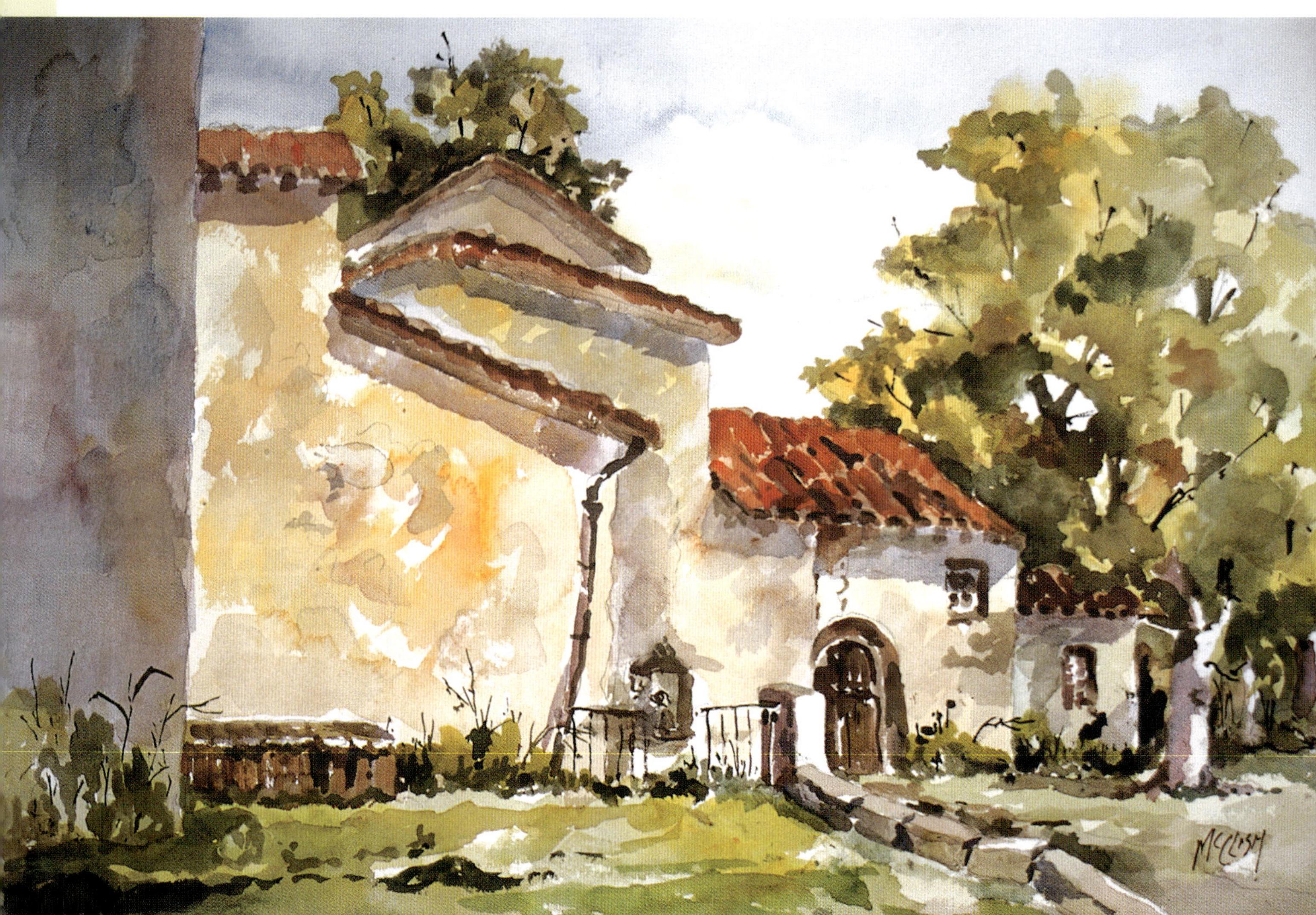

Umbrian Monastery, (Abbazia Di Sassovivo, Umbria, Italy), 15 x 22", 140 lb. Arches

Little sprigs of grass and weeds overlap building setbacks. Using Thalo Green that I've darkened with Burnt Sienna, I put variation patterns in the forward grass area and the row of stones along the walkway. Somehow, the sunlight coming in from the left did not appeal to me. While it gave cast shadows for the building indentations it also created too many vertical lines. I moved the sun over to the right side and painted the shadows using one-quarter right front light. The warmest color was used for the nearest shadow. Cooler shadows were used in the more distant areas. I painted tree trunks and several small limbs in the tree foliage. Some were painted in holes in the foliage letting sky show through while many of the smaller branches were painted in at random.

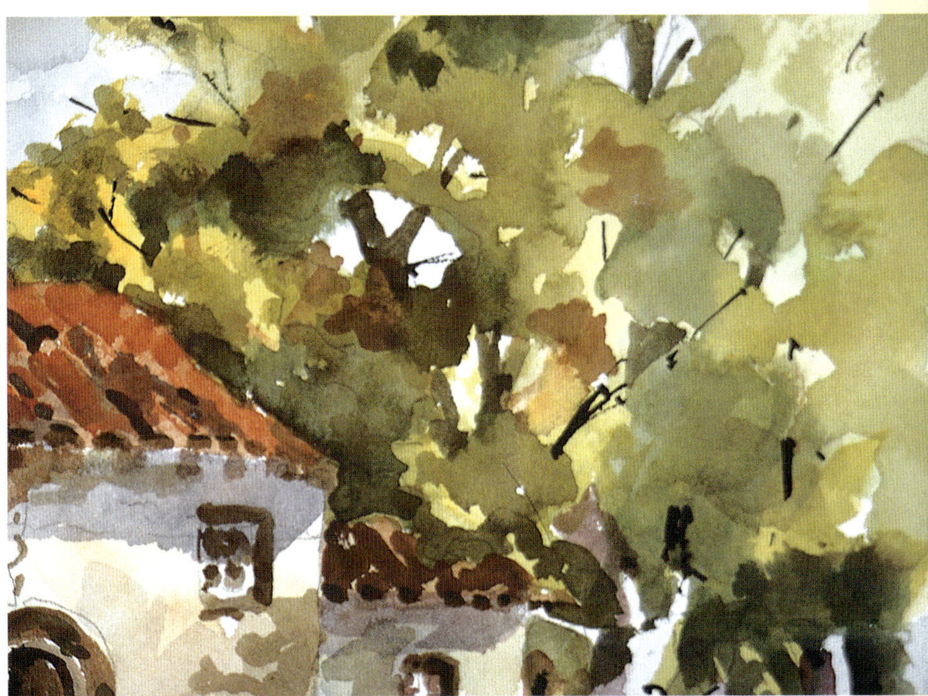

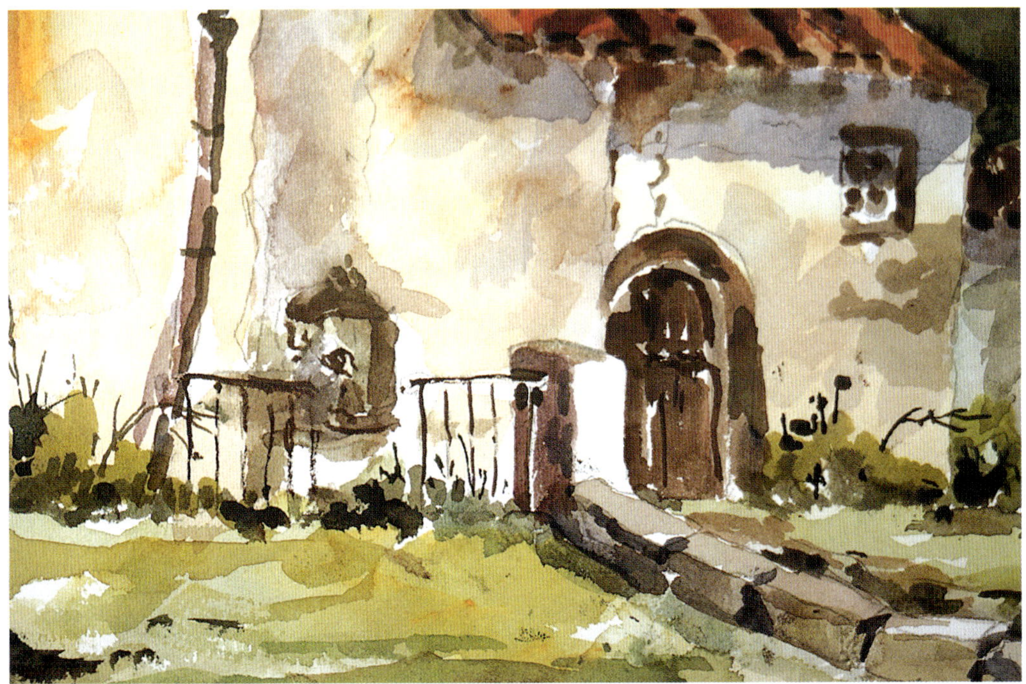

When I painted the textured and mottled walls, the most colorful wall was the main one on the left but the lightest value area was the wall around the doorway and the post to the left of the door. This became the center of interest area. I put little details hinting at some sort of statue in the little alcove behind the iron fence.

Make a "Patch" Painting

Back in the late 1930s I was a radio officer with the United Fruit Company, otherwise known as the Great White Fleet. Their ships were all painted white and were on regular runs to ports in the Caribbean and South America. Their cargo: loads of golden yellow bananas, brought back to stock food markets all over the United States.

The thrill I've always had when visiting a port is still with me. It's a wonderful reminder of that sea-going time in my life. This one day, while strolling through Port Manatee, which is not far from my home in Bradenton, I saw this scene that took me back to those times at sea. Directly ahead of me was a small coastal freighter that was docked in the foreground. She had a fairly brilliant yellowish band painted on her topsides just above the waterline, which added color to the scene. On my right side was a large modern freighter, and behind her at some distance was a smaller ship. The message that came through to me was, simply, "Ships." Out came my sketchbook; my value drawing was on the way.

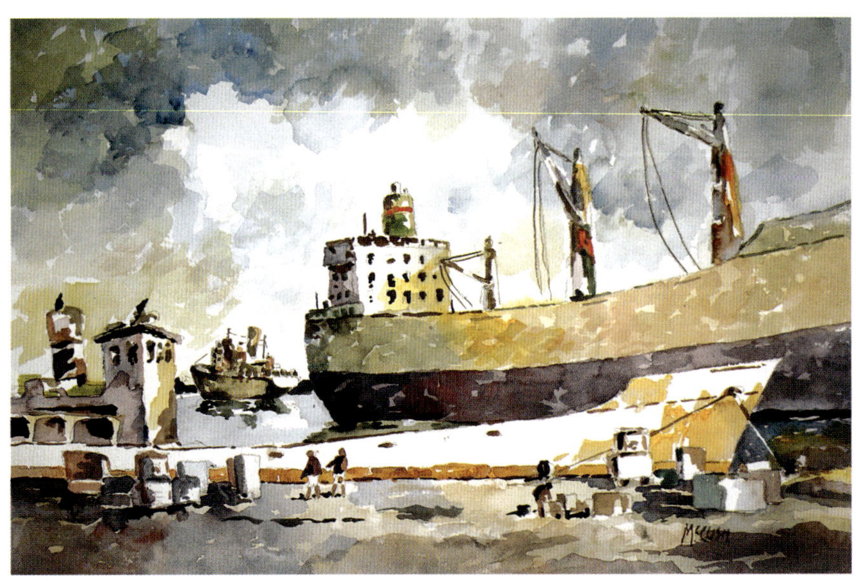

16

A Ship in Port Manatee, Florida

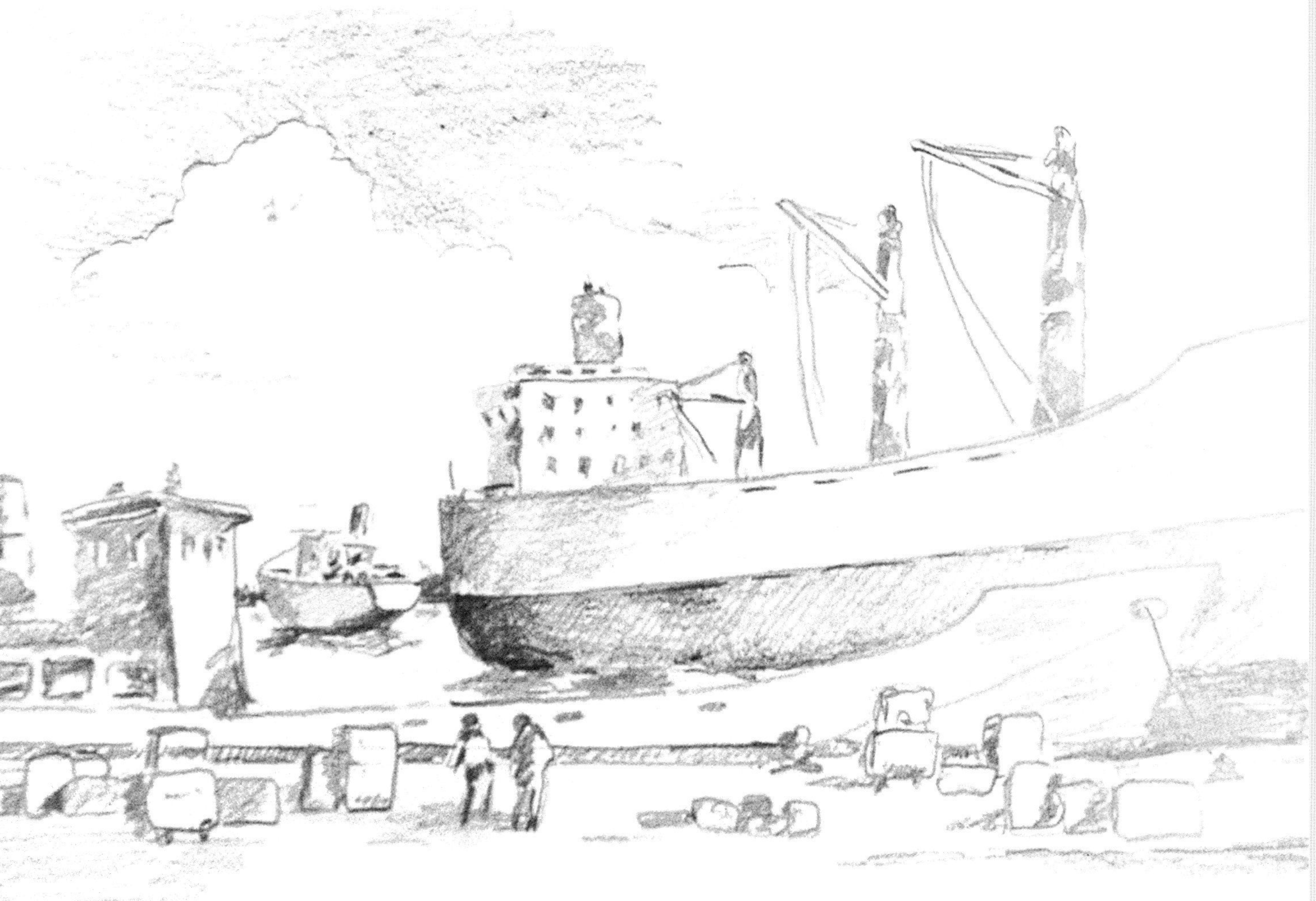

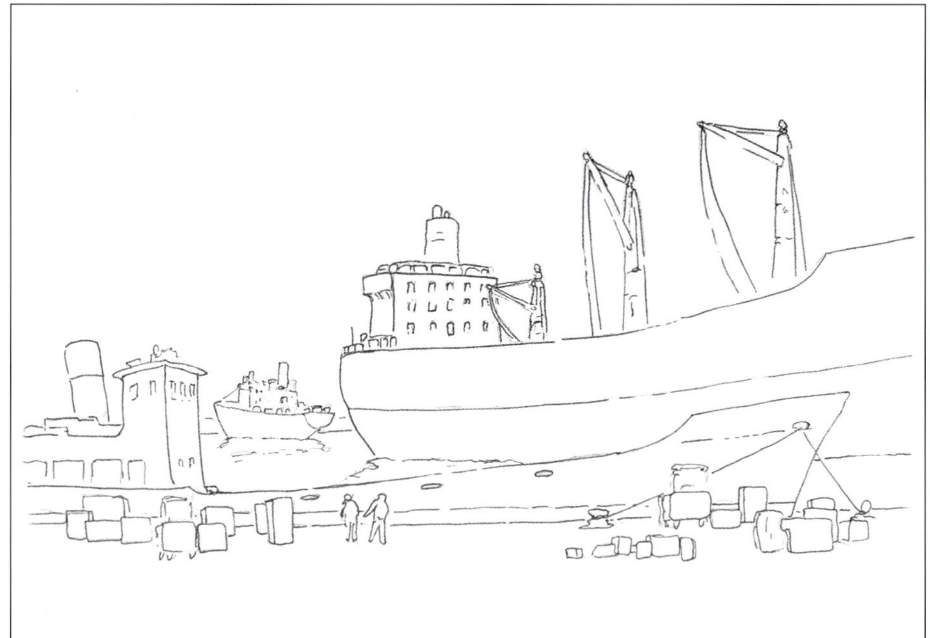

STEP 1 ▼

After transferring the sketch to a line drawing on a half-sheet of Arches cold-pressed watercolor paper, I took a long look at it. This would make a good "patch" painting, I thought, because the technique of applying loose and varied size patches of paint instead of a plain watercolor wash would be ideal for the type of composition and subject matter that I had in mind.

I began by brushing a light blue background wash across the sky. I then gave the large ship to the right a light yellow-orange coating down to the dark line on the hull. From there, I painted the darker area with a background color that used Thalo Blue and Alizarin Crimson as a base. I added bits of Burnt Sienna and New Gamboge to tint it in spots. On the foreground vessel, I dabbed in the yellow stripe with just a tinge of Cadmium Red Light in the central area. You can see this line in places between some of the boxes on the dock. I painted the shadow superstructure planes of the ships with dark lavender. Finishing this initial step, the ship in the background received a splash of a mixture of Thalo Green and Burnt Sienna. It was rather dark at the bow and also under the stern or back of the ship. At this point, the picture starts to say, "a port with ships."

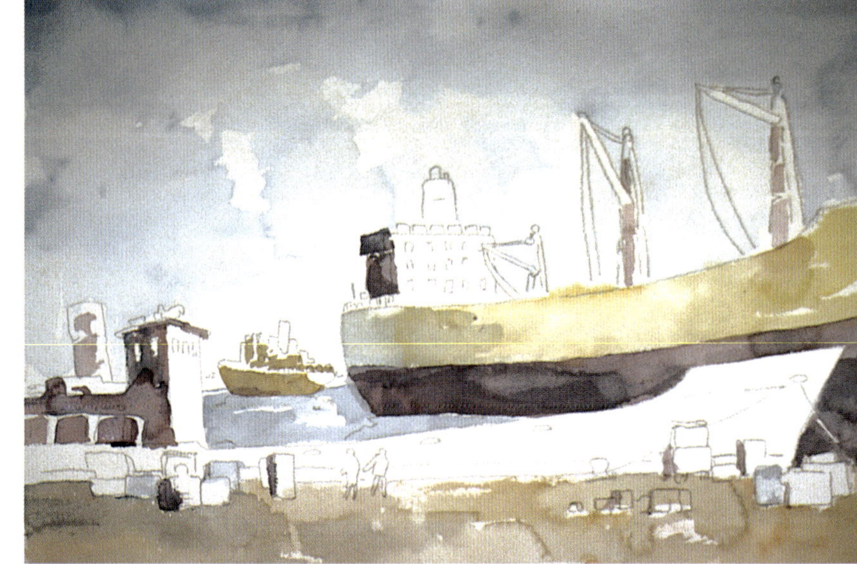

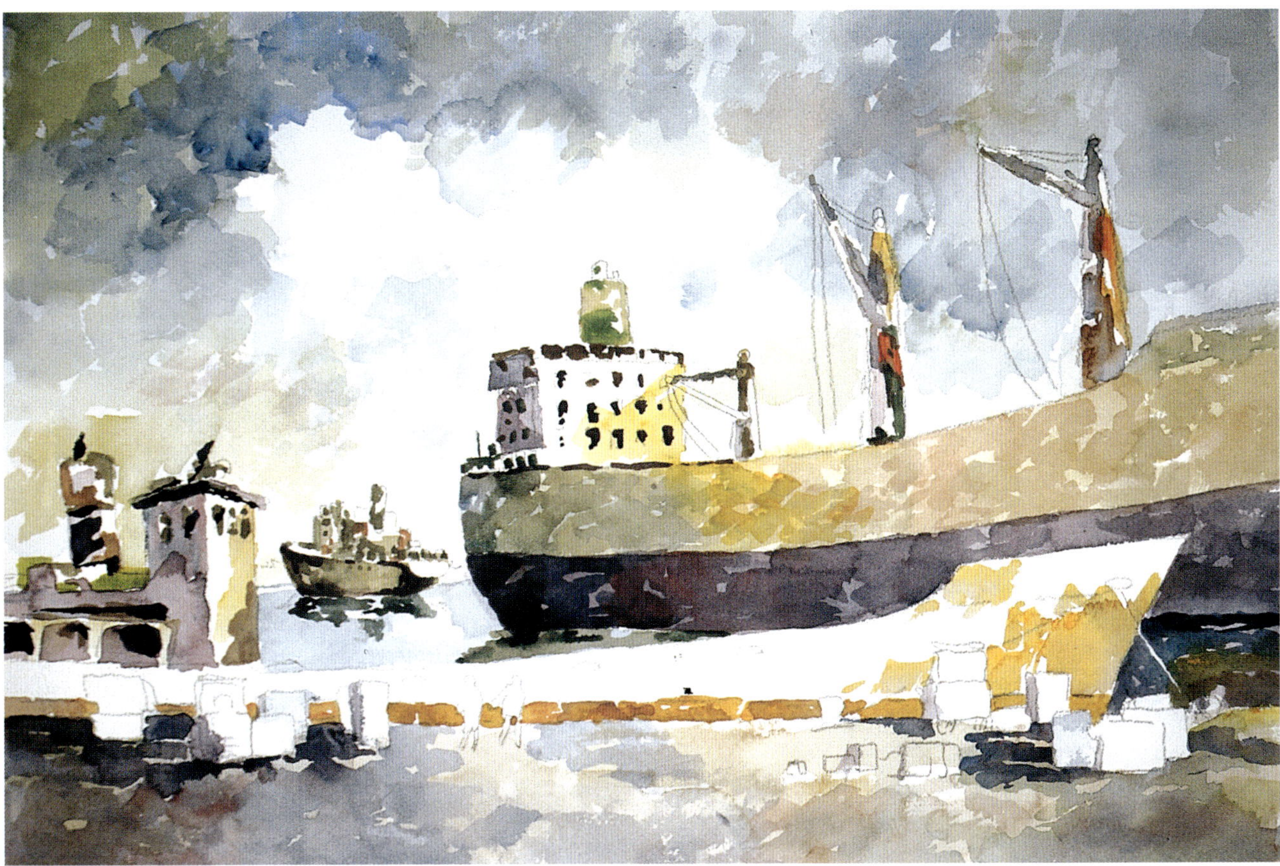

STEP 2 ▲

Using a mixture of Thalo Blue, New Gamboge and Thalo Green, I started what I call patch painting (you might call it dabbing) in the upper left-hand corner of the sky. As I worked down through and across the sky, the puddle changed color several times. I added a deeper value blue to paint across the tops of the clouds. New Gamboge was added lower in the sky. A hint of Cadmium Red Light appears in some spots. I gave the upper side of the large ship the patch treatment, using light varied colors. Below that, in the wide dark band stretching down to the waterline, I varied the values from dark at the stern to lighter colorful applications in the center section and on to a little darker color in the bow. I noticed that the blue color in the sky had paled when it dried and I was not happy with it. I mixed up Thalo Blue, Thalo Green and a small accent of Burnt Sienna and went over the upper left section of the sky with special attention to the tops of the clouds as they marched across the sky. The new patches that I painted did not line up with the ones underneath but they created an interesting random glaze pattern on top of the previous patches. It looked better. The increase in value helped out a lot in the composition. A light group of color patterns seemed to fit on the bow of the small freighter. The foreground dock looked a little lonesome so I reinforced it with varied textures of cool darks on the left side, with a smaller area and not so dark on the right. I painted the center area, using warmer colors.

It was time to paint the dock-hands. I assumed the two of them were discussing something about the job so I added a third fellow off to the right. I had him bending over examining one of the crates. (When you add people to a scene have them doing something; it's better than just making stick figures.) I added various colors and values to the boxes and crates on the dock. Moving up to the cranes on the large ship, I accented them. They seemed to be a little colorless until I added a splotch of Cadmium Red Light. That addition plus spots of dark value accents made them look more like cranes. The white vessel in the foreground needed to be moored properly, so I put in the dock lines with a script brush. With the same brush, I added the crane rigging lines. The large funnels on most ships usually have an insignia or a distinctive decoration painted on them. Using color, I indicated some details on the stacks, and it worked out fine. Pictures are said to make a statement and I think that this one is no different. It says, "busy port."

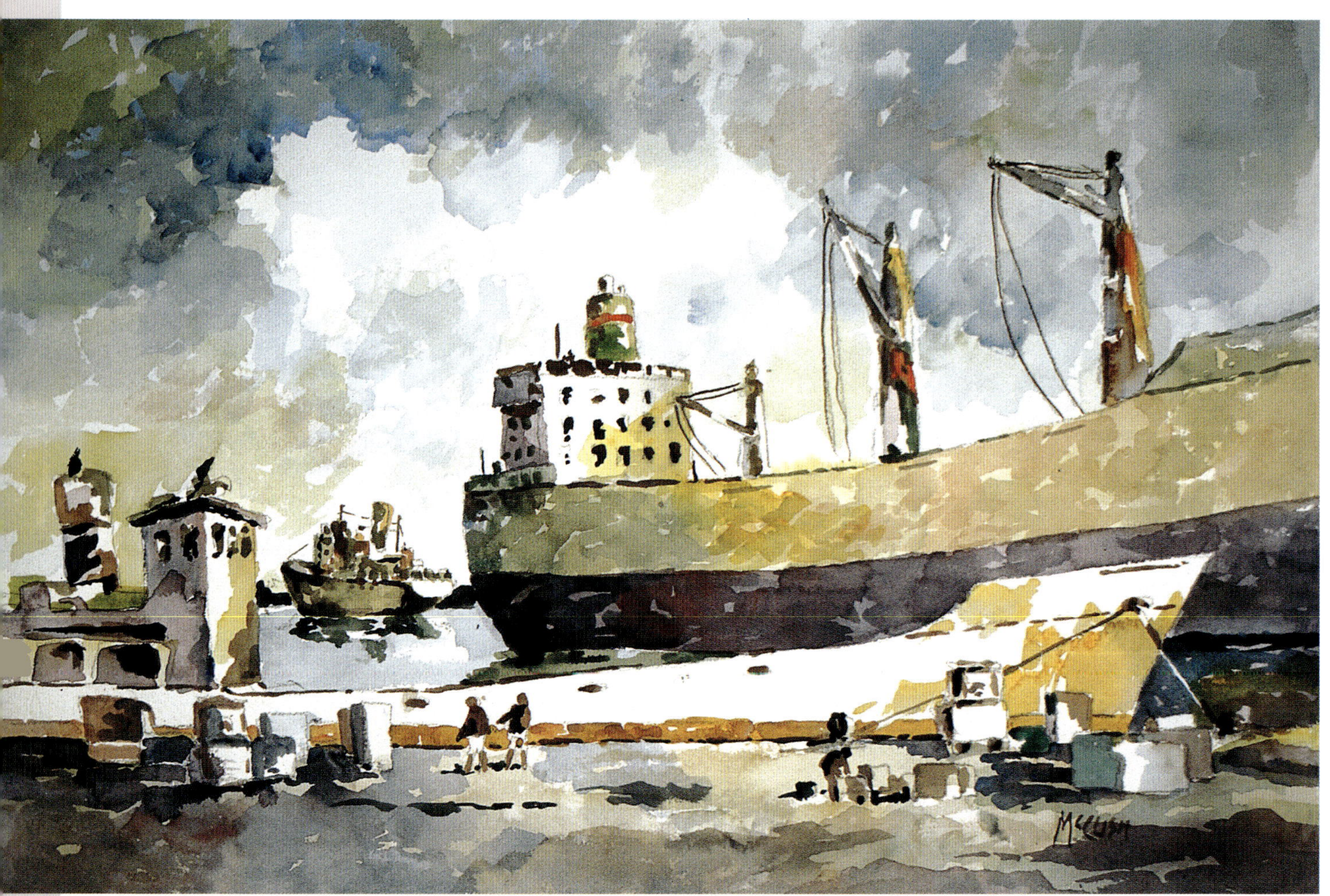

Busy Port, (Port Manatee), 15 x 22", 140 lb. Arches

In this close-up of the
sky, you can see the
blue patches that were
glazed over the initial
sky wash.

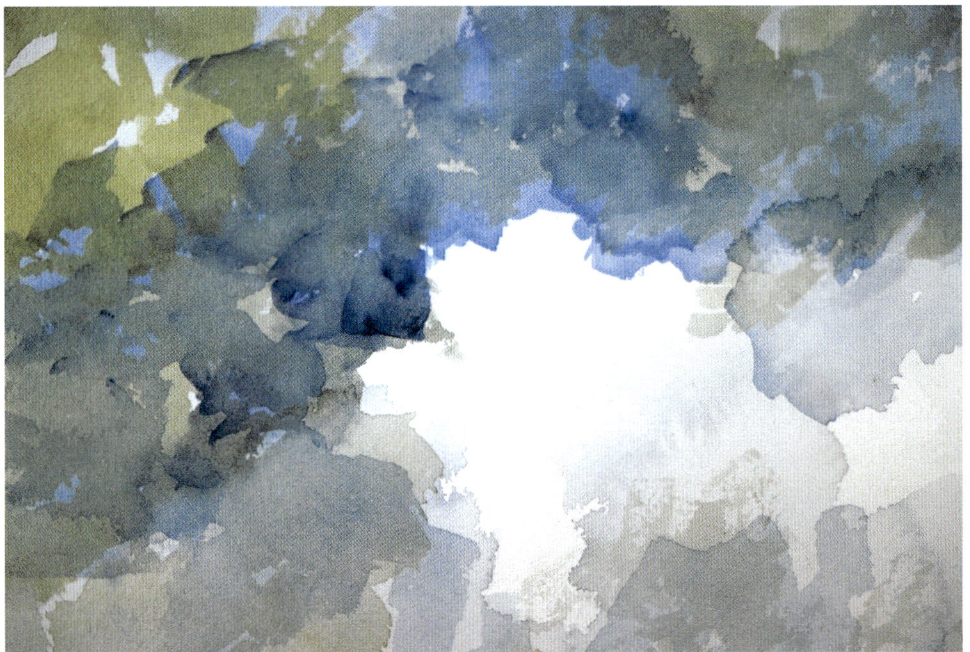

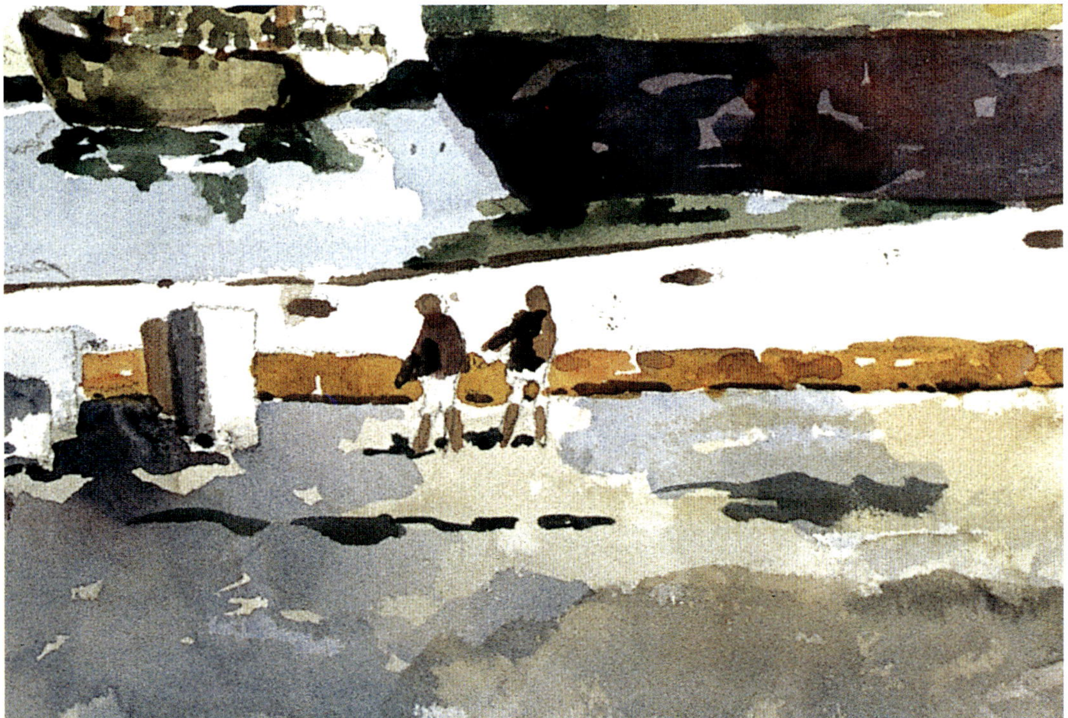

The two dockhands are shown busy at work.
When you add people to your paintings, have
them doing something rather than hanging
around like stick figures.

The Anatomy of Waves

When my 43-foot ketch, *Ona,* left Chicago and sailed down the Illinois Waterway, it was the start of an odyssey that many people dream about, but few experience. *Ona* traversed the muddy Mississippi, the Gulf of Mexico and the ever-changing Gulf Stream to finally end up in the crystal clear waters of the Bahamas. Nassau, the capital and our first port in the islands, was a laid-back island town. Dockage and other expenses were minimal, which contributed toward making it a fun, relaxed place to be. When the Out Islands beckoned, *Ona* turned southeast and headed down the Exuma chain of rock and sand cays. Incidentally, cay is pronounced key in the local King's English. At the south end of Exuma was Georgetown, noted for the annual regatta of Bahamian workboats, or smacks, the name they go by locally. It was here that we became acquainted with the Bahamian crews and their boats. I brought out my sketchbook and camera, and with thoughts of Winslow Homer, I went to work. Here is one of the value sketches of the workboats. I regret to say that there are not many of these workboats left in the Bahamas. They were replaced by flashy, fast, modern outboards.

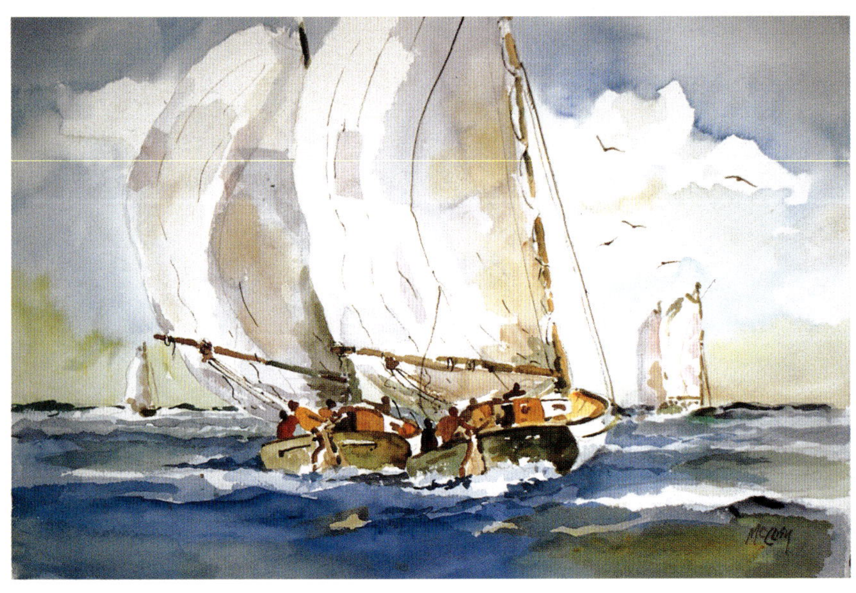

17

A Regatta
in the Bahamas

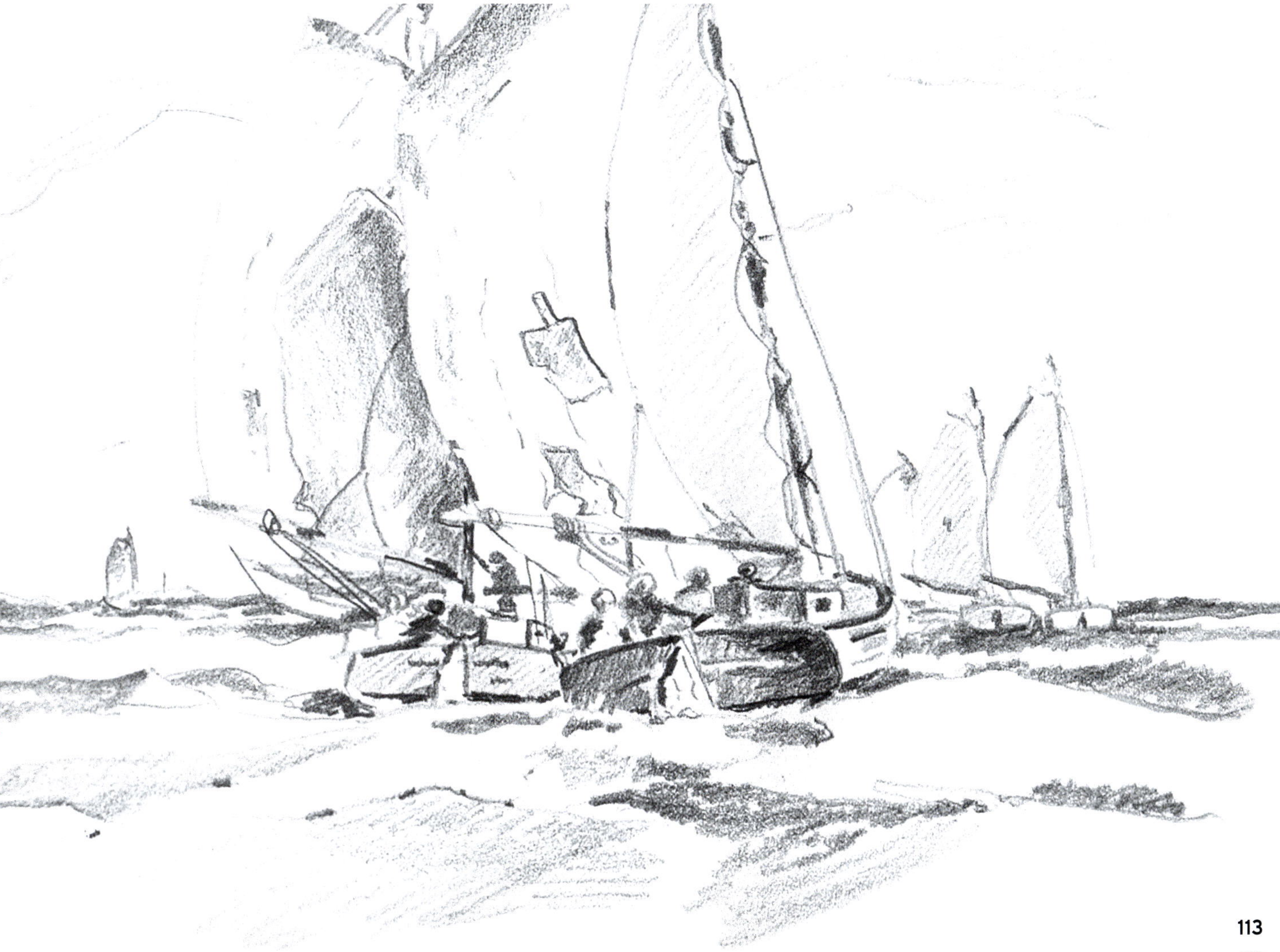

This is the value sketch of workboats
that I made on location in The Bahamas.

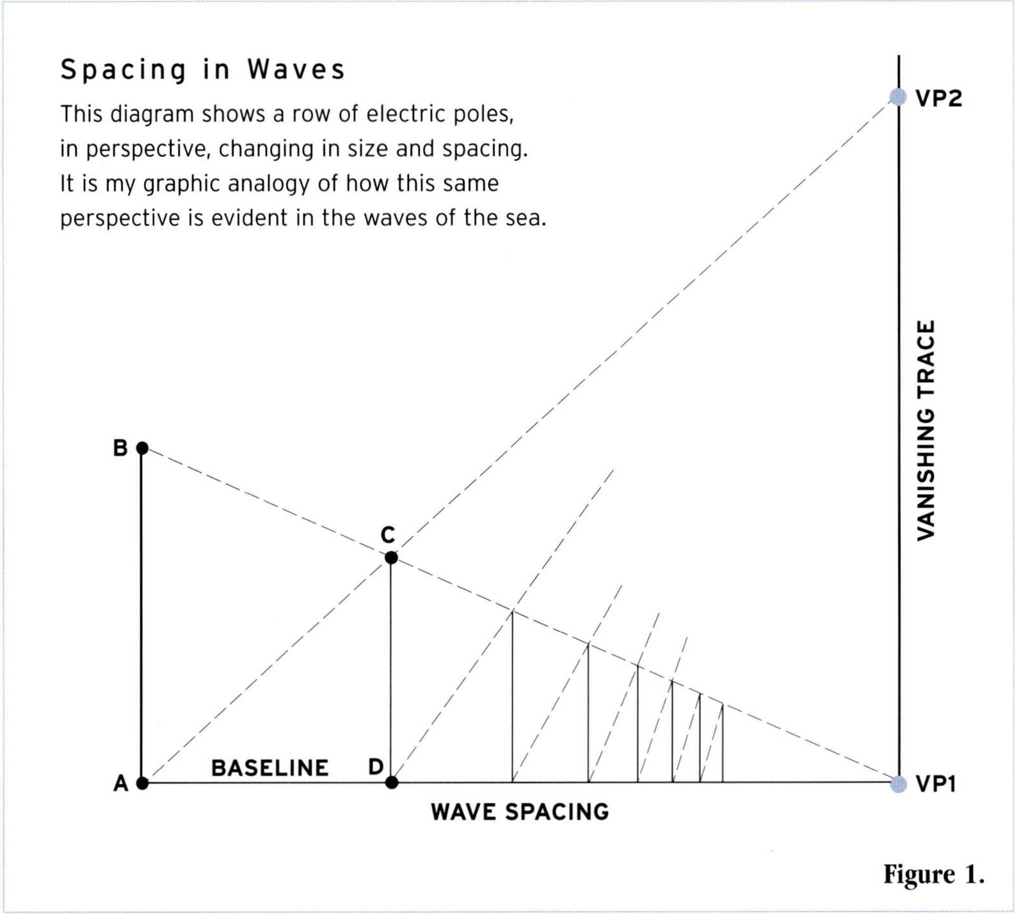

Figure 1.

In Figure 1, the line **AB** could be an electric pole or fence post. Its height is not relative. I drew a line from B down to the vanishing point on the right. This sets up the heights of the succeeding posts. The distance **AD** is an arbitrary spacing that sets up the scene for the following perspective spacing of poles. I then drew a line from **A** through **C** and on to the vanishing trace to establish a second vanishing point. Notice that the spacing between poles gets smaller as they recede. Since spacing in waves is somewhat equal, they can be compared to the change in equal post spaces when placed in a perspective drawing. The far waves are very close together and we look out across the tops of those waves. In the view of the foreground waves, we are looking somewhat down on them and they have flattened out and are much longer.

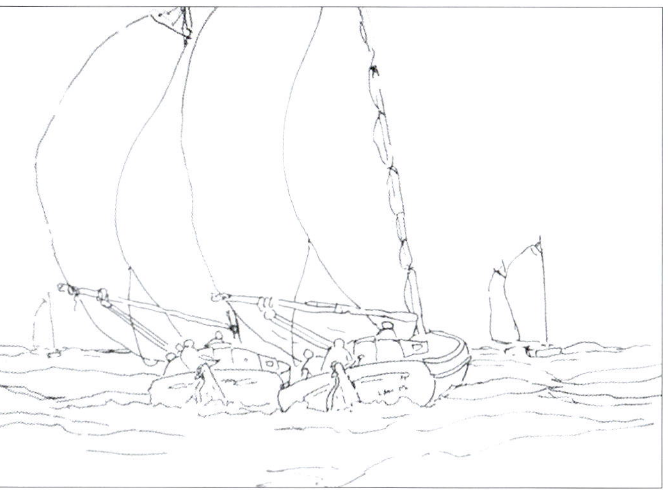

STEP 1 ◄

I edited the 8 X 11½ inch sketch by trimming about ½ inch from each side and an inch from the bottom. I then made a line drawing from the value sketch on a half sheet of watercolor paper; I was now ready to paint. Even though there are very few straight lines in this scene, perspective is evident in the boats and also in the waves. The mass of the boat recedes as is evident by the drawing of the major foreground vessel, but there are no customary lines of perspective going to an established vanishing point. The height of the masts and size of the sails also decreases in perspective as the boats move further into the background. The design of the six boats in this drawing is based on a ratio of 2-2-1. This means that there are two boats, one primary and one secondary, in the foreground. In the middle ground is a grouping of two boats, and, finally, there is the single, far distant one on the left. There is also perspective in the waves. The spacing and size decreases as the waves become more distant.

STEP 2 ►

With a large number 18 round brush, I dampened the sky area except for the major clouds. They are about two-thirds of the way up in the sky area. I didn't want them to go much higher on the sheet for fear that their dominating white areas might drag a viewer's eye to the top and right out of the picture. I painted the sky with a watered-down Thalo Blue. It was darkest at the top of the sheet and got lighter as it receded in the distance to meet the horizon. In this instance, eye level coincides with the true horizon. Any time that you can see the sky and distant water line meeting, that line will be eye level and horizon. The tops of the clouds had a definite line and that was accented with the addition of a touch of Thalo Blue in the sky to darken it. The bottom lines of the clouds were softened. On the left side, I added some New Gamboge into the wet sky where it meets the horizon. The sky is a receding plane and changes in color and value as it recedes. On the right side, I added a touch of Burnt Sienna at the horizon. The sky was painted around the sails and boats. Water in the Bahamas is so clear that you can see bottom in 40 to 50 feet of water on a calm day, so it many times alters the surface colors. A pure sandy

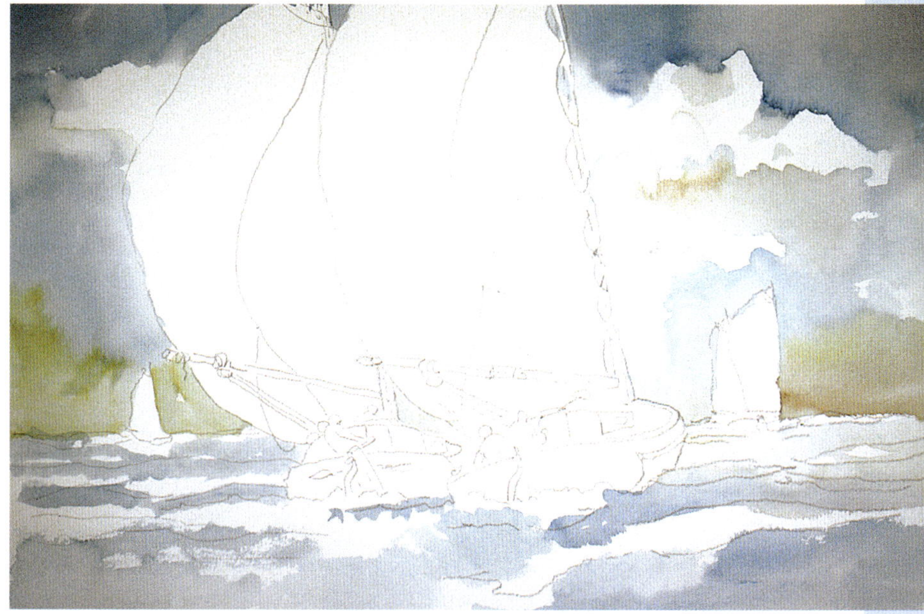

bottom in some areas makes the water almost transparent reflecting that light sand bottom while other areas are very dark from a reef or grass bottom. Looking across the tops of the more distant waves, the sky was reflected and the surface became rather dark. I gave varied lines of under painting washes to the water surface as it receded. The wake of the boats had some bubbling of foam that I left as pure white of the paper.

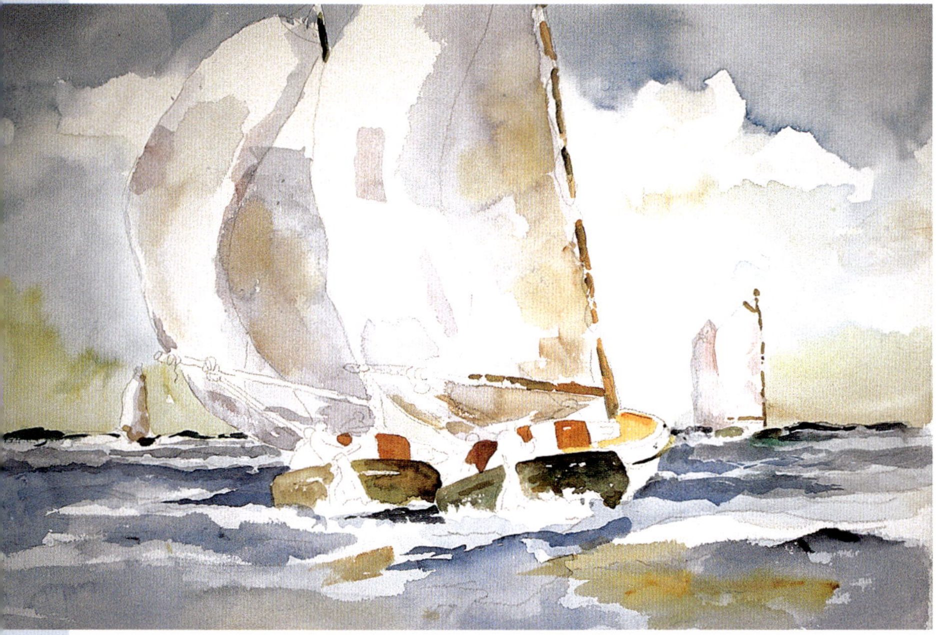

I mixed a lavender and painted the shadow area where the sail bellied out. The front boat's sail was casting a shadow on the sail behind it. I dropped just a tinge of New Gamboge and Cadmium Red Light into the wet pigment in some areas of the sails to liven them up. An accent of Thalo Blue was added to the rollicking water where it abutted the boats. The darker this accent became, the more I got of a third dimension feeling. The two small boats on the right and the far distant one on the left had a very loose wash of leftover lavender on their sails. I gave a wash to the foreground water all the way down to the bottom of the paper. I used Burnt Sienna to paint the back of the boat cabins, then added New Gamboge and painted the deck of the right boat. I had fun painting the boom on the forward boat. Since these are workboats, there is a box filled with sand sitting on the deck just forward of the cabin. They build a fire in this box to cook for the crew, and every once in a while it flames up, burning the boom. They use a splice to repair this. I have shown it here.

STEP 4 ▼

When putting people in a scene, it is good to have them doing something, even if it's only to tie a shoe. In this case, I painted crewmembers engrossed with the excitement of the race. All of them were busy on the boat, including those just looking up at the set of the sail. I used a positive and negative painting technique. By this, I mean that some of the crew were painted positive and I painted around the others, leaving them as negative or merely suggestions of people. Decks on these vessels are traditionally painted a buff color and that was what I used on the deck of the left boat. The entryway into the dark cabins was painted with a Thalo Green-Burnt Sienna puddle that I mixed on the palette. I used a Burnt Sienna mixture to paint the booms and masts. A little green and yellow was dropped in various areas that were still wet. I used a watered-down lavender to emphasize the sails on the distant vessels. The foreground water was next. It was the widest wave of all; I simplified it with practically no details except for a very dark blue on the top of the wave.

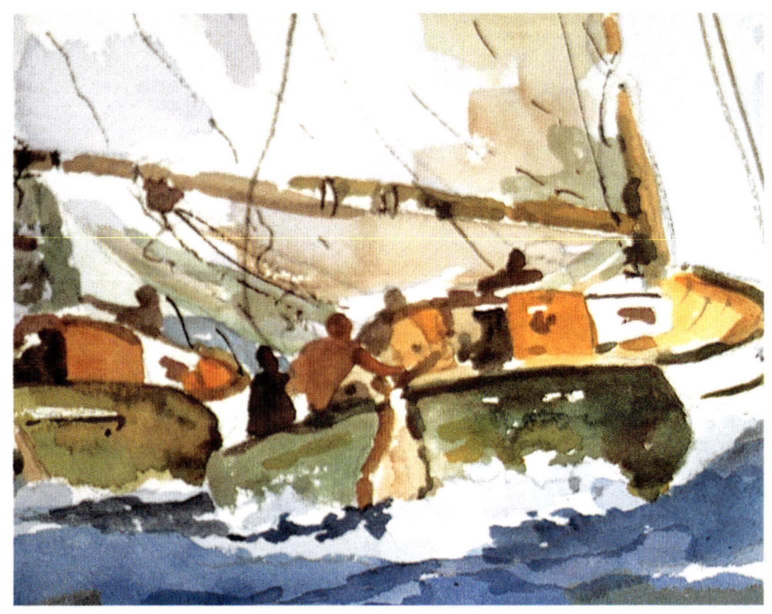

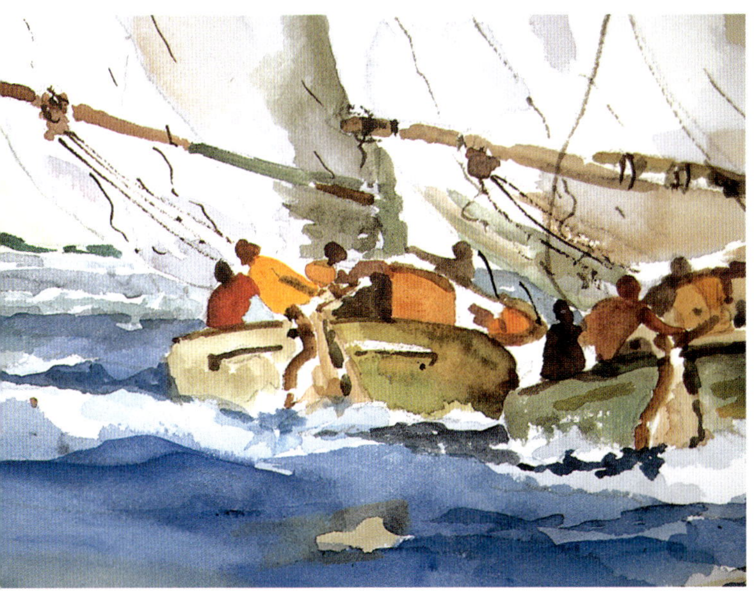

This detail of another boat is a good example of loose, spontaneous watercolor painting.

I sat the picture up and took a look at it. There was some space between the foreground boats. I felt that the background water should show through so I filled in the openings with a light wash of Thalo Blue. Since the sails on the vessels were hand stitched, the seams had to show. I took my rigger brush filled with Thalo Blue and Burnt Sienna and put in the seams in a lost-and-found technique. By this I mean that there are only suggestions of the seams with breaks in the seam lines. They helped to accent the bellied shape of the sail. In the bottom of each sail there were wrinkles and I simulated them in the stitching seams. The shadow that the forward boat's sail had cast on the sail of the left boat looked a little weak, so I reinforced it. A line hanging from the top of the mast draped loosely in the face of the sail splits and then goes under the bottom of the sail and up on the backside forming a pocket or holder when the sail was dropped. Rigging to hold up the mast was very simple. I stroked it in with the script brush. Next, I had to paint in the birds that are ever-present in almost every nautical scene. Remember that birds flap their wings up and down and soar with them more or less level. I noticed some competing whites in the painting; I minimized them with a little dirty water. I looked once again and saw that there was nothing more to do to "Bahamian Odyssey."

Bahamian Odyssey, *22 x 30", 140 lb. Arches*

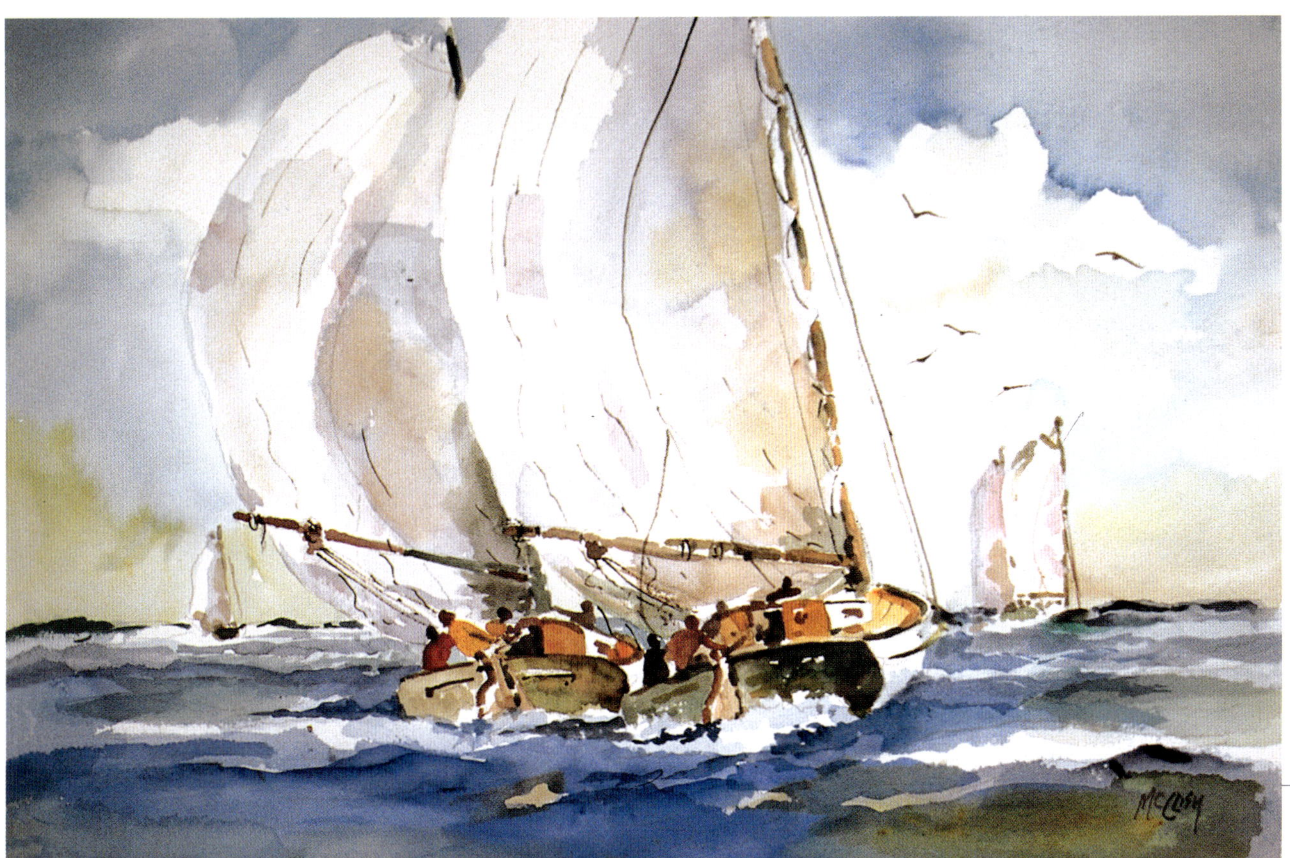

Boats—Important Elements in Marine Paintings

After presenting you with a step-by-step demonstration of a boat race in the previous chapter, I thought it would be appropriate to follow up with some hints about drawing boats. As a subject for drawings and paintings, boats have fascinated artists over the centuries. And they were beautifully presented in the various schools of painting. Boats are still popular today among many traditional painters, especially, of course, those specializing in seascapes and marines. They, too, have done admirable work in portraying boats of all types, shapes and attitudes. However, on my visits to a number of amateur art shows, and even in professional art galleries, I have seen paintings of boats that really should have been drawn and painted with more care devoted to the construction and accuracy of the boats. I know a lot about boats because I have owned and sailed many kinds and even built several. The first was a 28-footer of wood and the second was a 43-foot ketch that I designed and built using steel for the hull. I also was a marine surveyor and a boat designer for a number of years. That taught me a lot about different kinds of vessels and I have made it my business to learn all about them. I'd like to share some of this know-how with you.

The first thing you have to think of is making the boat that you draw a plausible one. One of the ways that you accomplish this is by getting the perspective correct, because doing this will make your boat look right when sketched or painted, in or out of the water. It's easy enough to put a box in perspective, but you can't fit a boat in a box and then chisel away its elements until nothing but a boat is left. Every line in a boat seems to be curving or slanting in some direction, or perhaps, in a constantly changing direction, but they still have perspective. We can't readily see that because almost none of the lines follow through to a conventional vanishing point, as the mass of the boat does. Here are a few hints that might help you to draw a small wooden boat with classical lines. This approach uses what I call a *book* to draw a boat in almost any

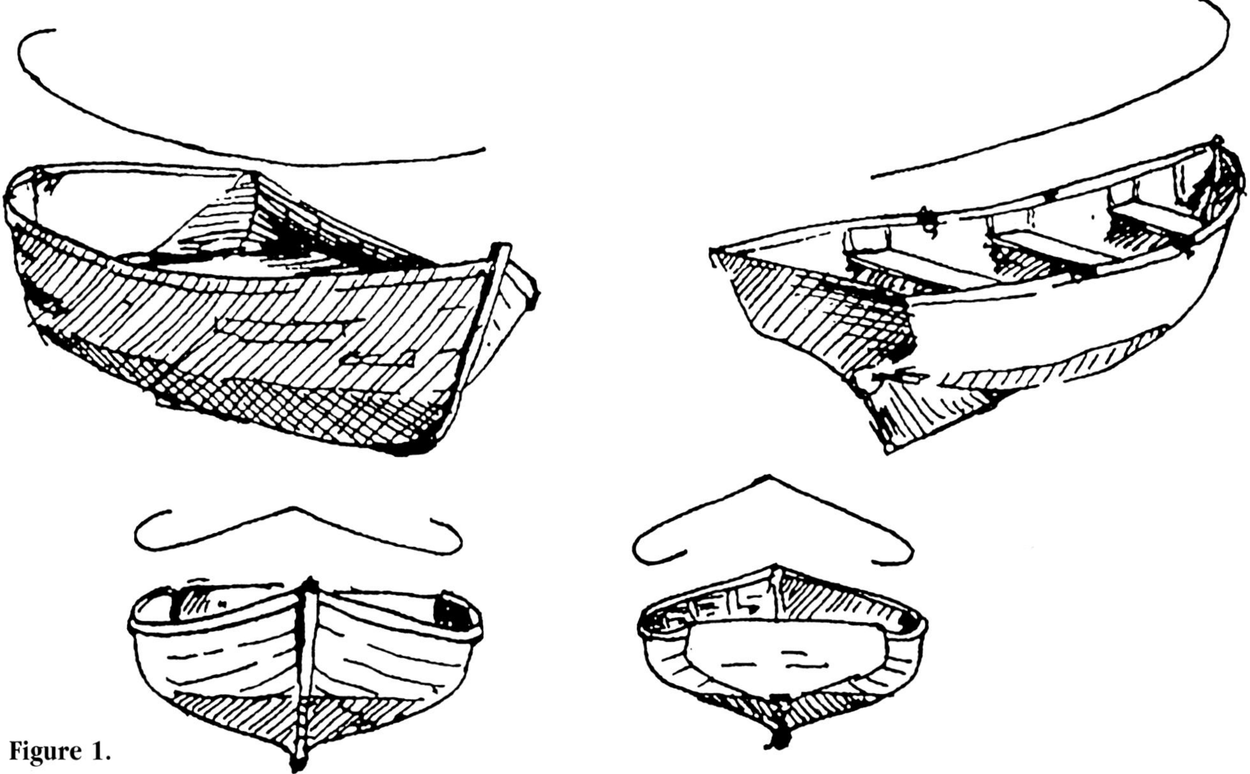

Figure 1.

configuration. The hook says, "I am curving and still going around as I disappear." This is true whether you use it to draw a very small boat or an ocean liner. You just use it differently for various-sized vessels. To draw the sweeping hook, raise your hand from a writing position that's free of the table and use your arm to contribute to the drawing.

In other words, loosen up! When the freehand hook looks good, finish drawing a boat.

It is usually best to draw a boat using a view from the rear. From the bow, normally the highest point on a boat, all you see is the bow. When trying to draw a boat with a stern view, some students in my watercolor classes have ended up with it standing on end with the bow sticking way up in the air. I would get them to lay the boat down in a normal position, by just having them move the bow down and redraw the sides to meet that point. The seats in a small boat are about the only perspective lines that are parallel; they go to a common vanishing point. This includes the top of the transom or back end. If the top of the transom has a slight curve, use the two end points to form a perspective line, and they will be parallel with the seats.

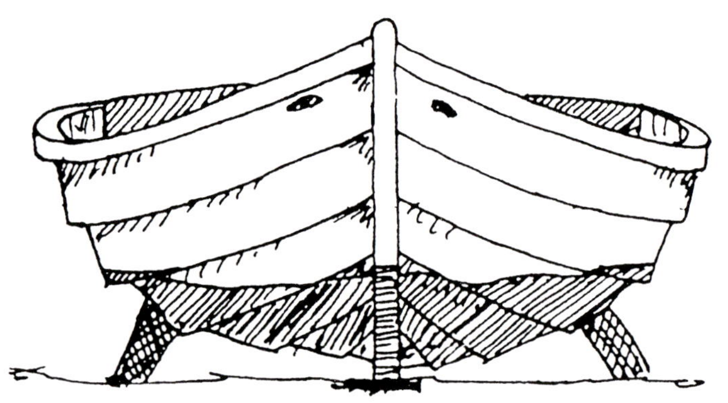

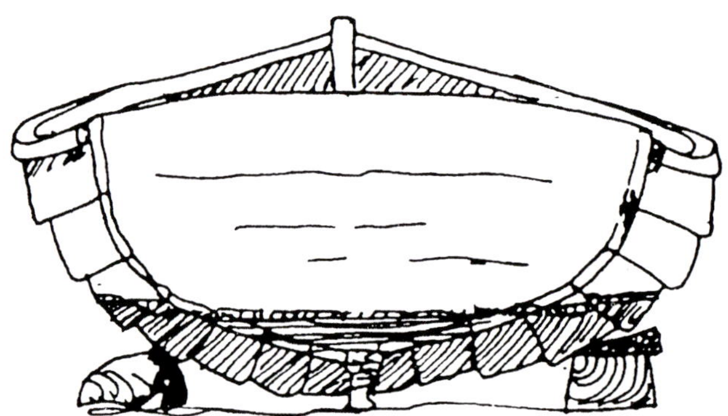

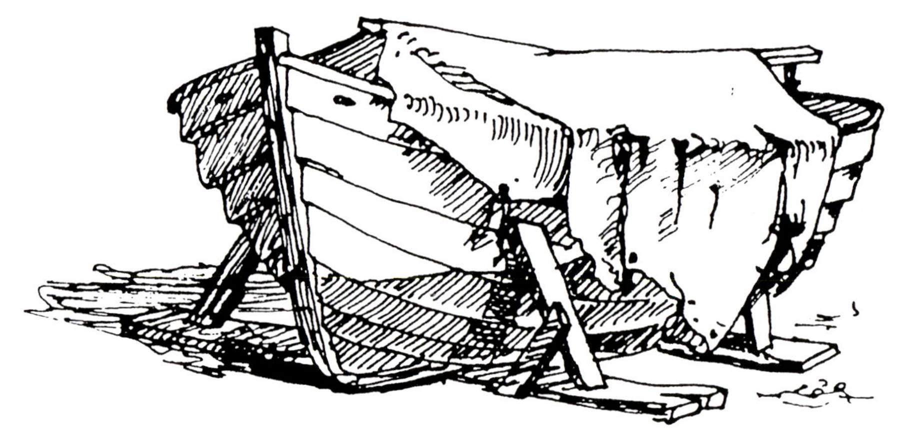

Figure 2.

Showing the Shape of a Boat

Here is a drawing of a small boat that has overlapping planking. The lines of the planking help to show the rounded shape of a hull.

A way to show the shape of a boat

The sides or planking of the boat take on many variations. If the boat is a plastic or glass fiber construction, it can be very smoothly molded with little or no interior framing. There are ways, too, to construct a boat of wooden planks that are so closely fitted that the look is the same as that in plastic siding.

One of the more interesting and artistic ways to indicate the side of a boat is to overlap the planking. This is called "clinker" or "lap strake." The planking adds a bit of intrigue to what may be a plain area in the painting and it also helps to show the shape of the boat a little better. The addition of shadows under the overlapped planks may also be used to good advantage. When drawing the planking lines, it could be compared somewhat to an orange peeling section, since the side of the boat is also rounded. The lines start out at the front and then have to expand to go around the larger center, or belly, of the boat before starting in at the back.

Boat things to remember

Boats have been built in every shape including a transom that is reversed slanted, or perpendicular along with other configurations of the hull. But when you draw it as shown, it seems to say, "Boat" just a little better. In this classic, or more nostalgic boat, the bow has a slant, the fattest or widest portion of a boat is usually just a little over halfway from the bow to the transom. This point also conforms to the lowest portion of the deck. The bow is the highest, midship or center is lowest and it sweeps up to the transom. Some boats have sides that are straight up and down but on others, the topsides may lean in or out. I guess that there is no really correct design for a vessel regardless of its size. The hardest composition that contains a boat in it is a broadside view. Always turn the boat a little and the composition will improve because you have added a third dimension. At the waterline going all around the boat hull is a stripe of anti-fouling paint called a "boot top." It helps to stop the growth of grass or other marine organisms. The boot top is usually on boats that stay in the water all season.

The Rigid Road to Loose Watercolors

No matter how you look at the title of this chapter, you can't escape the contradiction in its premise. And yet, these words are true. Over my many years of teaching, the first thing many students expressed to me were their ambitions to paint as freely as I did. Freedom, I told them, comes from discipline. That discipline includes learning the basics first and then applying them. If you have the basics, it seems that the brush floats with a freedom all of its own over the paper. I call it an educated brush. I don't think they liked hearing this. To them, the freedom in the work of contemporary painters, especially those working in the abstract mode, had to be the result of their carefree life.

They learned soon enough that this is not so. I showed them my black-and-white pencil sketches and the paintings I made from them. The sketches, reproduced on these pages, along with the paintings that they inspired, helped me to capture each particular scene while I was on location. My detailed sketch was usually accompanied by a half sheet (15 x 22") watercolor. Later back in my studio, I would implement many of these sketches and watercolors, sometimes with photographs that I would use for color notations, to direct me in painting studio watercolors. Exact color is not really relevant and many times I took freedom in my color selection. With all of the values worked out in my sketches, I was free to express myself with paints on the watercolor sheet. The detailed sketches in no way hindered me in my quest for a loose approach in painting my landscapes. On the contrary, I truly felt free; after all, the big problems were solved for me when I first drew the sketches at the site.

I'd like you to study the sketches and paintings that I've presented here. They are of places in New England, Italy and France, three of my favorite areas.

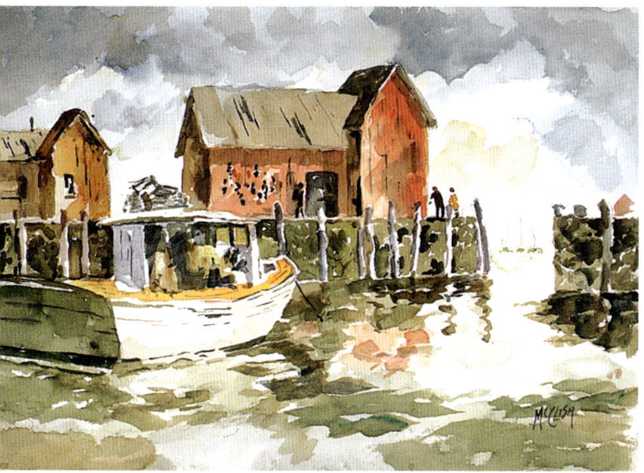

Motif #1, Rockport, Mass.

The old fishing shack that's known as Motif #1 was so named because many artists regard this structure as the most painted building in America. Whether that's true or not is unimportant. No artist's trip to Rockport is considered complete without seeing and sketching or painting Motif # 1. The red shack is the third Motif, the first being lost to fire, the second having been devastated in a punishing blizzard. Motif #1 is a fading red building that prominently stands on the end of a dock dominating the harbor entrance. Hanging on the wall facing the harbor is a colorful display of fish floats. Like many other artists, I just had to make a sketch and painting of the historic structure. I added a moored boat to complete the harbor scene. The changes that I made, in transferring the sketch to the paper, were indeed infinitesimal. You can see how spirited the painting is despite the tight handling of the pencil sketch.

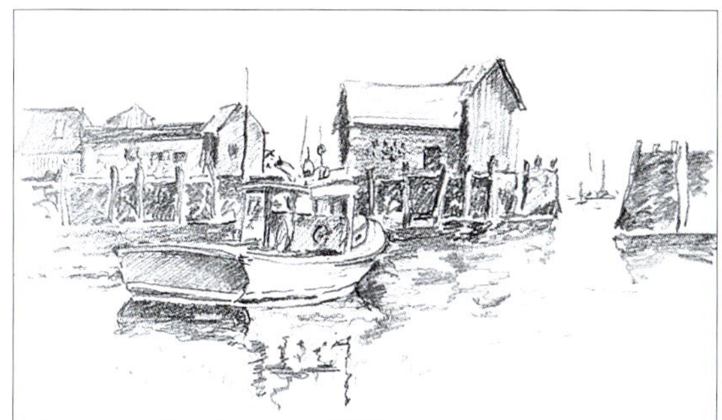

Maine Boatyard ▶

I took a turn down a little traveled road in Southport, Maine, and came upon this small boatyard. There were a few yard hands working on boats and none of them paid any attention to me. I guess that it is the down-east way of being friendly. I parked, got out my art tools and went to work. Being president of the International Society of Marine Painters at the time helped my enthusiasm for picturing the marine scene.

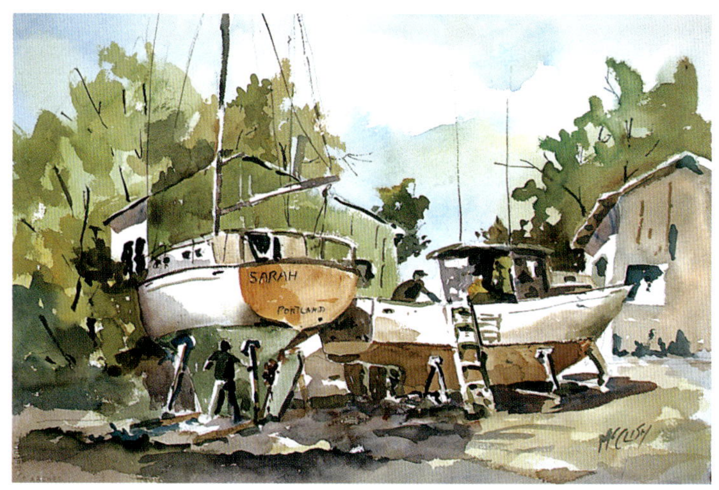

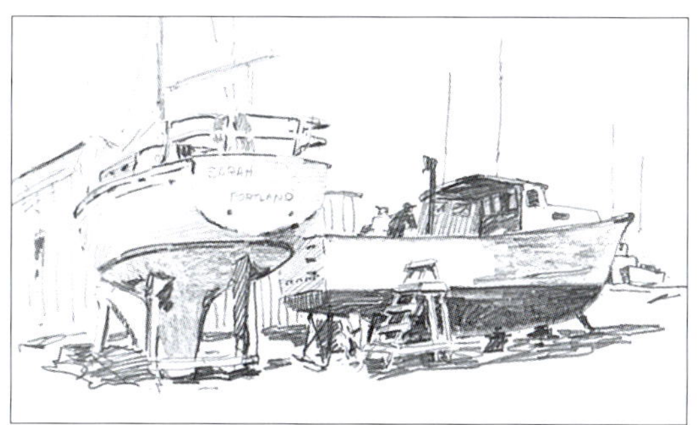

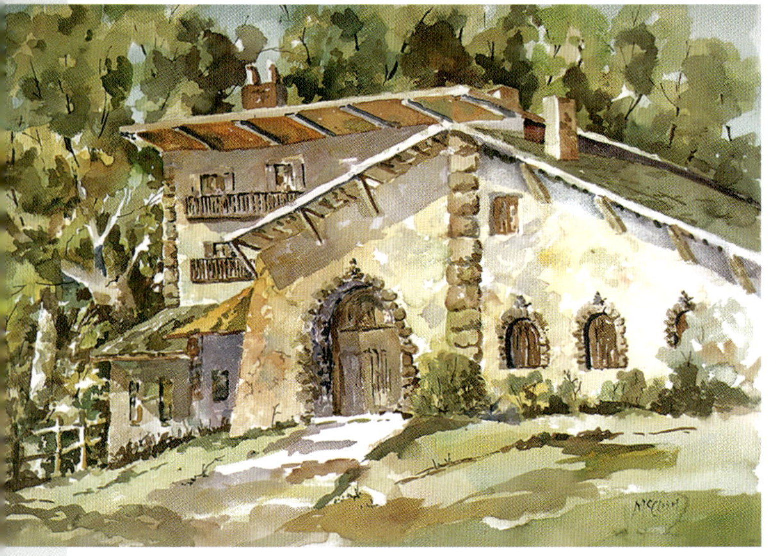

◄ Arnaga Estates, France

Our bus, filled with ready-to-paint artists, turned in at Arnaga Estates somewhere in central France. The main house was a fairly large castle with the typical turrets and other castle amenities. It was just too much to paint on the spot. However, I did make a sketch of it, hoping to make a painting some time in the future. As we were leaving the castle area, I saw what was called the Gardener's House. It basked in the sunlight, with interesting effects being created on its balconies, its attractive entryway and interesting roof shape. They all combined to make the house a fascinating subject. I opened my sketchbook and made a second sketch, which enticed me to stay on and paint a half-sheet watercolor. I assembled my tools, sat down on my stool and went to work. In painting the picture, the sketch was a big help to me.

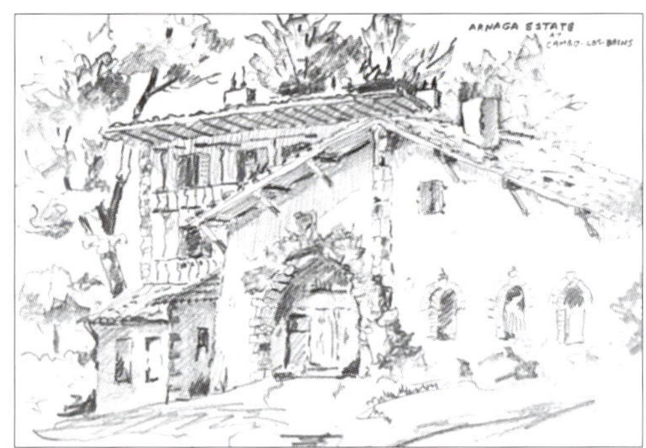

Boothbay Harbor, Maine ►

Located on the rocky shores of Maine, Boothbay Harbor fairly screamed to be painted in a very loose technique. I parked and strolled down the main street that was filled with wall-to-wall people. Looking ahead, I noticed the footbridge that spanned the lower end of the harbor. It looked inviting and, what's more, it was tourist free so I ventured across it. About halfway across I turned, looked back and decided to paint the backside of the buildings which were along the main thoroughfare. Since I was looking at the town from the seaside, there were many pilings at the water's edge with buildings of different kinds and shapes sitting on top of them. At this juncture, there were no tourists. They were all on the other side, walking the shops. I returned to my car, grabbed my painting gear and returned to the bridge, which would become a little crowded whenever someone walked by. I had no trouble; all of them were courteous, each taking a quick look and going on. Here is the result of my work, which, you can see, is a literal paint version of my value sketch.

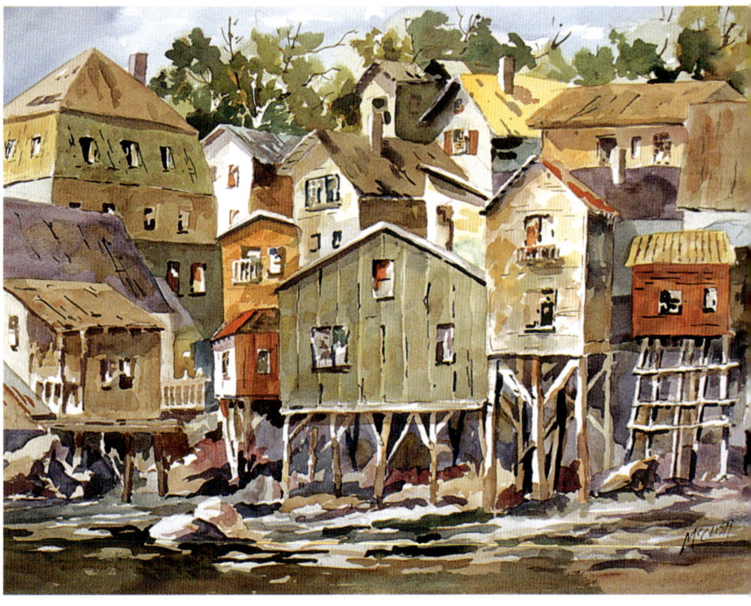

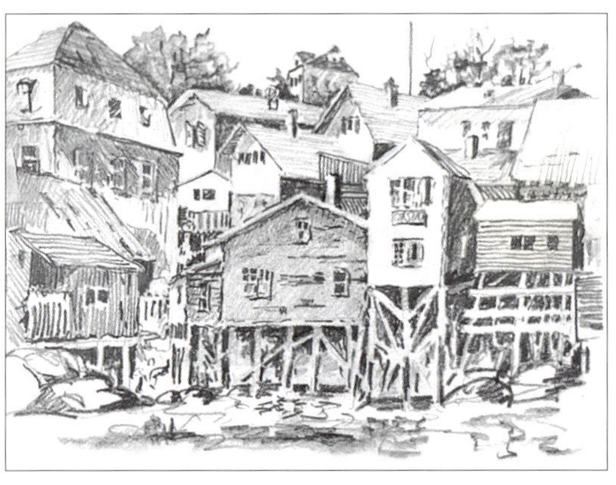

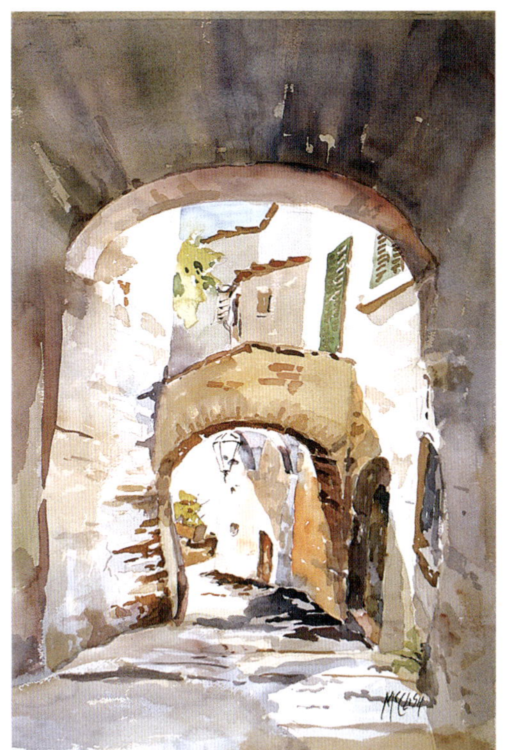

◀ Arches in Italy

Ever since the ancient Romans discovered how to built arches,
builders in Italy went crazy with their construction. The important
function was their use to brace buildings, but the builders also found
them useful as roadways that sometimes doubled as overpasses for
pedestrians, carts and, in the case of aqueducts, the carrying of
water. As a result, in my trips through the hill towns of Italy, I came
across a wealth of arches that served one purpose or other. What
was important to me, though, was that they provided me with interestingly shaped structures and fascinatingly rustic subjects for loose
watercolors. I saw this beautiful view from my vantage point that
happened to be under a large arch. The sunlight streamed down,
highlighting buildings with three-quarter back light, which left the
arch in shadow, a sort of partial sil-
houette. It was too beautiful to pass
up. It was the classic composition, a
dark foreground going into a blaze of
sunlight and then back into at least
partial shadow in the distance. There
is reflected light on the left foreground building from the brilliant
sun's rays on the building on the right.
My palette and brushes were soon at
work. Incidentally, the vertical format
of this painting is one I rarely use for
landscapes. I chose it because of the
vertical nature of the subject matter.

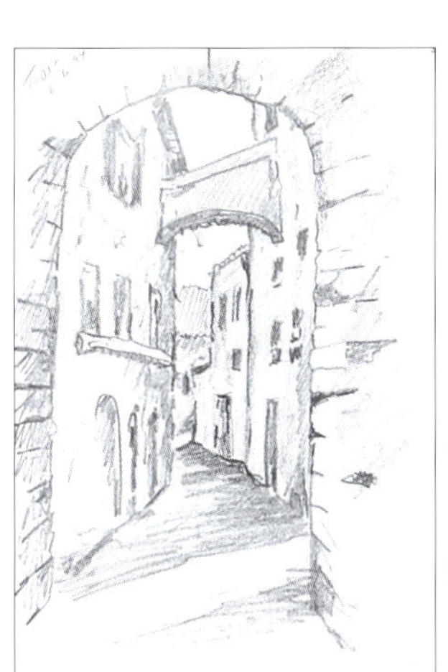

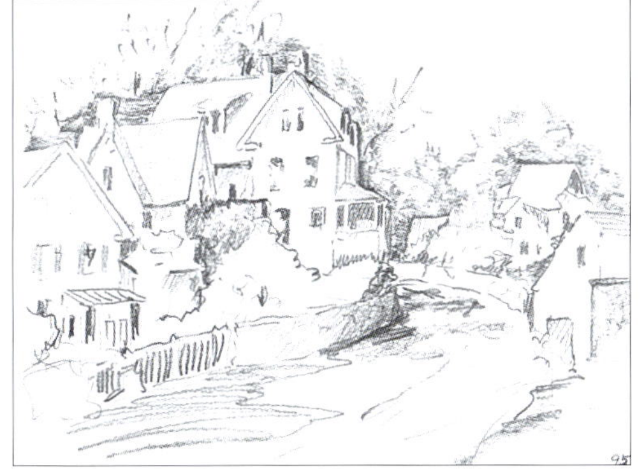

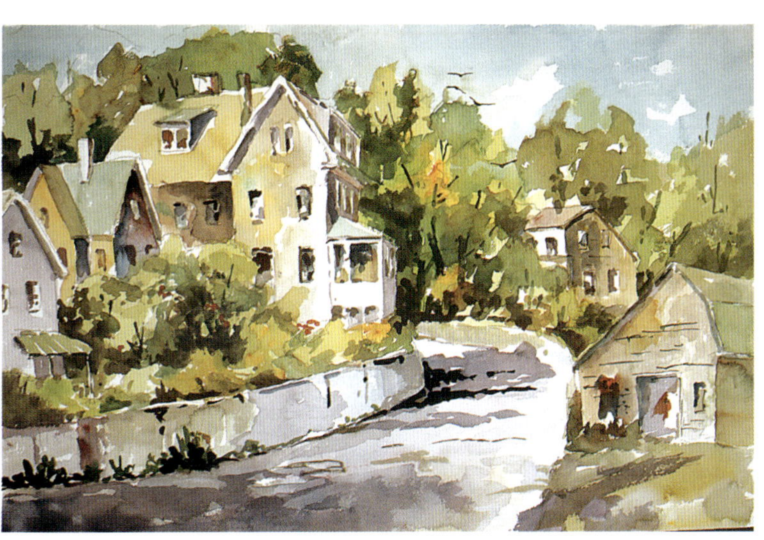

◀ East Gloucester, Mass.

Leaving the Rocky Neck Art Colony, I turned
right instead of left to follow the shoreline
on my return to Rockport. One block passed
and I saw this typical New England scene.
It is a quaint street with equally quaint older
type houses jumbled together in a group.
I increased the curvature of the road just
a little and even might have narrowed it
at the same time. Some of the homes also
were moved a little closer together to give
a more intimate feeling. I guess those slight
changes made it say "New England" just
a little bit easier. Most of Gloucester is just
filled with scenes of vintage homes with
many on curving streets that go up or down
hill. Even though there is no water in this
scene, water dominates most of the views
in this seaport and fishing center.

Montmarte, Paris

This area is an artist's delight. It is a large hill accessible both by a funicular and curving roadways and affords a breathtaking view of Paris. The Sacre Coeur, a beautiful church, occupies part of the top of the hill, and an art colony took over the little park in its center that is surrounded by shops and restaurants. I painted the Sacre Coeur a few years ago and used the painting as my annual Christmas card. The area is literally swamped with tourists, as is shown by the value sketch and a watercolor that I painted. I find it so much easier to inject a loose character to any scene that has crowds of people in it.

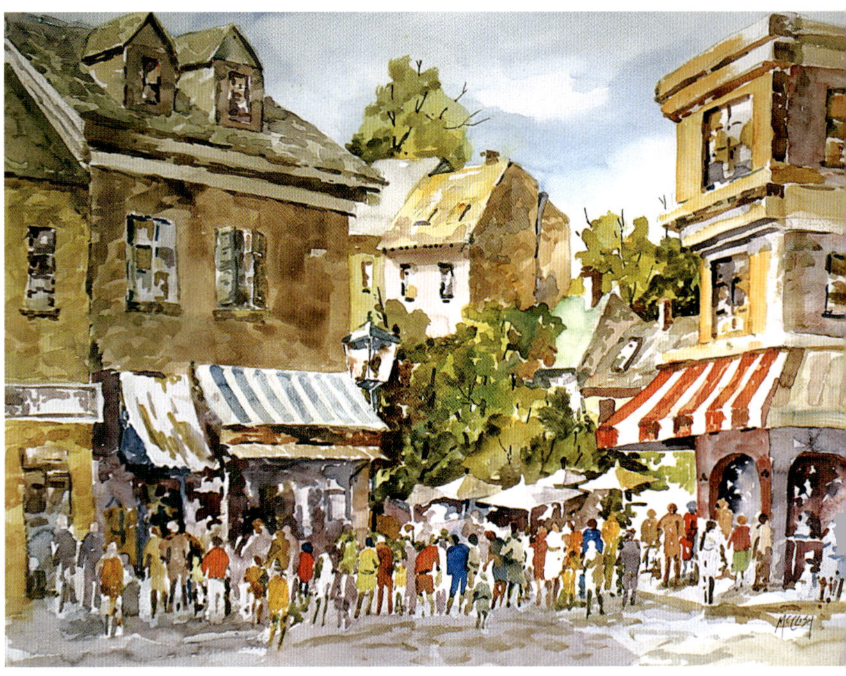

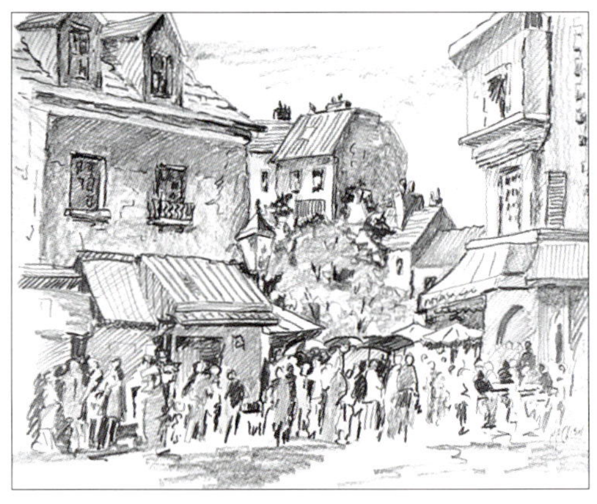

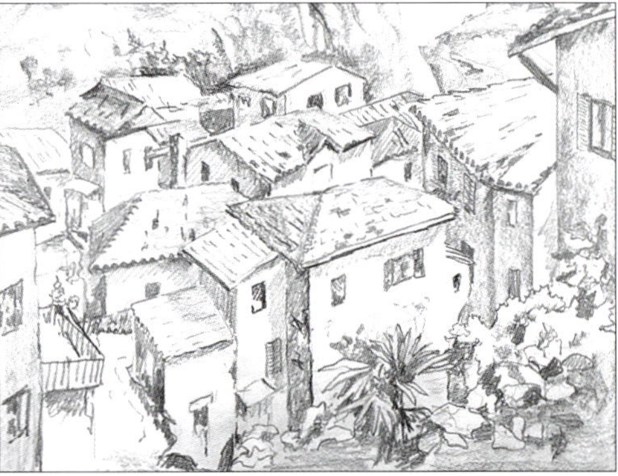

Looking Down in Italy

In Arrone, my group of students was trudging up a steep hill with me when we ran out of breath and stopped. Looking back over where we had been, one student commented on the perspective as it appeared on the buildings below us. It was a scene with a very high horizon that was above and out of the picture frame. I liked it. After the value sketch, it was fun to paint. It is a unique and different view. You can see in the painting that I greatly simplified the cluster of buildings.

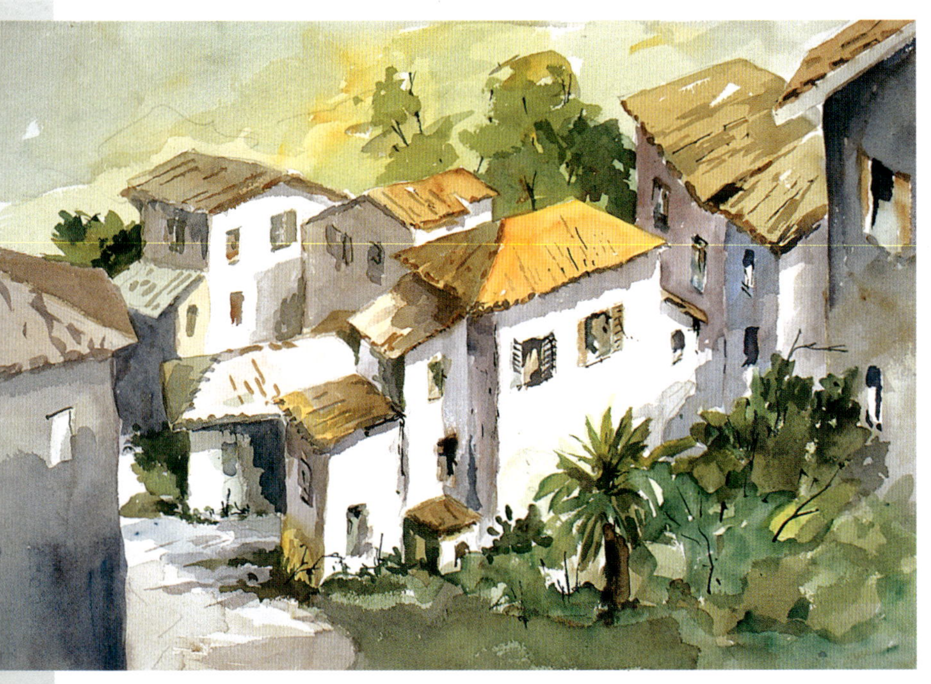

Final Thoughts

wo very sound reasons made this book a special delight for me to edit. One of them was Jerry McClish's evident endearment for Cape Ann, that beautiful, enchanting spot that's located about forty miles northeast of Boston and which is home to Gloucesterites and Rockporters, of which I was one for thirty-one years. His watercolor renditions of scenes of the area's sea and land jogged back memories of the experiences I enjoyed with friends and loved ones for a large portion of my life.

The other reason was Jerry McClish himself. When I met him I knew he could paint; that was obvious for all to see. What I learned, during the preparation of this book, was that he was a very bright guy and a far cry from the curmudgeon I was sure I would be dealing with. I enjoyed the time that I spent on this project, a lot for the reasons I spelled out, but mainly because this is a very good book, about a valuable painting medium and with magnificent instructions by a dedicated and extremely knowledgeable artist-teacher.

Herbert Rogoff
Editor

Index